CRITICISM WITHOUT BOUNDARIES

University of Notre Dame
Ward-Phillips Lectures in
English Language and Literature

Volume 12

Criticism without Boundaries

DIRECTIONS AND CROSSCURRENTS
IN POSTMODERN CRITICAL THEORY

EDITED BY

Joseph A. Buttigieg

UNIVERSITY OF NOTRE DAME PRESS
NOTRE DAME, INDIANA

Library of Congress Cataloging-in-Publication Data

Criticism without boundaries.

(Ward Phillips lecture series ; v. 12)
Bibliography: p.
1. Criticism. I. Buttigieg, Joseph A. II. Series: Ward-
Phillips lectures in English language and literature ; v. 12.
PN85.C7   1987   801'.95'0904   86-40593
ISBN 0-268-00762-4

Manufactured in the United States of America

Contents

Preface

The English Department at the University of Notre Dame in-
augurated the Ward-Phillips lectures in 1966 during the chairmanship
of Professor Ernest Sandeen and named them to honor two deceased
members of its faculty. Professor Charles Phillips had, by the time of
his death in 1933, spent no more than nine years at Notre Dame but
in that relatively short period he established himself as one of the University's most distinguished teachers. He also worked hard to help found
the University Theatre. Reverend Leo Ward, C.S.C., another exceptional teacher, chaired the English Department from 1936 until his death
in 1953. Through their teaching, writing, and administrative efforts,
Charles Phillips and Leo Ward contributed immensely to the growth
and distinction of the English Department.

The Ward-Phillips Lectures held in April 1984 differed significantly
from the previous series. Whereas in the past a single visiting scholar
delivered four formal lectures, this time nine distinguished speakers addressed a broad topic from a variety of standpoints. The extensive discussions that accompanied the lectures gave the three-day event the aspect
of a symposium. All the participants on both sides of the podium share
the credit for making the occasion memorable.

The majority of the speakers are associated with the journal *boundary 2* which since its inception under the editorship of William V. Spanos
has provided a valuable and influential forum to countless poets, fiction writers, critics, and theorists interested in exploring and analyzing
the possibilities, the implications, and the significance of postmodernism.
The presence of the *boundary 2* "group" helped in no small measure
to give the 1984 Ward-Phillips Lectures their distinctive character.

Equally valuable and innovative were the contributions of Professor Fred Dallmayr and Professor Fabio Dasilva from the respective
faculties of the Departments of Government and Sociology at the University of Notre Dame. They were the first scholars from an academic
discipline other than Literature and from within the Notre Dame com-

munity to deliver Ward-Phillips Lectures, thus adding a new cross-disciplinary dimension to the series.

This volume gathers the essays originally prepared for the Ward-Phillips Lectures of 1984. Some of them have been substantially amplified or modified for publication while others retain their original form. Still, they all convey, as faithfully as can be expected, a sense of the issues and debates that dominated the occasion of their original presentation. Professor Donna Przybylowicz was prevented by force of circumstance from coming to Notre Dame to deliver her lecture. Since her essay formed part of the original program, however, it too belongs in this collection.

A large number of individuals collaborated and worked hard to organize and promote this lecture series. To thank them all is practically impossible but one cannot help mentioning the special generosity and support of a few. Professor Robert Burns as Acting Dean of the College of Arts and Letters and Professor Edward Kline, Chairman of the English Department, provided the institutional and financial backing that made it all possible. Their encouragement and advice was invaluable. The graduate students in the English Department helped in many ways to put the program together. Among them, Sheila Conboy and Melita Schaum devoted countless hours to many tasks which they tackled with fervent enthusiasm. Professor Teresa Phelps from the University of Notre Dame Law School, Professor Stephen Watson from the Philosophy Department, Professor Edward Vasta and Professor Eileen Bender, both from the English Department, made my organizational work easier and more pleasant than it would have otherwise been. I also relied heavily on the assistance of Mrs. Connie Maher and Mrs. Georgeanna Caldwell who, as always, were unusually adept at coordinating the efforts of everyone involved. Mr. Michael Garvey contributed his expertise to promote and publicize the lecture series. My friend and colleague John Matthias has supported all my efforts generously and with enthusiasm. Dr. Richard Allen of the University of Notre Dame Press improved several facets of this volume through his professional and tactful advice. Above all, Dr. Jennifer Anne Montgomery is owed very special gratitude for helping with every phase of planning, organizing, and successfully carrying out the necessary arrangements.

The Ward-Phillips Lectures of 1984, apart from stimulating the Notre Dame community to reflect on the import of postmodern critical theory, also provided a forum for friendly but keen discussions among colleagues who in their busy everyday academic lives have few occasions for such sustained exchanges.

1. Introduction: Criticism without Boundaries

JOSEPH A. BUTTIGIEG

> O madness of discourse,
> That cause sets up with and against itself.   *Troilus and Cressida* (V:ii)

It may, at first sight, appear odd that a collection of essays dealing with contemporary movements in critical theory and practice should be gathered together under a rubric that relies on a spatial metaphor. The term "boundaries" evokes images of mapped territories, a panoptic view of artificial divisions replete with echoes of a renounced version of history. It begets memories, perhaps, of some history teachers in grammar school who unfurled their maps and waved their pointers with the aplomb of military strategists. Those same teachers often regarded the historical atlas as the most basic textbook, containing as it does within its covers a visual and, in a sense, stabilized survey of shifting boundaries, of expanding and shrinking empires, of successive centres of power. After the assault on the Modernist propensity for spatializing time and following the urgent calls for a return to "history," it does indeed seem incongruous to employ a spatial metaphor in conjunction with postmodern criticism. Yet, the image of boundaries must be retained, not as a holdover from a discredited though persistent historiographic habit but rather to signal an intent to examine the territorial claims, the disciplinary authority of critical discourse.

In order to steer clear from the seductive notion of regarding contemporary critical theory and practice as the most advanced stage of some abstract progressive urge towards greater refinement and sophistication, or as the product of a disinterested intellectual endeavor in singleminded pursuit of "Truth," or even as the degeneration of a self-evidently glorious tradition—in order to avoid such naive views and approach criticism critically on the terrain of worldly interest, it helps to employ the boundary metaphor with all its attendant connotations of territoriality, sovereignty, dominion, provinciality, and so on. The

1

point of such an exercise, of course, is not to perpetuate a "boundary" mentality in criticism, or in any other form of discourse, for that matter, but rather to reveal and recognize the existence of boundaries, their artificiality, their debilitating effects, and above all the interests they stake out. Discovery and recognition mark the first necessary stage in any effective effort launched against discursive boundaries with the goal of abolishing them or, at least, dislodging them and loosening their constraining power; otherwise, they will remain concealed by the misleadingly attractive humanistic rhetoric of intellectual objectivity, disinterestedness, serene irony, and impartiality.

To refrain from discussing disciplinary boundaries, to refuse to acknowledge their existence, to proceed as if they were immaterial would be tantamount to an abdication of critical responsibility and maybe even to an abandonment of the task of criticism itself. So, the advocacy of a criticism without boundaries does not entail the endorsement of a free-floating, metaphysical, Olympian stance that places the critic above the contentious fray like some sagacious judge endowed with the aloof authoritativeness of cultivated indifference. Instead, it seeks to engage the dominant discourses of criticism and their objects on the terrestrial plane of history through the sustained and persistent scrutiny of the relationships among literature, criticism, other disciplines and their discursive regularities, Academe, cultural institutions, alternative modes of inquiry, political and civil society, oppositional voices, and a myriad of related movements and forces. Spatial metaphors enable the disclosure of the vast and complex economy of power that informs these relationships. They bring to the surface the nexus between knowledge and power, and make possible the retrieval of the study of critical discourse from the history of consciousness in order to ground it in worldly (i.e. genealogical) history. In other words, the adoption of spatial, geographic metaphors can help bring to the fore the historical character of the history of criticism by indicating, as they do, how the establishment of boundaries or frames under the guise of ever more complex systems of differentiation serve to circumscribe, limit and, ultimately, control the play of difference.

The writings of Michel Foucault contain some of the most convincing examples of the usefulness of spatial metaphors to any critical study of discourses that endeavors to retain its primary focus on history and the processes of power. In an interview with the editors of *Herodote*, a journal of Marxist geographers, Foucault explained why his "spatial obsessions," as he called them, feature so prominently in his investigations of the relations between knowledge and power. If one were to rely exclusively on metaphors of time, according to Foucault, one would end up "erecting a great collective consciousness as the scene of events."[1] Treating discourses in terms of temporal continuity, in other words, prevents the analyses of discourse from taking into account the historical process of power, that is, the mundane interplay of individual and collective interests. Hence the need for metaphors of space, metaphors that appear to be borrowed from geography but which upon closer consideration, Foucault observes, turn out to have juridico-political, military, fiscal, economico-juridical, and administrative derivations. The list of terms Foucault discusses in this interview does not include "boundary." Nevertheless, what he has to say about the pertinence to his project of words like "field," "territory," "displacement," "domain," "region," and "horizon" applies also to "boundary" with most of its attendant connotations:

> Once knowledge can be analysed in terms of region, domain, implantation, displacement, transposition, one is able to capture the process by which knowledge functions as a form of power and disseminates the effects of power. There is an administration of knowledge, a politics of knowledge, relations of power which pass via knowledge and which, if one tries to transcribe them, lead one to consider forms of domination designated by such notions as field, region, territory. (PK, 69)

In his interview with *Herodote*, Foucault discussed his work in very broad, general terms. As one would expect, the move from this level of generality to the actual identification of the various loci where knowledge functions as a form of power can hardly be simple or direct and requires long, painstaking research—especially since the Foucauldian project does "not concern itself with regulated and legitimate forms of power in their central locations" but rather "with power at its extremities, in its ultimate destinations, with those points where it becomes capillary, that is in its more regional and local forms and institutions" (PK, 96). The difficulty of such an undertaking is further compounded when one deals with literary critical discourse and the institutions that simultaneously support it and receive support from it. The revered tradition of disinterested aesthetic judgement, reinforced by the claims made for the autonomy of art and the credibility habitually granted to literary critics' proclamations of detachment from worldly, extraliterary considerations—this tradition stands as a formidable bastion against the intrusion of such mundane concerns as discursive power, institutional authority, administrative controls over fields of knowledge, disciplinary boundaries, and so on. Questions of this nature, the orthodox response would go, properly belong to other spheres of knowledge such as sociology, political science, or social history but have nothing to do with the realm of literature and literary criticism *per se*.

Nevertheless, on occasion, the solemn facade of objectivity, detachment, intellectual tranquillity, and ascetic fidelity to universal Truth breaks down, exposing the power structures and hierarchies that by defining and protecting the boundaries of discursive disciplines perpetuate the centralization and administrative control of knowledge. These occasions arise in times of crisis when critical criticism—the voice of what Foucault calls the "subjugated" and "disqualified" knowledge through which "criticism performs its work" (*PK*, 82)—threatens to disrupt the entrenched order and orderliness of a discursive domain. In the face of what he may perceive as a severe crisis, the traditional intellectual sometimes feels compelled to set aside his reserved *hauteur*; he suspends his composed air of a neutral spectator and issues an urgent rallying call to fellow members of the profession, to the appointed guardians of their institutions, and even to all enlightened supporters of the cultural patrimony, enjoining them to defend and protect not merely the power, privileges, and interests ensconced in the *status quo* but Western Civilization itself. When this happens, one need not possess the gifts of an exceptional genealogist like Nietzsche or a thorough archaeologist like Foucault to recognize that "devotion to truth and the precision of scientific methods arose from the passion of scholars, their reciprocal hatreds, their fanatical and unending discussions, and their spirit of competition—the personal conflicts that slowly forged the weapons of reason."[2]

Talk of crisis seems to be a permanent feature of the humanist's repertoire and all too frequently it serves as a convenient rhetorical device to lend a sense of urgency or immediacy to the humanist's work. In the last few years, however, the more or less routine lamentations have given way to shrill calls for remedial intervention and even for disciplinary measures. The customary moans of the humanists' jeremiad have been replaced by a stentorian chorus clamouring for a return to the proven standards and values of the old dispensation. The present Secretary of Education, formerly the presidentially appointed Maecenas at the National Endowment for the Humanities, demands the restoration of sanity in the nation's educational system. His simple prescription: a core curriculum that would expose students to the great documents of Western civilization.[3] Meanwhile, from the halls of Harvard University—the belated American version of the imperial Museum at Alexandria—Professor W. Jackson Bate issues an appeal, *urbi et orbi*, urging the faithful—in this case, university administrators, alumni, and educated people generally—to rescue "the whole cultural heritage" from strangulation at the hands of the experts—that is, university professors—and re-establish the Renaissance ideal of *litterae humaniores*. The barbarians must have broken down the gates and entered the citadel, so that now one must face the enemy within. (Perhaps to circumvent the enemy, Bate wrote "The Crisis in English Studies" not for a professional journal but for the generally educated readership of *Harvard Magazine*.)[4] William Bennett and W. Jackson Bate probably have different ideas about the precise values embodied by the "great tradition" they appeal to, but both of them share a nostalgia for the threatened certitudes of the past and a readiness to recuperate a bygone era through administrative *fiat*.

The high office held by Secretary Bennett guarantees that his words and deeds have the most direct and visible impact on the administration of knowledge at all levels of the educational system. Yet, the views of W. Jackson Bate and his prestigious academic peers may ultimately prove more important and influential since they confer the authoritative stamp of approval, the certificate of legitimacy upon the pronouncements of the State's chief educational officer and effectively conceal the ideological agenda of his humanistic discourse. Moreover, the distinguished humanist speaking from within a university of Harvard's calibre generally commands greater respect, especially within academic circles, because of the presumption that the humanist-scholar harbors no interest other than the furtherance of knowledge whereas the politician seeks to satisfy the conflicting demands of many different constituencies. W. Jackson Bate's bleak assessment of the current state of the humanities, while only one out of many proffered by alarmed academics, vibrates with uncommon resonance for another important reason besides his eminent position in a most prestigious university, his remarkable scholarly output, and the great number of impressive honors and awards deservedly heaped upon him by the *cognoscenti*. Unlike several others who have vehemently expressed views similar to his, W. Jackson Bate cannot be fairly identified with the New Critical old guard against whom much postmodern criticism has been specifically levelled. One cannot adequately dismiss W. Jackson Bate's outburst as the expression of personal resentment by a disgruntled scholar who sees his preeminence subside with the emergence of a vigorous new faction within his discipline. As the range of his published work and his urbane style amply demonstrate, W. Jackson Bate never quite belonged to a specific dominant faction within the literary critical establishment, nor has he been generally associated with a narrow polemical position for or against a particular school of thought. Indeed, he can with full justification lay claim to that most benign epithet so highly prized by the liberal intelligentsia—*pluralist*.

W. Jackson Bate shapes his account of the current crisis in the humanities within the framework of a historical narrative—a clever and elegant move wholly in keeping with his insistence in the course of the essay on the crucial importance of history for the entire humanistic enterprise. What exactly Bate means by history needs to be examined and questioned, but first one must recall the main contours of his broad historical outline. The story of the present crisis, in Bate's version, starts in the 1880s with the widespread adoption by American universities of the German model of academic specialization. Ever since then humanistic studies have been steadily regressing to the point of utter disintegration. The decline originated with the division of the once unified humanities into separate departments; the center lost its solidity as each subdivision of disciplines generated further fragmentation. "Between 1880 and 1920 the humanities, now several departments, found themselves in the peculiar federation of states (and, very soon, counties and townships) that characterizes the modern university, held together less by loyalties to the institution and to the broader ideals of education than by the desire to be left alone to 'cultivate one's own garden' " (CES, 46). For a while, though, the humanistic ideal still had a home, for English departments took over the responsibilities shirked or neglected by other departments. Until 1950 or so, English departments addressed a broad spectrum of interests and attracted large numbers of students; they thus became "the flagship of the humanities." The fate of the humanities is now linked to that of English departments: "If English departments falter badly, all humanistic departments will suffer . . .'English' is a barometer and measure for other humanistic fields . . ." (CES, 47). In order to fully appreciate the nature and depth of the crisis in the humanities, then, one should look at the crisis in English studies. So, Bate turns his attention to the history and character of English departments, again starting his account with the 1880s.

W. Jackson Bate identifies two phases in the modern history of English departments. From the 1880s until the mid-1950s two sets of conflicting tendencies somehow coexisted within English departments. On the positive side, English departments assumed custody of the Renaissance concept of *litterae humaniores*. Unlike other branches (or counties, or townships, or horticultural preserves) of the humanities, English studies retained a broad base; unencumbered by the difficulties of a specialized vocabulary and free from the unavoidable limitations that accompany the study of foreign languages, English departments continued to provide access to the glorious tradition that stretches back to ancient Greece and Rome and that "carried Europe through the Renaissance with brilliant creativity, and, in the process, also produced the Enlightenment" (CES, 48). On the negative side, English departments also absorbed the deleterious tendencies of the late nineteenth century: the retreat, in the wake of Romanticism, by literature and the arts from the public arena to the restricted sphere of personal, idiosyncratic experience, and the increasing emphasis on the specialization of learning in a misguided imitation of the natural sciences. Adherence to the Renaissance legacy of *litterae humaniores* provided English departments with a sense of allegiance to a communal overarching ideal, whereas, at the same time, the new emphasis on the specialized organization of knowledge with its corollary stress on detailed scholarship and formalist analysis engendered within the same departments a sense of fragmentation. Yet, this "centrifugal heterogeneity," as Bate calls it, "was kept in precarious balance. Though actively practiced by only one in twenty, the Renaissance ideal of *litterae humaniores* was at least given lip service. Even militant specialists half sensed that it was the only umbrella under which their subjects could unite. And it still allowed the academic 'humanist' to feel that his or her subject was of central importance to life" (CES, 50).

The center could not be expected to hold forever, though, especially with the great changes that took place after 1955 when colleges and universities have had to cope with two unprecedented sociological phenomena. First came a period of tremendous growth during which the number of doctoral candidates increased more than tenfold in certain State universities. (Harvard, we are assured, was guilty only of a

much less drastic expansion.) In order to cope with these numbers, Bate
maintains, English departments gave up teaching the history of criticism
and literary theory, abandoned the task of transmitting the idealistic
legacy of *litterae humaniores*, and relied instead on the practical approach
made readily available by the New Criticism. "What quicker way to
'train' them—get them into the profession—than to junk, quickly, all
but the rudiments of the New Criticism (people concentrating on a text
or two, and pushing aside everything else)? For twenty years (though
there are notable exceptions), the profession engorged a huge group—
mostly all tenured by now—who regarded literature as a private preserve,
and were themselves innocent of history, of philology, of 'ideas' generally" (CES, 50). After two decades of seemingly unbridled expansion
came the inevitable bust: a disastrous crash in the academic job market,
a steep decline of undergraduate enrollments in liberal arts courses, and
a blind search for remedies which forgetful or ignorant of the guiding
ideals of *litterae humaniores* only plunge the humanities into a deeper
chasm. Now with the devastation nearly complete, the humanities face
self-destruction unless university administrators heed Bate's urgent alarm
signal and charge immediately to the rescue. Who knows?—maybe they
will rouse themselves to action and reprieve the desperately distressed
Mnemosyne and her daughters in the nick of time, before their predicament becomes truly hopeless!

W. Jackson Bate's appeal to university administrators raises an exceedingly baffling question. Why should he turn for help to the very
same elements that, as he himself explains in the body of his essay,
presided over the demise of *litterae humaniores*? Are the present administrators he addresses any different from those who for the past three
decades have been infatuated with notions of productivity, visibility,
specialization, prestige? Does he, perhaps, see evidence of a new administrative breed emerging that will reverse current trends by giving
preference to the wide ranging, broad-minded humanists who devote
their lives to studying and teaching over the busy entrepreneurial researchers who obtain large grants, regularly publish books and articles,
are omnipresent at large conferences, and have achieved superstar status
in the profession and beyond? W. Jackson Bate knows only too well
how and on whom current administrators lavish their universities'
resources to really believe that they have lately undergone a change
of heart. The reason for the surprising direction of Bate's exhortation
must be sought elsewhere in his essay: not in what little he has to say

about administrators, but in the way he couches his whole account of the disintegration of the humanities in the form of a potted history of the modern university as an institution. One must needs recognize, in other words, that W. Jackson Bate's concern centers not so much on knowledge as on the institution of knowledge, not on *litterae humaniores* per se but on the way they are administered, not on what individual scholars and researchers actually do but on how to ensure that their work retains its organic links to the purposive structuration of learning and the normative pedagogical function of the university. Only administrators sitting at the very center of institutional power can exercise without too many encumbrances the direct regulative control that would preserve the unity and integrity of the official domain of knowledge. The "unity of knowledge," in defence of which W. Jackson Bate writes, faces its severest challenge from within, from those scholars and researchers who have actively questioned the tradition of *litterae humaniores*, who have countered its claims, and who have consciously abjured the duty to uphold it or abide by its sanctions. Against these refractory members of the profession, against these heretical renegades of the intellectual clerisy, only the supreme authorities of the academic hierarchy can summarily intervene by issuing edicts of interdiction and excommunication. W. Jackson Bate, therefore, implores university administrators to preserve unity by once again exercising their rights of veto over appointment and tenure decisions.

W. Jackson Bate attenuates the harshness—indeed, the authoritarian viciousness—of his stance by his profession of fidelity to the memory of the Renaissance humanistic ideal, his devotion to the inherited tradition of Western civilization, and his purported attachment to history. He presents himself as the embattled custodian of an endangered memory, an abandoned sense of history, and a well-nigh forgotten literary tradition. Yet, ultimately, what Bate and the administrators he hails endeavor to salvage from what they regard as the ruins of the current crisis in the humanities cannot possibly be Mnemosyne, Clio, and her siblings. Nobody, not even a well-educated Harvard alumnus, seriously believes that the fate of memory, history, and the arts depends solely upon the state of affairs at American universities; no university has ever been mistaken for Mount Helicon. Bate's real worries are about the Alexandrian Museum, the legendary prototypical university, the place built by the dispensers of learning with monies provided by the emperor to house the Muses, as in a gilded cage, in order to contain, control, and administer them. As for Mnemosyne, her vagaries too can be held in check within the Museum where she is reduced to voluntary memory. "This is the uniform memory of intelligence," as Beckett puts it in his discussion of Proust, "and it can be relied upon to reproduce for our gratified inspection those impressions of the past that were consciously and intelligently formed."[5] Inside the walls of the Museum serenity normally prevails; the turmoil of history yields to the tranquil dignity of the orderly arrangement and memorization (or, should one say, memorialization?) of monuments which both singly and as a collection attest to the wisdom bequeathed us by the past and mock the efforts of the latecomer to forge history differently. In his anxiety to maintain the peacefulness of the awe-inspiring halls of the Museum, Bate requests the endorsement of its caretakers to expel and bar from future admission those raucous, disputatious voices clamoring for a reassessment of the value of the monuments, the rearrangement of the orderly display, and the introduction of new exhibits. One need not be an alarmist to realize that if the parvenus take over or have their way, not only will the Museum lose its character, not only will history look different, but the very nature of the Museum itself will be undermined and the governing concepts of history will undergo radical revison. For this reason, Bate seeks to rally support for his version of history through his version of history.

In some respects, W. Jackson Bate's narrative bears a close resemblance to fable and derives its broad outline from the structure of basic myths. To start with, he divides the history of knowledge into two parts separated by a fall. In the prelapsarian era "a unity of knowledge and learned concern was taken for granted" (CES, 46). During this golden age, the values of *litterae humaniores* held undisputed sway. After the fall, occasioned in the 1880s by a craving for the forbidden fruit of the German model of specialization, there has been a steady deterioration towards chaos. Redemption and salvation, however, remain possible if sufficient determination can be mustered to cast out the false prophets and embrace once more the teachings of the old masters. Now that we have reached the nadir of Western civilization and are wearied by a hundred years of aimless, guideless wandering through a decentered wasteland, now more than ever we need to re-establish our ties with the intellectual giants of the prelapsarian past. In fact, Bate prescribes a heavy dosage of history to cure the current doldrums. The present craze for critical and literary theory, he believes, resulted from the vacuum created by the fall into specialized fragmentation and more specifically by the antihistorical bias of a degenerate New Criticism. Hence, the need to return to history. But what does Bate mean by history in this case? He means the history enshrined in the Museum, a history that presents itself as already complete. Strictly speaking, this conception of the past cannot properly be called history since it already contains within it all the answers for the present. "Scarcely one approach to the arts has been advanced during the last twenty years that—in its essential premises—has not been examined and answered (often profoundly) in the previous two thousand years" (CES, 50). Why should humanists bother with Derrida, much less allow themselves to be intimidated by his vaunted "deconstructionism"? Anyone familiar with the history of philosophy knows that his questions are "old hat"; they were raised by the pre-Socratics and later by David Hume and the answers are still available in Plato's dialogues and in Kant's tomes. Besides, Hume "would doubtless consider the deconstructionists premises and certainly their conclusions to be of kindergarten nature" (CES, 52). The past, thus conceived, becomes the preemption of history, the burial ground of the present, the grimmest memorial to the vanity of all human effort, the aprioristic erasure of change and difference.

Elsewhere, W. Jackson Bate has written brilliantly and persuasively on the burden of the past; in this essay, however, he uses the past as a club to smite all who doubt the efficacy of litterae humaniores. He also manages to convince himself that the exponents and followers of contemporary criticism and theory are ignorant of history, that they have not read the old masterpieces. Of the structuralists he says that "they were fundamentally historically innocent" and that "philosophy from the beginning to Kant, and even after Kant, was a nearly closed book to them" (CES, 50-51). To be sure, there is ample evidence that many structuralists, like countless others before and after them, paid scant notice to history and that philosophical training, especially in the Continental tradition, has all too often received short shrift in Anglo-American universities. Nevertheless, this should not obscure the fact that structuralism and poststructuralism have provided a major incentive for many to read philosophy. If one were to study Claude Lévi-Strauss' work attentively, for instance, one would certainly end up reading Kant, among many other old masters.[6] Bate similarly distorts the facts when he declares that "Derrida significantly never turns to the really major philosophers except to snatch at stale pessimisms (e.g.

Nietzsche), which appear to deny the possibility of finding truth" (CES, 52). In fact, Derrida impels one to read or reread Plato, Descartes, Kant, Hegel, Husserl, and a host of other "classics" apart from Nietzsche. And what about the attentive re-examination of the entire Western philosophical tradition instigated by hermeneutics, which Bate declines to mention? Bate cannot admit to any of this because his case rests on the presupposition that a true knowledge of the past, a thorough grounding in the tradition cannot but lead to an affirmation of the unity of knowledge and a reinforcement of the structure of its Museum.

W. Jackson Bate identifies the abandonment of the Renaissance ideal of *litterae humaniores* as simultaneously a major cause and a devastating consequence of the retreat by the humanities, and more specifically literary studies, from the larger arena of public issues and values. The aesthetic emphasis on personal experience, the insistence on the autonomy of literature, the ever narrower focus of specialized scholarship, the increasingly complex and inaccessible "jargon" of humanistic disciplines—all these factors have, in Bate's view, deprived the humanities of their rightfully central place in human affairs. Fragmentation, that is to say, rendered the humanities marginal, it sundered their relationship with the world. Bate compares the situation in the humanities with the predicament of Antaeus who derived his strength from direct contact with his mother Gaea. Once Hercules lifted him off Earth, Antaeus became powerless and was easily strangled. For their survival, the humanities must remain in touch with history—history, here, meaning not so much the past as the "common experience of life."

Taken in isolation, Bate's injunction that the humanities take possession, once again, of their prominent role in the public forum may be regarded as an encouragement to cultivate an open exchange with the world beyond the confines of academic institutions—the world of social concerns, political struggles, economic exploitation, and so on. Unfortunately, as Prufrock feared, "That is not it at all,/That is not what I meant, at all." Bate's vision of earthbound humanistic studies has nothing in common with, say, Edward Said's concept of worldliness or Frank Lentricchia's notion of the necessary historicity of literature, although it does seem to bear, vaguely, some remote resemblance to Gerald Graff's desire to recuperate realism. In fact, Bate evinces his minimal interest in the world outside the university by the way he excludes almost completely from his account of the regress of *litterae humaniores* any serious consideration of economic, political, and social factors. He alludes in passing to the great shortage of teachers in the post-War period that led to the rapid expansion of American universities and to "the draconian effects of inflation [and] public disillusionment with widespread higher education as the key to a new society" (CES, 50) that contributed to the collapse of the academic job market in the 1970s. He makes no mention of the relationships between universities and corporations, the government, the military, and the culture industry; he provides no sense of the changing role of intellectuals in society during the last hundred years; he does not acknowledge the importance or the impact of technology, national and international politics, the cold war, and the many other obvious phenomena that have shaped this century. While he objects strenuously (and justifiably, one must add) to the way in which literature has become the private preserve of specialists, Bate with his blinkered view of history contributes nothing at all to the removal of those protective discursive boundaries that keep the rest of the world at bay.

What is worse, when Bate encounters evidence of legitimate contemporary socio-cultural-political concerns making their mark upon the university curriculum, he considers such evidence indicative of the fragmentation and lack of seriousness that bedevil the humanities. He finds no justification for the introduction of courses in women's studies and "ethnic" literature into the curriculum; they simply pander to "current enthusiasms"; the issues they address would be better treated within the context of the lost tradition of *litterae humaniores*. "Women writers who had worked, with pride, in larger literary traditions, were snatched arbitrarily—whether major or minor—and a field overnight was created in 'women's studies' " (CES, 51). Setting aside the fact that anyone who believes that "women's studies" appeared suddenly one fine (or benighted, depending on the point of view) morning must be historically blind, the notion that women were snatched arbitrarily from a larger tradition is ludicrous since women never had a voice in that tradition to start with. Indeed, if the humanistic tradition that Bate extols contained within it the history of women's struggles, then the emergence of women's studies would hardly have come as a surprise. How could women have worked "with pride," as Bate contends, in a tradition that not only ignored them but demeaned them? The great tradition of which Bate writes empowers and legitimates or, at the very least, lends a measure of respectability to all the forces of resistance lined up against women's demands for their rightful place in society. For just as Rev.

Jerry Falwell quotes the Bible to sanctify his antifeminist crusade, others could invoke Xenophon's *Oeconomicus*, Aristotle's *Historia Animalium*, Juvenal's *Satires*, Aquinas' *Summa*, or even Rousseau's *Emile*, to mention a few random canonical texts where woman's "proper," subordinate domestic role and her inferiority—depravity, even—are taken to be obvious, incontrovertible features of the *natural* order and, further, apparently unsusceptible to cultural remedy.

W. Jackson Bate's fierce opposition to and denigration of women's studies and "ethnic" studies reveals the real exclusionary limits of liberal pluralism. He strongly favors a diversity of points of view and a variety of methods and approaches within the humanities only insofar as they reinforce the "unity of knowledge." Through diversity, he thinks, one can appreciate the range, the richness, the all-absorbing, all-embracing power of the capacious humanistic tradition. Diversity of this kind eschews real difference, it serves only to accommodate the largest possible number of elements within a homogenous whole. The humanistic pluralist feels impelled to enlarge the circumference of *litterae humaniores* as much as possible, but only in order to extend the authoritative reach of its stable center. Excessive specialization tends to bring about a shrinkage of the circumference. The growth of women's studies and "ethnic" studies, however, presents a much more serious danger because they directly challenge the authority of the dominant tradition by preparing the ground for the formation of a counter-tradition. Contrary to what Bate asserts, women have not "snatched" anything away from the tradition; instead, they have deemed it necessary to articulate their counter-memory, to produce their own history, to feminize Clio. The pluralism of liberal humanists wedded to the old dispensation cannot countenance with equanimity such expressions of radical difference; it cannot allow Mnemosyne to run loose or Clio to leave the precincts of the established Museum.

Although W. Jackson Bate characterizes the history of literary studies during the last one hundred years as one continuous drift towards greater and greater fragmentation, the crisis he descries reveals some crucial discontinuities, certain important cleavages which he chooses to ignore. One simply cannot lump together philological excess, literary antiquarianism, the New Criticism, "ethnic" studies, women's studies, and deconstruction and offer them all as examples of the same incremental tendency towards "centrifugal heterogeneity." The New Criticism, for instance, with its dogma of the autonomy of the work of art, far from being inimical to *litterae humaniores*, stemmed in good part from an effort to protect the metaphysical ideal of the humanistic tradition from the perceived materialistic onslaught of positivism. The widespread adoption of the procedures of practical criticism admittedly contributed, together with numerous other factors, to a significant diminution of emphasis on the historical and philosophical education that normally accompany literary studies. Nonetheless, this should not be allowed to obscure the fact that the New Critics subscribed to a great many of the basic goals and values that Bate attributes to the Renaissance ideal. Notwithstanding the early work of I.A. Richards, the New Critics upheld literature as "a form of knowing" and preserved faith in "the moral and educative effort on human character of knowledge" (CES, 47)— just like erstwhile humanists eulogized by Bate; they strove to hone the faculty of judgment in their students, they were deeply suspicious of what they took to be a drift towards subjectivism in the Romantic tradition, and they highly admired Coleridge's declarations (a sample of which Bate quotes approvingly) on the unifying power of the imagination. One need only recall T.S. Eliot's essays to dispel any notion that the New Criticism represented a flight from the classical core of the tradition.

The New Criticism, specialized though it was in a given sense, stands as an example of consolidation rather than fragmentation of the humanistic tradition. W.K. Wimsatt, for instance, relied on Aquinas and Kant to support his view of aesthetics as an "impractical stasis."[7] Cleanth Brooks accorded literature and literary criticism the status of metaphysics,[8] thus placing literary discourse in a tradition that stretches back, at least, to Aristotle. Further, all the major New Critics although profoundly suspicious of the merits of the historical approaches to literature prevalent in the late nineteenth and early twentieth centuries, nevertheless betrayed a deep interest in (monumental) history in their preoccupation with establishing or revising the literary canon. For abundant evidence of their general adherence to the values and, in many cases, the vocabulary of the mainstream theological tradition one need only turn to their major works. They may have promoted the idea of reading and interpretation as a private, unworldly activity, but they cannot be counted among those whom Bate accuses of giving up their loyalty to the institution (i.e. the university) and of fostering a "desire to be left alone to 'cultivate one's own garden." Far from allowing anyone to solitarily cultivate a private patch, the New Critics succeeded in putting into place the disciplinary machinery that would ensure the en-

forcement of conformity. For a few decades their systematic demarcation of the terrain of English studies denied status and legitimacy to
the disruptive and unsettling discourses of women's studies, "ethnic"
literature, and so on. While the grip of the New Criticism remained
firm, the operations of English departments fully supported the putative
humanistic goals of their institutions and occupied a central place within
them. If, as Bate claims, English studies have reached an impasse because
the professors are now "leaving it to the untutored student to try to
find the answers, and to try to put it all together into meaning (an in-
tolerable burden on students of college age)" (CES, 53)—if this is the
baneful consequence of contemporary criticism, then the New Criticism
must be seen to contain the paradigm for a solution and certainly not
be condemned as a major cause of the present crisis in the humanities.
For the New Critics spoke with surety; they offered complete knowledge
to counter the doubts raised by positivism; they reaffirmed the miracle
of communication against the grim materialism of science; they posited
universal values and normative judgment in the face of the supposedly
relativistic temper of their times.[9] The New Critics were definitely not
guilty of inducing "centrifugal heterogeneity" and fragmentation; true,
they narrowed the boundaries of literary discourse, but by doing so they
reinforced its homogeneity and, above all, its disciplinary authority.

"Disciplines," Foucault has demonstrated, "constitute a system
of control in the production of discourse, fixing its limits through the
action of an identity taking the form of permanent reactivation of the
rules."[10] The debate between traditional humanists like W. Jackson Bate
and the New Critics arises out of disagreement over where and how
the limits or boundaries of literary discourse ought to be fixed. Both
camps, however, share a conception of their field as a discipline, as a
system of control over the discursive practice that constitutes their sphere
of knowledge. Moreover, each side believes that its own definition of
the discursive boundaries of the discipline ensures the authoritativeness
of the discipline itself, while the opponents' misguided demarcations
endanger its very survival. Hardly ever missing from these disputes are
displays—sometimes restrained but at other times histrionic—of the exclusionary willfulness from which the discipline derives its character
and by means of which it exercises supervisory power over its terrain.
To be sure, the humanistic rhetoric of openness, the declarations of
commitment to the free exchange of ideas almost always accompany
and frequently camouflage the disciplinary demarcation of boundaries.

Just as Bate emphasizes the breadth and the inclusionary nature of *litterae humaniores* while insisting on the need to exclude certain topics or courses and to prohibit the "wrong" type of scholars from university appointments, so also Cleanth Brooks declares himself in favor of the "free trade" of ideas and "free passage" across the boundaries while defending the need for "a clearer marking of boundary lines" and condemning the "muddling of the boundary markers."[11]

The adjustment or realignment of the extant and generally accepted boundary lines inevitably provokes howls of "Crisis!", premature obituary notices about the profession or discipline, demands for a return to the *status quo ante*, and even nostalgic appeals for a great leap backwards to the *status quo* that preceded the *status quo ante*. When such an atmosphere prevails the custodians and beneficiaries of the established order tend automatically to identify the agitators favoring change as a revolutionary *avant-garde*. Paradoxically, the agents of change often turn out to be quite conservative, not to say reactionary, as was the case with many New Critics. In many other instances, new movements or schools of thought that promise to bring radical transformation in their wake end up merely as instruments of a superficial *aggiornamento*. Such movements, which can normally be accommodated within the dominant discursive order without excessive difficulty, help (in a sense) to reinvigorate the discipline by giving it the appearance of dealing with new problems and by supplying it with urgent reasons for further elaborating its already mightily elaborate discursive rules and procedures. The term "crisis" when employed to describe these phenomena loses much of its meaning; it implies that a discipline is undergoing a critical change, that a threshold, a decisive turning point has been reached when, in fact, no more than a renovation takes place. Genuine disciplinary crises are rare; truly critical criticism seldom achieves widespread currency and when it does almost never lasts too long before being assimilated by the very same discourse whose regulative authority it initially challenges. In a different and perhaps somewhat cynical perspective, all of this may be taken to suggest that crises, in certain ways, must be induced in order to make criticism possible, or else to ensure the perpetuation of critical activity.

One need not be either a sympathizer or a denigrator of postmodern criticism to agree that the great changes wrought on the landscape of the humanities in general, but most particularly in literary studies, since the middle of the 1960s were occasioned, to a very significant extent, by the exhaustion of overworked and outworn practices. An intricate conjuncture of circumstances, much too complex to unravel here, induced a number of critics, historians, and theorists, many of them employed by English, Modern Languages, and Comparative Literature departments at American universities, to give serious consideration to some exciting European developments in the human sciences. The breach in geographic boundaries widened as Paris, Geneva, Heidelberg, Marburg, Frankfurt, and other centers of intellectual ferment attracted increasing attention from across the Atlantic; the blurring of disciplinary demarcations grew as the vocabularies of phenomenology, hermeneutics, structural anthropology, linguistics, psychoanalysis, and so on gradually came to form part of the literary critics' discursive repertoire. During the last five years of the 1960s it was exceedingly difficult for Anglo-American litterateurs to determine what all these newly imported enthusiasms or "discoveries" had in common other than their esoteric, alien character and their destabilizing influence. The terrain of the humanistic disciplines and their discursive regularities came under assault from so many different directions that for quite some time little effort was made to conscientiously identify the various enemies and to carefully distinguish them one from the other. Many of those who remained attached to the endangered order and were determined to uphold its values resorted to blanket condemnations and excoriated "theory" and "criticism," *tout d'un coup*. The staunch defenders of the Museum, no less than its purported invaders, benefited substantially from the commotion—the new polemics offered a welcome diversion from the repetitive boredom of old debates, the combative atmosphere infused the normally stodgy discussions among experts with fresh spiritedness, the inflamed rhetoric of scholarly battles breathed new life into academic journals, conferences, and conventions that had been struggling against the *ennui* generated by pedantry and predictability. Almost twenty years ago, Paul de Man asked: "What interest can this Gallic turbulence have for literary studies in America?"[12] Looking back one can say that at least part of the interest rested in the opportunity to generate new interest in a somnolent discipline and provide its practitioners with a reason to keep busy and remain productive.

By no means does this signify that *all* the throes of crisis experienced over the last two decades have been spurious. The discursive boundaries and disciplinary authority of the humanities have been and remain today under considerable strain. In literary studies, for example, Paul de

Man's assessment, by and large, still holds true: "The trend in the Continental criticism, whether it derives its language from sociology, psychoanalysis, ethnology, linguistics or even certain forms of philosophy, can be quickly summarized: it represents a methodologically motivated attack on the notion that a literary or poetic consciousness is in any way a privileged consciousness whose use of language can pretend to escape, to some degree, from the duplicity, the confusion, the untruth that we take for granted in the everyday use of language."[13] Nevertheless, the critical thrust spurred by the advent of Continental trends has been dulled, the attack on privilege largely blunted, the threat to discursive regularities and disciplinary authority rendered marginal. Once the various oppositional voices were grouped, categorized, named, and their positions systematized, they could be managed and to a very large extent accommodated within the persistent institutional order. The brief trajectory of structuralism across the American academic horizon stands as a useful illustration of this process. The initial furor directed towards structuralism while it served as a convenient catch-all label for the many ideas emanating from Paris quickly died down after one of its most articulate Anglo-American proponents presented a discriminate, systematic version of its sources and tenets in such reasonable terms as to render it innocuous. Jonathan Culler persuaded many skeptics that structuralism posed no radical threat to anything but the most inflexible orthodoxies; he reassured the readers of *Structuralist Poetics* (1975) that their received notions may be couched in a new vocabulary without abandoning any of the most cherished fundamental dogmas and hierarchies. The fact that by the time Culler published his soothing account structuralism had already been overtaken by the more rigorously antihumanistic stance of deconstruction was, for the time being, set aside. Indeed, Culler sought to further assuage any lingering doubts when, addressing the topic "Structuralism and Grammatology" at a *boundary 2* symposium in 1979, he affirmed that even though deconstruction had displaced structuralism which itself had succeeded the New Criticism, the basic project for criticism remained substantially unchanged, for what lies beyond formalism is still more formalism.[14] Subsequently, Culler caught up with semiotics and deconstruction and guided his readers through those labyrinths with similar tranquillizing effects.

Jonathan Culler's work represents only one, albeit prominent, example among many others that together contribute to the preservation of institutionalized disciplinary boundaries, the continued impervious-

ness of much discursive practice to the impingement of worldly concerns, the persistent resistence of the discourse of criticism to the critical
demands of a troublesome history that remains unarticulated and un-
authorized. One may be dazzled by the interpretative acrobatics of J.
Hillis Miller, or mesmerized by Geoffrey Hartman's seemingly endless
meanderings through the uncharted textual wilderness, but in the end
one cannot fail to notice that notwithstanding their professed devotion to de-mystification, de-authorization, de-privileging of the institutions of reading, they remain strangely cut off from the arena of history;
that in spite of their reiterated oppositional stance, it remains virtually
impossible to determine what precisely they are opposed to. Many deconstructors seem to be so entranced by their "joyous affirmation[s]
of the freeplay" of texts that they have little time to consider the deprivation of another sort of freedom suffered by those who are not blessed
by the cultural consolations of irony. The interminable debates among
critics have, by virtue of their endlessness, frequently contributed to
the preservation of criticism as a distinctive form of discourse within
the academy. These debates have also totally absorbed the interest of
most participating critics; an overwhelming fascination with contrariety
in itself seems to govern the indulgence in contrariness. Criticism has
had much of its energy spent in the power struggles among different
theoretical camps, and the struggle itself has acquired greater importance than its outcome. As long as the vigorous competition among
critics continues, critical discourse displays its autotelic character but
at the same time conceals its inconsequentiality from itself.

In the meantime it would be redundant to argue simply that the
power struggles within the discipline are irresponsible; it is much more
important to urge a renewed avowal of the critical task of criticism.
This entails taking action against the erection of exclusionary disciplinary
boundaries, challenging the authority embedded in discursive regularities,
militating against all institutionalized configurations of power, resisting
the seductive allure of the rhetoric of ironic detachment, giving voice
to the histories suppressed by and excluded from the "official" memory
of the inherited tradition. Above all, in order for criticism to retain
its critical edge and not become itself disciplinary, its practitioners must
work incessantly against all those barriers that diversely shield intellectuals, individually and collectively, from the major social, cultural,
political, economic, and moral struggles of their times.[15] The humanistic
tradition does not face imminent collapse, as W. Jackson Bate fears;

the Alexandrian Museum in the shape of the modern university shows even fewer signs of damage to its foundation than it supposedly incurred fifteen or twenty years ago. If there ever was a serious crisis in the humanities, it is now surmounted as criticism has been largely (though not yet entirely) absorbed and accommodated within the secure boundaries of the terrain it may have momentarily threatened with upheaval.

The critical attitude needs to be revivified as a different voice that is intent on making a difference. The papers gathered in this volume exemplify various ways in which the critical intelligence can exercise itself in the effort to remain open to the concerns normally bounded off by disciplinary demarcations, to disclose the economy of power and privilege camouflaged by the rhetoric of scholarly discourse, and to create space through genealogical critiques of the monumental tradition for the articulation of critical versions of history.

NOTES

1. Michel Foucault, *Power/Knowledge*, ed. Colin Gordon, trans. C. Gordon et al. (New York: Pantheon, 1980), 69. Hereafter cited in the text as *PK*.

2. Michel Foucault, *Language, Counter-Memory, Practice*, ed. Donald F. Bouchard, trans. D. F. Bouchard and Sherry Simon (New York: Cornell Univ. Press, 1977), 142.

3. See William J. Bennett, *To Reclaim a Legacy* (Washington, D.C.: National Endowment for the Humanities, 1984).

4. W. Jackson Bate, "The Crisis in English Studies," *Harvard Magazine* 85 (Sept.-Oct., 1982): 46-53. Hereafter cited in the text as *CES*.

5. Samuel Beckett, *Proust* (New York: Grove Press, 1931), 19.

6. For Claude Lévi-Strauss' description of his work as "Kantism without a transcendental subject," see "Overture" in *The Raw and the Cooked* (New York: Harper & Row, 1969), especially p. 11.

7. Cf., for example, W. K. Wimsatt, *The Verbal Icon* (The Univ. of Kentucky Press, 1954), especially pp. 272ff.

8. For one of Cleanth Brooks' most straightforward appeals to metaphysics, see *The Well-Wrought Urn* (New York: Harcourt Brace, 1947), 264ff.

9. Cf., for example, Cleanth Brooks, "Preface" in *The Well-Wrought Urn*.

10. Michel Foucault, "The Discourse on Language" in *The Archaeology of Knowledge*, trans. A. M. Sheridan Smith (New York: Harper & Row, 1972), 224.

11. Cleanth Brooks, "Foreword" in *Critiques and Essays in Criticism*, ed. R. W. Stallman (New York: Ronald Press, 1949), xxi.

12. Paul de Man, *Blindness and Insight* (New York: Oxford University Press, 1971), 5.

13. Ibid., 9.

14. Cf. *The Question of Textuality*, ed. W. V. Spanos, P.A. Bové, and D. O'Hara (Bloomington, Ind.: Indiana Univ. Press, 1982), 75-85.

15. On this topic see the superb analysis provided by Paul A. Bové in his *Intellectuals in Power: A Genealogy of Critical Humanism* (New York: Columbia Univ. Press, 1986).

2. The Function of the Literary Critic in the Postmodern World

PAUL A. BOVÉ

I

The major modern forms of aesthetic and moral literary criticism are now illegitimate. The professional study of the "form and meaning" of enduring works of "great beauty" and "moral value" can no longer be justified in those terms alone. Those who feel it can (or should be) need to explain the declining role of poetry and literary education in America and must, in so doing, confront the fundamental political and economic forces which marginalize the humanities and the poetic imagination. They must not do this only in theory, so to speak;[1] they must also lay down a practical plan which they can show has some chance of succeeding in the face of all the cultural and institutional forces which oppose the continuation of critical intelligence and imagination in what many like to call our "postmodern world."[2]

These residual humanists—they must *prove* they are more than residual—should also confront the all-too-painful personal realities of the profession, especially the intellectual and pedagogical inertia and irresponsibility of those very common professorial figures who not only fearfully mock serious intellectual practice as "theory," but retire into the semiemployment of their "teaching," "scholarship," and above all "*ADMINISTRATION*," safely away from hard work, the public-intellectual sphere, and the intransigent political and cultural issues facing our society. There is a nearly endless list of these issues which quite specifically impinge on the skills and supposed values of literary criticism: one thinks of such immediately "critical" topics as the "death of the subject," narrative problematics, the instabilities of interpretation, etc.,

23

to say nothing of the socially more important but professionally more distant issues of the culture industry, the colonization of the unconscious and the "third-world" by the new "information industries,"[3] the ever-increasing ties between knowledge and research and the military,[4] the challenges to the great explanatory models of the modern period, and the need to find ways to theorize the decentered politics of the age of internationalized capital.

Even though we live in an age which increasingly exercises both hegemony and domination in and through sign-based structures, the literary academy not only has failed to reorganize itself to address the new social and intellectual problems created by these structures; it also has returned to "core-curricula" and tried to minimize the influence of "radicals" within the academy.[5] Even worse, so-called "men and women of the sixties" have adopted a high moral tone (exploiting the communal rhetoric of the sixties?) and speak of their "love of literature" to justify their own decisions to operate the most repressive and anti-intellectual elements of university bureaucracy—often as failed critics whose professional survival has been a fluke of demographic history: that is, they were hired and tenured at a time of teacher shortages, have accomplished little, and block the way of other better trained, more intelligent, less self-centered, and politically more concerned scholars.

Of course, when speaking of the profession as a whole, my description of this situation is exaggerated and requires considerable amplification to be demonstrative; nonetheless, (especially when speaking of very many academicians who have made their careers by running programs), it is, I feel, reasonably accurate. When one considers, for example, the existence of a group like Physicians for Social Responsibility adapting traditional medical concerns for health and life to counter the campaign of misinformation undertaken by bureaucrats, manufacturers, and others who profiteer in the "rearming of America," the absence of an institutionalized (and often even individual) response by literary humanists who are—supposedly—most caring of humane values and most able to examine the workings of sign systems, history, the creation of images, the manipulation of audiences, etc.—this absence is most amazing, but also understandable.

Of course many (but I think not most) literary scholars and cultural critics do address these and related issues in their work and do help their students to acquire the skills and knowledge to treat them as well, but we must keep in mind the force of Louis Althusser's remark: "those teachers who . . . attempt to turn the few weapons they can find in the history and learning they 'teach' against the ideology, the system and the practices in which they are trapped . . . are a kind of hero . . . [the majority] do not even begin to suspect the 'work' the system . . . forces them to do, or worse, put all their heart and ingenuity into performing it with the most advanced awareness. . . ."[6]

In a recent conversation with a distinguished critic who chairs a comparative literature program and directs an undergraduate human- ities program, I rediscovered an all-too-common anticritical dimension to so-called American pluralism. This critic was willing, he said, to allow those he calls "deconstructionists" and others who "do that kind of stuff" to join the literature faculties of his university as long as they did not become dominant, as long as no "critical mass" was established which would shift the "balance of power" in the faculty. Why? Because he and his friends believed that all literary critical points of view should be represented on faculties; that no single point of view has a monop- oly on the truth; and that it is only collegial that everyone should be allowed to do their own thing. A majority of "contemporary" critics would not be acceptable, he felt, because they would attack pluralism itself (it is not clear that he has not overestimated his differences from the majority of "contemporary critics").

I refer to this incident not to illustrate the sad state in which we find liberalism in this unaware critic's pluralism, but to draw attention to his anticritical position: no possibility exists, as far as he and others like him are concerned, to demonstrate the greater desirability of any crtical position over another; they are all equal as forms of professional practice. This is the sort of position we are accustomed to associate with the careerist antitheoretical defenders of a pragmatic professionalism. What is interesting about this conversation is that it suggests that such pragmatic positions give ideological voice to the "silent majority" within the profession itself. What is most disturbing about this convenient ar- rangement between the leading representative figures and the purchasers of their books is its reduction of the critical mind to a nihilistic ascesis which is largely explainable in class-terms. Since such an explanation would take more space than I have available, let me simply say that this "critic" had reduced the value of critical reason in intellectual life, education, and culture to a consumeristic aesthetic of personal taste, "tolerance," and competition for rewards. He articulated a position as likely, I submit, to threaten civilization as any of the so-called "ad-

vanced" theories of contemporary criticism. Above all, his words represent the dominant institutional attitude toward literary criticism, an
attitude which has become its purpose: gratification and the acquisition of exploitable skills.

II

    American literary critics are not very likely to study or to write
much about the purpose and nature of their institutionalized discipline.
Texts like Ohmann's *English in America*, Graff's *Literature Against Itself*,
Said's *Orientalism* and *The World, the Text, and the Critic*, parts of Hartman's *Criticism in the Wilderness*, or Lentricchia's *After the New Criticism*
and *Criticism and Social Change*[7] are not only an odd lot, but noticeable
because to varying degrees they all attempt—in their different ways—
to relate the ends of literary study to the important social and intellectual issues of the time as these are reflected in the works and practices
of other disciplines.

    One might be able to imagine an occasion when texts of Wolfgang
Iser or other so-called "reader response" critics interested in interpretive
communities and competence models could be useful in addressing such
issues; but until today no one has found a way to overcome the essentially ahistorical, professionalistic, and idealistic tendencies of these
"methods" and "positions" and turn them to any social, critical purpose.[8] The task of making such texts useful is complicated by the existence of books like Culler's *Structuralist Poetics* or *On Deconstruction*.
Yet without critical reflection on the history and practice of institutional literary study and scholarly production within modern and
postmodern societies, humanistic educators and intellectuals will be of
no help in our current cultural and political crises. No matter whether
one believes, like Gramsci, in the formation of organic intellectuals
for revolutionary purposes or, like Habermas, in inventing principles
of organization to adapt our system to its problems—or in some other
similar position—the critic or literary intellectual must establish connections with others whose work can help us understand and act on
our present situation.

    Unfortunately, North American literary criticism has very few prac-
titioners whose stature is such that their work is of significance to many
scholars in other fields or who are important originary figures within

our general culture as are Marx, Freud, Keynes, Dewey, and perhaps even Chomsky. One can even suggest that barring the non-academic Edmund Wilson and with the partial exception of Lionel Trilling, no literary critic has achieved the position of general cultural significance enjoyed, for example, by Reinhold Niebuhr from the 1930s to the 1960s. Of course, we must admit that it seems unlikely that our more techno-cratic society could ever again need a general intellectual[9] to elaborate the ruling class's ideology as Niebuhr once did or as Croce did even more clearly in Italy.[10] But it seems strange that in an information-based society—which relies increasingly on the manipulation of symbols, signs, and testing data to control and exploit political and economic oppor-tunities, often to the detriment of less powerfully placed people at home and abroad—literary critics, those most thoroughly trained in and sup-posedly committed to the study of such semiotic processes, have not seriously taken up a position of opposition to their repressive use.[11]

Academic literary study is, in some ways, of very recent vintage[12] and appears destined to a short life. It may well go on for years as a self-renewing professionalized institution often can—despite its difficulties in reproducing. Perhaps all the recent agony over and theorizing about the profession suggests that its contradictions and distortions have become so pressing as to leave its more anxious members little to ab-sorb their energies except efforts to find what can at best be a merely verbal legitimation of their position and function. Of course, there are those who feel no anxiety at all: these are either the habituated time-passers whose "common sense" keeps them going or the unsuccessful professionals who might be established figures in elite universities or well-funded specialists in composition and pedagogy. At times all of these shadows combine in one misty figure.[13]

A thorough and convincing explanation of how and why the legitimacy of academic literary study has come to require this profes-sionalized apology would demand a very long story, indeed. Now it is enough to remember the originary work of I. A. Richards and to recall how "practical" criticism cultivated the delicate sensitivity necessary to the fine art of balancing paradoxes and other forms of verbal instability in a pattern of critically resolved or suspended stress. We should remember that Richards called this cultivation "training in discrimina-tion" and that as a form of professional and cultural specialization it contributed to the division of labor. We might also agree upon one result of this divisive training: it took critical thinking up into "lit. crit."

Despite the New Criticism's antagonism toward "positivism," it is possible to argue that the assumption of criticism into "English studies" corresponds to a renewal of positivist tendencies in the social sciences[14] and a reduction in its critical heritage.[15]

All variations on such an analysis would have to end by saying that eventually this division of intellectual labor, so easily institutionalized in the American bureaucratic university, helped produce an anemic institution largely bled of critical purpose by its isolation from the increasingly semiotic and informational cultural and political issues which, paradoxically, critics were best trained to analyze.[16]

Literary criticism's doubtful legitimacy can perhaps best be seen in the results of its persistent strategy: questing for the "new" as a way of reinvigorating and restoring itself. That this strategy is itself a sign of the decay of literary criticism out of the contradiction of its origins can be seen in any quick survey of its forms.[17] A very preliminary categorization suggests that contemporary literary critics can be divided into three groups by virtue of the differing relations of their practice and ideology to the active forces of anomie and repression in our civilization. In the first of these crude categories we find those who know not what they do when they ignore the anomalies of their professional and social situation and train their students—or hope to—in the no longer marketable skills of their own specialized paradigm. Such educators are functionaries of an ideology they do not perceive as such: they take their position to be natural and unquestionable, although mysteriously and sadly under attack. They grow depressed.

The second group is allied to the first: they are the priests of the dominant ideology engaged in defining its power and expanding its influence. They study the "crisis" of our culture and profession but do so only to reform the "flaws" and "misdirections" that have, as they see it, led to the loss of stability, order, values, and "common sense." They frequently mistake elements of the third group—if I may be allowed a prolepsis—for the *cause* of the crisis they perceive. They cannot seriously think through the idea that the questioning existence of those they call "radicals" or simply "barbarians"[18] indicates the real illegitimacy of the social organization and cultural values they defend or, in their fantasies, hope to "return to." The members of this second group are, of course, the ideological favorites of the first group, at least of those in the first group whose intellectual life has not ceased altogether. The first group values the high priests of the reaction just to the degree that the latter deny the importance of the questioners or find a way to domesticate them. Not surprisingly, often the priestly class sustains the tillers of the first group by misinforming them. Two of their functions, in clear words, are to simplify and to lie.

Of the third group—which is multifaceted—many descriptions might be offered. I am most interested in one feature which easily distinguishes this third group from the other two: its members often critically study the history and structure of intellectual language and practice to draw attention to its effects and to the traditional intellectuals' interest in playing certain roles. At times they go beyond even such critical history and suggest different kinds of language and work more likely to be of use, especially to others, in their struggles against power and domination.

Such critics try to invent new tactics to reduce the ease with which intellectuals can be taken back up into the hegemonic institutions that, in large part, have formed them. Because of this need to resist the "acceptable" forms of language and practice, critics of the third group often produce work others call "alienating," "elitist," "threatening," or simply "absurd." Of course, much "theoretical" work in criticism and composition is simply narcissistically obscure or pretentious and prissy. But the simultaneous complaint that such "difficult" work—for which their leaders tell them they need "guides"—is (bizarrely) "reductive," "egotistical," hateful of literature, or "ideological" suggests how contradictory is the majority position.

This tripartite schema is very crude. Not only does it leave out of account those "heroes," as Althusser calls them,[19] who work anonymously to alter the ideology and practice their institution embodies, but it also does not consider those (few) members of the first group who change, who are open to a discussion of issues, and who try to acquire the skills needed to see the social order around them and their professional function within it. Most important, however, is this schema's failure to describe how and to what extent the work of the third group is caught up in the dominant culture's defining practices and languages, which taken together, are precisely those realities which most make possible critical work. Needless to say, my categories would have to be refined to account for those whose work, while appearing to place them in the third group, is actually merely subjective and sometimes exploitative private enunciation.

Of course, there is always the question of uniformity of views within each group. This question is an admirable extension of pluralistic[20] middle-class concerns for the individual as well as an important call for scholarly responsibility. Unfortunately, I cannot assume that responsibility here. Although specificity and precise detail are always crucial, I feel that in this case it is even more important to understand the role and ideology of contemporary literary critics by seeing how they represent and practice their intellectual functions. Within the third group this becomes a central question because one must make judgments on the relative effect of the various critiques and tactics suggested to resist and modify the ruling but illegitimate ideology of domination.

III

Any discussion of the role of the intellectual must begin with Gramsci who, recasting Marx's *The German Ideology*, best explains how the praxis of both the detached, disinterested mandarins and bureaucratic, technological functionaries supports the "hegemony" of the ruling class. Every emergent social group "creates together with itself, organically, one or more strata of intellectuals which give it homogeneity and an awareness of its own function not only in the economic but also in the social and political fields" (*PN*, 5). He goes on to suggest how useful this ideology is to the ruling class:

> every "essential" social group which emerges into history out of the preceding economic structure, and as an expression of a development of this structure, has found (at least in all history up to the present) categories of intellectuals already in existence and which seemed indeed to represent an historical continuity uninterrupted even by the most complicated and radical changes in political and social forms. . . . Since these various categories of traditional intellectuals experience through an "*esprit de corps*" their uninterrupted historical continuity and their special qualification, they thus put themselves forward as autonomous and independent of the dominant social group. (*PN*, 6-7)[21]

Gramsci's comments help us to see that modern idealism and American pragmatism have their historical origins in the social practice of traditional intellectuals whose misperception of their own "autonomy" legitimates their claims and actions and so their cultural force and value. In addition, this misprision blocks any investigation into the historical, social origins and positions of their own functions in society: they are, on this matter at least, ahistorical and nonreflexive. Since in literary study these idealist and pragmatic intellectuals are in a dominant position, I want to stress both this point about their blindness to the social origins of their beliefs[22] and the range of possible critiques which can be made of it. For example, when we invert what seems to be the direction of cause and effect, we discover, as Nietzsche had prefigured in *On the Genealogy of Morals*,[23] that to maintain their legitimacy these intellectuals must create a defense which blocks their own and others' investigations into their origins and purposes. In other words, in purely functional terms, traditional intellectuals are not and cannot be "autonomous" because to protect the illusion of their privilege and the structures it assures and depends upon they must rule out of play certain areas of investigation and so restrict the development of critical, especially, political knowledge. (There are many ways in which they hinder others' research. Essentially they all come down to denying their legitimacy.)[24] It follows from this that idealist theories of knowledge are among the highest and most necessary defenses of such intellectual functions: the illusion of traditional intellectual autonomy "can be connected," Gramsci suggests, with "idealist philosophy" (*PN*, 8)[25] Habermas helps us to see how easily intellectuals tend toward an idealism: their social legitimacy depends upon the illusion of autonomy, and since, as Habermas insists, we make a validity or truth claim simply whenever we make an assertion, intellectuals can make legitimating representations of themselves (and their group's interests) only to the extent that they can claim them to be valid products of autonomous seekers after truth.[26]

Gramsci's concept of the intellectual corrects this representation in two ways: first, by referring all intellectual activity to "the ensemble of the system of relations in which these activities (therefore the intellectual groups who personify them) have their place within the general complex of social relations" (*PN*, 8); and, second, by reversing the division of labor:

> The problem of creating a new stratum of intellectuals consists therefore in the critical elaboration of the intellectual activity that exists in everyone at a certain degree of development, modifying its relationships with the muscular-nervous effort towards a new equilibrium, and ensuring that the muscular-nervous effort itself,

in so far as it is an element of a general practical activity, which is perpetually innovating the physical and social world, becomes the foundation of a new and integral conception of the world. (PN, 9)

Gramsci's notes are a valuable practical-historical formulation of the material power of intellectual activity in domination and resistance. More specifically, Gramsci helps us see the importance of education, especially humanistic education in the reproduction of the dominant mode of production in modern societies, that is, the mode of exploitation.[27] In the notes gathered as "The Study of Philosophy," Gramsci argues that it is mechanistic to believe that the unilinear succession of modes of production will lead inevitably to the revolutionary displacement of the bourgeoisie by the proletariat. This at-one-time historically necessary concept must be superseded by a more voluntarist model of social change which, especially in theorizing the party and the role of intellectuals, recognizes the cultural battleground of revolution.

The growing role of knowledge in social exploitation furthers the division of labor and, only seemingly paradoxically, reifies the potential for intellectual work. Intellectual functionaries are essential—especially if they are liberals—to the operation of the information-based and sign-oriented structures of our culture.[28] They are present at all levels of our bureaucratized society: "at the highest level," writes Gramsci, "would be the creators of the various sciences, philosophy, art, etc., at the lowest the most humble 'administrators' and divulgators of pre-existing, traditional accumulated intellectual wealth" (PN, 13). Following Weber and Marx and working along a parallel line to the Frankfurt School, Gramsci stresses the organizational nature of domination as a condition for understanding the key role of education, the development of what Alvin Gouldner and others call "cultural capital,"[29] and the overproduction of intellectuals.[30]

The intellectual operation of the hegemonic organization requires a broad-based, humanistic education. But it also requires an elaborate structure of testing and tracking to elaborate "top intellectual qualifications" to distribute workers and rewards. The effect of this structure is to deny in practice what is claimed in theory: namely the illusion of democratic access to and control of technology and high culture. The administrative hierarchy of education is a primary mechanism for subjugation and subjection the reality of which should become obvious in its results: it promises access to and a share in the system, but also structurally "it creates the possibility of vast crises of unemployment for the middle-intellectual strata" (PN, 11). Gramsci goes on to draw the most important conclusion from his analysis of this structure: "The democratic-bureaucratic system has given rise to a great mass of functions which are not all justified by the social necessities of production, though they are justified by the political necessities of the dominant fundamental group" (PN, 13).

This means, of course, that the politics of culture is as important to revolutionary activity as the politics of economics. Culture, in other words, must be seen voluntaristically, as a mechanism for the defense of economic interest and political privilege. Not only does this insight imply that the battle ground of political struggle must shift from that economic arena in which traditional Marxists are most accustomed to struggle, but it also implies that the politics of culture must, in large part, be a politics of the humanities, of the control of sign-systems and their interpretation.[31]

Gramsci's analysis makes the inescapable claim that intellectuals are functionaries in class war. Humanistic discourses and practices, particularly those of philosophy and education, appear "above all as a cultural battle to transform the popular 'mentality' " (PN, 348). The aim of the hegemonic intellectuals is, in part through the middle-level functionaries, "to diffuse philosophical innovations which will demonstrate themselves to be 'historically true' to the extent that they become concretely—that is, historically and socially—universal" (PN, 348). The achievement of material and cultural priority ensures the "validity" of these concepts and the legitimacy of their practitioners.

The battle for domination depends upon the diffusion of organic intellectuals' concepts and their conflict with those of other groups. Another way of putting this is to say that language is an element in the political battle for hegemony—and, when put this way, it becomes clear how relevant Gramsci's remarks on the intellectual are to the practice of literary critics.

Gramsci's thinking about language begins from the American pragmatists and their Italian fellow-travelers. C. S. Peirce is especially important to Gramsci. Since the diffusion of philosophical concepts throughout society is essential to the establishment and maintenance of hegemony, "the question of language in general and of languages in the technical sense must be put to the forefront of our inquiry" (PN,

348). Gramsci modifies the Saussurian division between *langue* and *langage* in order to socialize and historicize the latter term especially: *langage* "is essentially a collective term. . . . Language also means culture and philosophy. . . . Culture, at its various levels, unifies in a series of strata, to the extent that they come into contact with each other, a greater or lesser number of individuals who understand each others' mode of expression in differing degrees" (*PN*, 349). Hegemony, then, is a function of language in its collective nature, or, as Gramsci puts it, "the general question of language" is "the question of collectively attaining a single cultural 'climate' " (*PN*, 349).

If culture is a question of language, as Gramsci suggests, and if hegemony and so politics is a question of culture diffused in and by language, then what shall we say is the role of the critic?[32] We can begin to answer this question by insisting that critical activity is more than "self-reflexivity," as many liberals would like to believe.[33] It should be always the dialectical reconsideration of concepts and methods based on the problems posed to criticism by the cultural environment. Critical education cannot be what it often sets out to be: the reproduction in the new generation of the knowledge, skills, values, position of the predecessors and teachers.[34] Not only do many objective conditions in fact prevent this traditional form of educational reproduction, but such reproduction is inappropriate to the critical enterprise: critical training should produce an intellectual, not restricted (except tactically) to ironic negation,[35] who constantly thematizes his or her work as a practical process of creating cultural unity.[36] Such intellectual work can emerge only from what Gramsci calls the "liberty of thought" which, in turn, requires knowledge gained in resistance to the hegemonic censorship of alternative concepts. Without such resistance, a positive political critique cannot be produced. From a Gramscian point of view we must say that all such critiques have one essential condition: a recognition of what we might call the "interface" between philosophy (conceived as the highest form of articulated humanistic knowledge) and history. With this recognition as a point of departure, a new kind of critic is possible: one "convinced that his [or her] personality is not limited to himself [or herself] as a physical individual but is an active social relationship of modification of the cultural environment" (*PN*, 350).[37]

Were literary critics to take Gramsci seriously, they would carry out a thorough critique of the basic paradigms of literary education and especially its relation to the university.[38] They would, in addition, attempt to reconstruct that education along different lines. Such a critique would have to begin with an institutional history of "lit. crit." as an aspect in the reproduction of the hegemony of modern technologic and cybernetic societies.[39] Critics would also consider what real social needs comparatively marginal figures like R. P. Blackmur and F. O. Matthiessen record and address in their work. In addition, one would have to judge the elements worth preserving in such hegemonic figures as I. A. Richards, W. K. Wimsatt, and Lionel Trilling.[40] In other words, taking Gramsci seriously would involve recasting critical studies so that they would engage constantly in dialectical self-revision and develop research strategies to study the ways in which the interrelated cultural strata of a society produce hegemonic and counterhegemonic representations in texts and other discursive systems.

A history of critical intellectual discourse and pedagogy might show, for example, that "lit. crit." institutionalized as "practical criticism" is one aspect of a disciplinary society which produces individuals who make themselves available to surveillance.[41] John Fekete has rightly suggested Richards' involvement with the defense of bourgeois interests and has begun an analysis of practical criticism's functionalism. His analysis might be extended, however, to trace the affiliations of practical criticism with not only the functionalist anthropology of Malinowski, but also with the sociology of Parsons and the proto-fascist elitism of Pareto.[42] Alvin Gouldner details just how, in its various forms, functionalism practically and ideologically defends the bourgeoisie during and after the crises of World War I and the Great Depression.[43]

Reading Richards and practical criticism after Foucault illuminates the specific ways in which the newly institutionalized "lit. crit." implements the functionalist project. Most important, such a reading shows how practical criticism creates the "reader" as an object of knowledge positioned by its discourse and pedagogy to be subjected and subjugated to discriminating training. In Gramsci's terms, we might say that "lit. crit." is a way of intervening in civil society to enable a mass interiorization of self-disciplining techniques derived from the structure of the classroom and the values and exercises of the student theme or protocol. We could justly extend our sketch to implicate the basic concepts of the American New Criticism. We would see, for example, why the New Critics so valued irony and the image: in their assertion of the priority of these aesthetic qualities in modern theories of the text and critical reading, the New Critics simply enacted the turn away from historical reflection which might have made their discipline less effective as a defense of the hegemonic order. As we have seen from Gramsci's work, historically reflexive thinkers (like Croce) become aware of their own social and political function and become either oppositional or idealistic intellectuals. In their elaborate ironic readings the New Critics enacted the turn toward idealism which remains the dominant mode of North American literary criticism.[44]

IV

Gramsci does not fully develop a theoretical model of how societies and their institutions survive so we are left with our specific problem: how can the institution of "criticism" modify itself to regain its critical purpose. The essentially liberal and idealist emphasis on self-criticism, on "reflexivity,"[45] is by itself inadequate: it is a necessary but not sufficient attitude. At best it testifies to the existence of demanding problems within the intellectual, cultural environment and the felt desire for change. Gramsci does not tell us directly, either how the capacity for nonalienated, positive, nonspecialised criticism might develop or how it will produce and disseminate a new ideological counter-hegemonic unity throughout culture. But from Gramsci's theory of cultural politics and his notes on the intellectual we can learn how to set a direction for theorizing the adaptability of cultural institutions: each successive crisis in the development of society requires an available reserve of cultural capital, a capacity to reorganize the institutions of language and discourse to control and regulate the forces of production to legitimate and nonrepressive ends.

As Gramsci sees it, counter-hegemonic forces always need an institutional structure to direct resistance and to reorganize the cultural possibilities of an old into a new and emergent society. For Gramsci the vanguard party was the vehicle which would give political direction to the forces reorganizing economic and cultural production.[46] The party would serve this function because only it can produce the kind of intellectual able to lead the opposition to capitalist hegemony: "leaders and organisers of all the activities and functions inherent in the organic development of an integral society"' (PN, 16). But it is precisely the role Gramsci assigns to the intellectual that suggests we should rethink the party's priority in his work.

In his post-1968 work, Foucault criticized the figure of the representative intellectual who might "speak for" and "lead" the "masses" as a potentially antidemocratic abuse of power. In what we might call "the structure of speaking for," the operations of power extend domination by making what is "known" into an object of science and an instrument of discipline.[47] Such "speaking for," we might say, reactivates the ideology of privileged subjects, points of view, and forms of language; it empowers certain determinations of will.[48] Foucault suggests that democratic forms require that the "representative intellectual" give way as a "representation" of intellectual authority and be displaced by the counter-image of the "specific intellectual." The latter, Foucault argues, always struggles against power locally, on a particular terrain, and does so in order both to sap and, if possible, take power.

I have argued elsewhere[49] that one task awaiting the critic as specific intellectual is to reveal genealogically the role of the humanistic discourses in the formation and maintenance of dominant ideologies in modern and postmodern cultures. The genealogically-trained specific intellectual can contribute an analysis of institutional discourses as these extend the disciplining power (which functions—at any given time— primarily in the interest of dominant groups) throughout an imperialist society and so the international order.

If Foucault is to be useful in refocusing these issues in Gramsci, one must keep in mind that after *The Order of Things* (1966) he thematizes neither the end of the subject nor the image of a new subject—much less a "method" to produce one. While the absence of such speculation might open Foucault to the charge that he undervalues the "utopian" element in culture or in forms of resistance on the part of the oppressed, it more importantly, I think, allows him to cast off the traditional intellectual's assumption of responsibility for imagining alternative subjectivities and to take up the task of the specific intellectual.[50] Such an intellectual must attempt to produce critical tools of use to those— on a national, local, or international level—who struggle against power as it subjugates them within constitutive systems of knowledge.

To be sure, these remarks inadequately represent both Foucault and his critics, but they do suggest one important democratizing modification of Gramsci's Leninist sense that the party alone can produce "leaders and organisers of all the activities and functions inherent in the organic development of an integral society" (PN, 16). A Foucauldian critique of this Gramscian figure would reveal its continuity with the often antidemocratic figure of the leading or representative intellectual to be found throughout high bourgeois humanistic as well as bureaucratic professional practice and ideology. "The intellectual," Foucault writes, "spoke the truth to those who had yet to see it, in the name of those who were forbidden to speak the truth: he was conscience, consciousness, and eloquence." Foucault concluded, on the basis of his analysis of May '68 and the development of new forms of political resistance outside the working class and the Party—for example, environmentalists, gay rights, minority, and womens' movements[51]—that these specific Western struggles—and this is a temporarily neccessary limit to the analysis here—no longer need traditional intellectuals "to gain knowledge" or produce representations (LCMP, 207). We might say that Foucault's theory, in contrast to Gramsci's, holds that in its historical specificity, a high-tech, information-based society, in which even the most advanced industrial economies are subject to the operation of the law of value, does not need "organic" intellectuals to provide leadership but rather requires specific intellectuals to provide expertise and to decode and control the discourses and technologies dominant in it. Foucault derives his claim that traditional or leading intellectuals are antidemocratic "agents of this system of power" from many historical and contemporary factors, but the claim especially depends upon and reveals the fact that these newer forms of political resistance arrogate to themselves responsibility for knowledge and consciousness in structures outside the "leadership" of both traditional and organic intellectuals. They are to a great extent "self-informing" and aspire to be "self-determining." Consequent on the democratic possibilities present in these new political forms Foucault offers the specific intellectual a new project: to name, reveal, and undermine the anonymous and obscure (although immediately present) operations of power as they negate such democratic possibilities.

Unlike Gramsci, and as we shall see unlike Habermas, for Foucault the intellectual's work must be regional and technical, specific and not totalizing; its aim is "to sap power, to take power" (LCMP, 208), not to represent others or bring enlightenment. Gramsci, we must remember, had insisted that "the new stratum of intellectuals" will lead to "a new and integral conception of the world" (PN, 9). While Foucault does not accept the leadership role assigned by Gramsci to the "organic" intellectual, his theory of the "specific" intellectual does coincide with the Italian's in one all-important regard, namely, in its stress on the way intellectuals join the service of the "truth of the collectivity" (*LCMP*, 208) by struggling against the forms of power.

In other words, the aim of Gramsci and Foucault, and, as I shall suggest, of Habermas as well, is to theorize (albeit in very different ways) an intellectual capable of practical political action against domination.[52] In post-'68 France, given the association of the PCF with the State and the critiques by Derrida and others of Foucault's own "representational" project in *Histoire de le Folie* (1961), Foucault was obliged to move away both from his own earlier problematic intellectual role as "archeologist" as well as from Althusser's party.[53] After May '68 Foucault was able to say that Deleuze teaches "us something absolutely fundamental: the indignity of speaking for others" (*LCMP*, 209). This self-revising statement, which moves Foucault away from the position of the representative intellectual implicit in his study of madness, can be seen as also a turn away from the Gramscian project. The positive element in such a revision is clear: we must draw the conclusion from that position metonymically associated with "Deleuze" and "appreciate the theoretical fact that only those directly concerned can speak in a practical way on their own behalf" (*LCMP*, 209). While it may be that, as some like Gayatri Spivak have tried to argue,[54] this model of "self-representation" effectively reimposes Western forms of subjugation upon the Third World in the process of theorizing it, it should be kept in mind that Foucault's idea is, in itself, a challenge to the often Gramsci-like position from which these critiques come. Even Gramsci's organic intellectual, we recall, spoke for "his" class (and the term was often gender specific in Gramsci) only from the basis of a complexly elaborated universalist position which grounded the considerable specific analysis that needed to be done.[55]

The practical project Foucault's work suggests could take the form of a demanding inquiry into the genealogy, affiliations, ideology, and structures of the institutions which form our critics—one which not only deployed already existing categories of critical thought but was able to invent new ones useful to the struggle to redirect critic energies. The interventions of the specific critical intellectual into the humanistic institutions of power should be aligned with the forms of resistance of those subjugated by the operations of power as they work (almost entirely—despite their Reaganite and Thatcherite populisms) in the interest of the dominant groups. Foucault's metaphor, drawn from the ideals of third-world nationalist struggles, has been too much sullied by first-world terrorism to be easily used,[56] but the democratic sense behind it bears being recalled: specific intellectuals must be like guerillas struggling with appropriate groups resisting on the local terrain of their domination. The object is "to attack an institution at the point where it culminates and reveals itself in a simple and basic ideology, in the notions of good and evil, innocence and guilt" (LCMP, 228). Despite the contrast between Foucault's concept of the "specific" intellectual and Gramsci's of the "organic" intellectual, the former's thinking does let us appreciate, in a slightly new light, both the values and limits of Gramsci's thought on this matter. It highlights one not-quite-so-Leninist aspect of Gramsci's thought: we can see that the concept of the "organic intellectual" not only demystifies the illusory role of the traditional intellectual, but in so doing it also potentially clarifies and approaches the recognition of the need for oppressed peoples to speak for themselves, to be allowed access to the acoustical systems, which, as Régis Debray might put it,[57] would allow them to direct their own cultures and to legitimate their subjectivities in resisting the subjugation of dominant discourses.

In theory, the association of the "organic" intellectuals with the bureaucracy of the vanguard party should not deny this need; but, as Gramsci develops the concept of the "organic" intellectual in relation to the intellectual potential of all human beings, it does tend, nonetheless, to reserve dialectical critical thinking to an elite representing the interests of the class in modifying the social environment. Although Gramsci insists that all human beings are intellectuals (PN, 9), his programmatic writing sometimes strikes a different and disturbing chord: "In the modern world technical education . . . must form the basis of the new type of intellectual" (PN, 9). Gramsci's theoretical commitment to the idea that all humans are intellectuals gives way to his political sense that resistance and the formation of a new hegemony require a leading elite, trained in science and other forms of technically-advanced managerial disciplines. This idea is not the same as that of the "specific" intellectual because such technological "organic" intellectuals provide not only leadership in directing the movement of the masses as they develop through education in the party toward socialism; rather they become, in themselves, the form and model of intellectual life per se. As I have already suggested, it is not only Foucault who is suspicious of the political consequences of this line of thought. Bahro, Konrad, Szelenyi, and Habermas have also made the point. But Foucault is particularly useful in suggesting how the possibility for reinscribing domination through the effects of knowledge and representation inhere even in the political structures of this organic model.[58]

Foucault's post-'68 conception of critical practice is more modest than that proposed by Gramsci. It is certainly less utopian than that suggested by Habermas or a number of American critics influenced by Anglo-American philosophical interest in consensus-making.[59] Foucault quite rightly insists that critical thinking should produce texts and analyses which name both the forms of knowledge and the institutions through which power is brought to bear, especially as it operates in the interest of the hegemonic. But this critical practice can only occur alongside the other actions of those struggling in their own ways to sap regulative power on a local level.

Gramsci has brilliantly seen that if the intellectual is to be conceptualized, the technical intelligentsia's role in the extension of state and civil oppression must be elaborated. But perhaps even this subtlety does not catch the manifold forms of power as they extend throughout society and across different societies in the structures of imperialism and neo-colonialism. It remains tied to an essentially hierarchical model of bureaucracy linking civil society and the state, to a basically macroscopic conception of oppression which, above all, fails to consider the complexities of power-knowledge in disciplining society to maintain its own subjectivity—a process which, of course, has consequences far beyond the limits of Western national boundaries.[60] One might follow the implications of both Foucault and Althusser and suggest that Gramsci remains, on this point, and despite his critique of imperialism, within the modernist metaphysical concept of a transpersonal subject. On this matter at least, Foucault's analyses of Western disciplinary practices for constituting the subject within the microphysics of power suggest that Gramsci's work locates itself on the periphery of the dominant discourse of disciplinary subjugation.[61]

Foucault's work on this point suggests that the critical project cannot be restricted to the dialectical debate with the social environment, which essentially is what Gramsci proposes. But the project must also take on the genealogical burden of aggressively inquiring into the institutionalized discursive foundations of key concepts, figures, and their effects in the various modalities of power which create and sustain them.

It would, in other words, mean giving a new seriousness and direction to Gramsci's notion of doing an "inventory" of the self.

In other words, Foucault's work extends Gramsci's insight into the centrality of language in social organization by stressing the necessity for the oppressed to speak for themselves, to produce their own representations, their own "subjectivities," "outside" the reach of subjugation or in resistance to it. While such a claim does not diminish the importance of the intellectual, especially of the critical intellectual struggling against an increasingly semiotic structure of dominance, it does change the intellectual's role. It suggests that intellectuals recognize that others can struggle to create their own subjectivity independently of intellectuals' power to produce representations and, indeed, try to gain control of the knowledge-producing apparatus of subjugation in order to be independent of it. Critical action can not only disclose and undermine the discourse of oppression, but it can open space to help others form their own subjectivities in opposition to the discursive and institutional definitions generated and affixed by dominant structures and their agents.

Habermas insists that such social subjectivities can emerge only in a space where meaningful and undistorted communication is possible. He follows Weber in two important ways: a critical concern for the anomie of public sector institutions and a distrust of the party's claim that the state seizure of power will end class divisions. As a result, Habermas sees certain tendencies in modernity and especially postmodernity as a retreat from rationality, or, as he puts it, as *"an outbreak of new contingencies."*[62] Simply put, Habermas's project stresses that history is developmental and that successful societies produce intersubjectively "recognized norms or *rules of communicative action"* regulating the economic and cultural "distribution of products" (HM, 132). Habermas complements earlier revisionists of historical materialism by emphasizing the importance, for this distribution, of rules for instrumental and strategic action. He goes so far as to assert that development of the forms of production depends, in large part, upon intersubjective communicative norms. (Unfortunately, this causes Habermas to be sympathetic to certain pragmatist moments in the conservative liberalism of Richard Rorty.) Different societies, of course, organize themselves differently, and Habermas wants to conclude from this that "unilinear" Marxist models cannot account for these various forms of organization (HM, 139). One might extend Habermas's argument into areas of imperialism and theories of colonial and neocolonial resistance; but Habermas himself refuses to do this.[63]

Habermas himself, however, is concerned to argue that modern Western societies cannot generate norms of intersubjective communication. His complex argument can only be briefly summarized: rules of intersubjective communication regulate the "specific forms of social intercourse, that is, the relations of production," but since these "express the distribution of social power . . . they prejudge the interest structure of a society" (HM, 138-39). In modern capitalist societies, Habermas concludes, such rules can only maintain economically exploitative relations (HM, 103). In postmodern societies, we might say (elaborating on Habermas's thinking), the primacy of science, technology, and education in the organization of the socio-economic system means the central problem is that of the relationship between society and what Habermas calls "internal nature" (HM, 165). And with this concern, Habermas converges with Foucault and suggests yet another necessary dimension for critical intelligence in postmodernity: the critique of administrative attempts to produce and control motivation and meaning in a culture made anomic by the difficulties of generating and sustaining nonsubjugating intersubjective rules for communicative action and resistance. Habermas would have it that we must develop public-sphere institutions while always recalling the distinction between the idea of their necessity, that is, the idea of democracy, and the formation of institutions which allow that democracy to exist.[64]

Foucault has already contributed substantially to our understanding of how, to maintain domination, power has formed and disciplined the Western subject. For Habermas, the intensifying (Western) transition from a classical, economically-based illegitimacy to an information-based one would involve an intensification of those kinds of techniques Foucault has in part analyzed: "In a future form of class-domination," Habermas writes, "softened and at the same time intensified, to socio-psychological coercion, 'domination' . . . would be refracted a second time, not through bourgeois civil war, but through the educational system of the social welfare state" (HM, 166). (It would also require extending this project to include questions of imperialism and gender.) Habermas envisages a chaotically vicious cycle of struggle "between expanded participation and increasing social administration" (HM, 166).[65] He pessimistically concludes this line of thought with a vision of the end of social evolution: "The structural scarcity of meaning" would, in itself, prevent the development of social adaptation. Learning would end, killed by subjugating representation. Societies could no longer form adequate motivations. Limits and contingencies—which Habermas associates with the postmodern—would increasingly appear as society failed to regulate communicatively its own relation to internal reality.[66] We might say that, for Habermas, the guerilla-like struggle to sap power so that the oppressed might speak for themselves is only one element in what one might call "an analytics of dissolution." Or, as I have tried to suggest elsewhere, we see that this line of thought brings Habermas to the point of calling seriously into question the adequacy of any critical practice which identifies itself solely with negation.[67] No doubt such a denial also, at one time, brought Habermas to charge indiscriminately that Foucault and Derrida "on the basis of modernistic attitudes . . . justify an irreconcilable antimodernism."[68]

Momentarily putting aside Habermas's defense of enlightenment reason[69] lets us develop a sense of what might be the composite aim of critical work today: critical intelligence involves a demystification of intellectuals' sense of their independence; a constant genealogical self-criticism; and research into specific discourses and institutions as part of the struggle against forms of oppressive power, forms of surplus-value extraction—if one talks about the international question in those terms. Yet critical intelligence should be all this with an eye to the possibility that such critique, in our time, may not get beyond an increasingly anomic struggle against more subtle but more powerful forms of domination and allocation of motive and meaning—especially within the worlds of Western intellectuals. This means, *inter alia*, that Western intellectuals must confront the historicity of the current surplus of ideological production as an essential condition both of right-wing authoritarianism and of the general critical inability to understand and destroy the system which depends upon that surplus as well.

Critical research should operate in this complex of problems because they are some of the issues which demand attention in our culture. They are increasingly linguistic-based problems of ideology and representation. They touch more and more the ability of intellectuals marginal to the dominant group and of subaltern groups to speak, to be heard, and to understand the discursive relation of the psyche or "internal nature" to society. If literary study affiliates itself with these other modes of critical work, not only will the profession and institution be modified but perhaps it will also help ease the shortage of critical intelligence in a society now so easily manipulated by the image-producing agencies of politics and corporations.

NOTES

1. See Charles Altieri, *Act and Quality* (Amherst: University of Massachusetts Press, 1983).

2. For some of the problems with this term see "An Interview with Paul de Man," *Critical Inquiry* 12, no. 4 (Summer 1986): 793.

3. See Jean-Francois Lyotard, *The Postmodern Condition*, trans. Geoff Bennington and Brian Massumi (Minneapolis: Univ. of Minnesota Press, 1984), 60-67; and Frank Webster, "The Saatchi Society," *New Socialist* 27 (1985): 3-4.

4. See the intense and unembarrassed competition among institutions, eventually won by Carnegie-Mellon University, to house the Defense Department's software development institute.

5. See Paul A. Bové, "The Barbarians Within: Xerxes' Hordes Are at the Gate," *Contemporary Literature* 26 (Spring 1985); 91-107.

6. Louis Althusser, "Ideology and Ideological State Apparatuses," in *Lenin and Philosophy and Other Essays*, 2nd. ed., trans. Ben Brewster (London: New Left Books, 1977), 148.

7. Richard Ohmann, *English in America* (New York: Oxford Univ. Press, 1976); Gerald Graff, *Literature Against Itself* (Chicago: University of Chicago Press, 1979); Edward W. Said, *Orientalism* (New York: Pantheon Books, 1976); Said, *The World, the Text, and the Critic* (Cambridge, Mass.: Harvard University Press, 1983); Geoffrey Hartman, *Criticism in the Wilderness* (New Haven: Yale University Press, 1980); Frank Lentricchia, *After the New Criticism* (Chicago: University of Chicago Press, 1980); Lentricchia, *Criticism and Social Change* (Chicago: University of Chicago Press, 1983).

8. For one of the best attempts to get beyond this trap, see M. Salvatori, "Pedagogical Implications of Reader-Response Theory," *Reader*, forthcoming.

9. Of course, some critics try to be "men of letters" in the service of the status quo. See for example the ubiquitous reviews and middle-brow collections by Denis Donoghue.

10. See Antonio Gramsci, "The Modern Prince," *Selections from the Prison Notebooks*, ed. and trans. Quintin Hoare and Geoffrey Nowell Smith (New York: International Publishers, 1971), 150f. Hereafter cited in my text as *PN*.

11. One must, of course, acknowledge the valuable exceptions: individuals like Edward W. Said and journals like *Jump Cut* and *New German Critique* which are at least in part concerned with such issues. Yet even in such publications one looks in vain for treatment of such matters of immediate

political concern as Central America and South Africa or of institutional importance as the history and function of media or popular culture studies in North America. The excellent essay by John Beverley, "El Salvador," *Social Text* 5 (Spring 1982): 55-72, is, in part, remarkable for being unusual. Beverley has combined history and political analysis with an understanding of the cultural role of poetry in the revolutions of Central America.

12. See Paul A. Bové, *Intellectuals in Power: A Genealogy of Critical Humanism* (New York: Columbia University Press, 1986), esp. Chapter 2, "A Free, Varied and Unwasteful Life: I. A. Richards' Speculative Instruments."

13. Consider, for example, Richard Lanham whose career began with traditional "lit. crit." and moved to the more lucrative areas of composition theory and "pedagogy," explaining the complexities of "theory," and mapping curricular reform. A full analysis of the ideological function of figures like Lanham would be mildly interesting since he so purely represents the "English Studies professional" in America. See his "Composition, Literature, and the Lower-Division Gyroscope," *Profession 84* (New York: Modern Language Association, 1984), 10-15; *Analyzing Prose* (New York: Scribner's, 1983); and *The Motives of Eloquence* (New Haven: Yale University Press, 1976). As of 1984 Lanham was also Executive Director of the Writing Program at UCLA.

14. Some small indication of the direction research should go in treating this question is provided by John Fekete, *Critical Twilight* (London: Routledge & Kegan Paul, 1977), 35-36; and Alvin Gouldner, *The Coming Crisis of Western Sociology* (New York: Basic Books, 1970), 333-37.

15. For an important comment on the failures of critical intelligence in the axioms of modern social scientific method and practice see Theodor W. Adorno, "The Sociology of Knowledge and Its Consciousness," trans. Samuel Weber in *The Essential Frankfurt Reader*, ed. Andrew Arato and Eike Gebhardt (New York: Continuum, 1982), 452-65.

16. Of course this point is not original with me. See Frank Lentricchia, *After the New Criticism*, and Edward W. Said, "Travelling Theory," *The World, the Text, and the Critic*, 226-47.

17. See Daniel O'Hara, *The Romance of Interpretation* (New York: Columbia University Press, 1985).

18. See Paul A. Bové, "The Barbarians Within."

19. For some sense of my suspicion of this choice of terms see my critique of the masterful intellectual, *Intellectuals in Power*, passim.

20. For another example of how like an incestuous carousel the pluralism debate can be, see *Pluralism and Its Discontents, Critical Inquiry*, 12, no. 3 (Spring 1986).

21. For recent testimony to the empirical accuracy of Gramsci's comment see Jurgen Habermas, "A Philosophico-Political Profile," *New Left Review* 151 (May/June 1985): 76.

22. See Cornel West, "The Politics of American Neo-Pragmatism," in *Post-Analytic Philosophy*, ed. John Rajchman and Cornel West, (New York: Columbia University Press, 1985), 259-75.

23. See Bové, *Intellectuals in Power*, chapter 1, "Mendacious Innocents."

24. See Charles Altieri, "An Idea and Ideal of a Literary Canon," *Critical Inquiry* 10 (September 1983): 51-52.

25. Lest it seem that the sociology of knowledge might be the key exception to what I am arguing, see Theodor Adorno, "The Sociology of Knowledge and Its Consciousness." See also Fritz Ringer, *The German Mandarins* (Cambridge, MA: Harvard University Press, 1969), 434, for a fine critique of Mannheim's project.

26. See Thomas McCarthy's discussion of this issue in Habermas, *The Critical Theory of Jurgen Habermas* (Cambridge, MA: The MIT Press, 1981), 300f.

27. See Pierre Bourdieu and Jean-Claude Passeron, *La Reproduction: elements pour une theorie du systeme d'enseignement* (Paris: Les Editions de minuit, 1970), esp. pp. 131-67.

28. For a concise sense of why liberal functionaries are essential to this operation keep in mind Cornel West's succinct explanation of liberal expectations: "The liberal response is to accept the commodification of culture and attempt to find some kind of authentic human existence within it. This response is naive and self-defeating. It is naive because it refuses to see this cultural process as a modern structure of domination and hence wrongly equates it with 'progress'. It is self-defeating in that it manages only to tease out of this culture some semblance of authenticity within a process that parades each new 'style' of authenticity for each succeeding market-season." "Harrington's Socialist Vision," *Christianity and Crisis* 43, no. 20 (December 12, 1983): 485.

29. See Alvin Gouldner, *The Future of the Intellectuals and the Rise of the New Class*, (New York: The Seabury Press, 1979).

30. As far as I know no one has discussed the growing interest among some younger American humanists, especially literary critics, in radical politics and the status of the profession in terms of the drying-up of the job market.

31. See Sacvan Bercovitch, "The Problem of Ideology in American Literary History," *Critical Inquiry* 12, no. 4 (Summer 1986), 631-53.

32. For one attempt to work out this question see Edward W. Said, "Secular Criticism," *The World, the Text, and the Critic*, 1-30.

33. It is also more than the professional self-celebration of those who joyously denigrate the value of critical self-consciousness as well.

34. That it is often consciously intended to be such see Frank Kermode's address to the Lionel Trilling Seminar at Columbia University, February 19, 1981, in which Kermode wrote: "Yet it must be obvious that the formation

of rival canons, however transient, is very dangerous; that in allowing it to happen we risk the death of the institution. Its continuance depends wholly upon our ability to maintain the canon and replace ourselves, to induce sufficient numbers of younger people to think as we do." See also Paul A. Bové, "Variations on Authority," *The Yale Critics*, ed. Jonathan Arac et al. (Minneapolis: University of Minnesota Press, 1983), 6ff.

35. See "Secular Criticism," *The World, the Text, and the Critic*, and Bové, "Criticism and Negation," *Intellectuals in Power*.

36. On the unifying possibilities of bloc politics see Paul A. Bové, "The Ineluctability of Difference: Scientific Pluralism and the Critical Intelligence," *Postmodernism and Politics*, ed. Jonathan Arac (Minneapolis: University of Minnesota Press, 1986), 3-25.

37. By inserting the female pronoun into Gramsci's text I do not mean to suggest that in Gramsci's revolutionary model men and women will occupy the same position in relation to discourse, nature, or power. One should see generally the work of Gayatri Chakravorty Spivak to understand the complexity of this problem.

38. I stress this because it is left largely untouched in the work of Said, who, along with Lentricchia and Joseph Buttigieg, has produced the finest theoretical elaboration of Gramsci in the literary academy.

39. For a discussion of some of the best work already done in this area see Bové, "Introduction," *Intellectuals in Power*.

40. On this last see Daniel T. O'Hara's forthcoming study of Trilling from the University of Wisconsin Press.

41. See Bové, "A Free, Varied and Unwasteful Life: I. A. Richards' Speculative Instruments," *Intellectuals in Power* chapter 2.

42. Fekete, *The Critical Twilight*, 35f.

43. Alvin Gouldner, *The Coming Crisis in Western Sociology*, 354-61.

44. The New Critics argued that their insistence on irony's formal characteristics was in opposition to the dominant modes of "linear" expression typical of the social sciences and the "declarative sentence." Nonetheless, despite this oppositional effort, it can be shown that the New Criticism was, at the same time, idealist, destabilizing of communal values, and a form of cultural subjugation which reinforced the dominant structure. The relation of Modern Anglo-American criticism to international forms of functionalism needs to be researched further to make all of this clear. See Paul A. Bové. "Cleanth Brooks and Modern Irony," *Destructive Poetics* (New York: Columbia University Press, 1980), 93-130. On the persistence of some of these values and functions around the concept of irony in contemporary criticism see Bové, "Variations on Authority: Some Deconstructive Transformations of the American New Criticism."

45. For a critique of the historically contradictory function of this term

see Paul A. Bové, "The Penitentiary of Reflection: Søren Kierkegaard and Critical Activity," *boundary 2* , 9 (Fall 1980): 233-58.

46. The vanguard party has been seriously critiqued by many who see it in fact or potential as an agency of domination threatening the possibility of the dialectical self-criticism which is the basis of all Gramscian theory and practice. Foucault and Habermas have also been persistent critics of the vanguard party. See also Rudolph Bahro, *The Alternative in Eastern Europe*, trans. David Fernbach (London: Verso Books, 1978), 307-14, and George Konrad and Ivan Szelenyi, *The Intellectuals on the Road to Class Power: A Sociological Study of the Role of the Intelligentsia in Socialism*, trans. Andrew Arato and Richard E. Allen (New York: Harcourt Brace Jovanovich, 1979), 156-83.

47. See Michel Foucault, *The History of Sexuality: Volume I, An Introduction*, trans. Robert Hurley (New York: Pantheon Books, 1978), 53-54.

48. Despite Foucault's fundamental differences with Louis Althusser it hardly seems possible to think that he was not influenced on this matter of "speaking for" by Althusser's theory of ideology. See Althusser's "Ideology and Ideological State Apparatuses," *Lenin and Philosophy*, trans. Ben Brewster (London: New Left Brooks, 1971), 123-73.

49. See *Intellectuals in Power*, "Introduction," and Chapters 1, 5, and 6.

50. I am aware that intellectuals of different gender are positioned differently within the structure of power and subjectivity. I thank Gayatri Spivak for drawing my attention to the need for such disclaimers in a discipline not yet aware of their obvious truth.

51. See Stanley Aronowitz, *The Crisis in Historical Materialism: Class, Politics and Culture in Marxist Theory* (New York: Praeger Publishers, 1981) for an extended treatment of this formation. Michel Foucault makes his argument in *Language, Counter-Memory, Practice*, ed Donald F. Bouchard (New York: Cornell University Press, 1977); hereafter cited in the text as *LCMP*.

52. See Frank Lentricchia, "On Behalf of Theory," *Criticism in the University*, ed. G. Graff and R. Gibbons. *Triquarterly Series on Criticism and Culture*, No. 1 (1985): 105-10.

53. See Jacques Derrida, "Cogito and the History of Madness," *Writing and Difference*, trans. Alan Bass (Chicago: University of Chicago Press, 1978), 31-63. Derrida originally presented this paper on March 4, 1963 at the *College philosophique*.

54. See Gayatri Spivak, "Can the Subaltern Speak?", forthcoming in *Marxism and the Interpretation of Culture*, ed. Cary Nelson and Larry Grossberg (Urbana: University of Illinois Press).

55. I say this not despite but because of Stuart Hall's insistence on the historically specific, moderately abstract nature of Gramsci's concepts. See, e.g., Stuart Hall, "Authoritarian Populism," *NLR* 151 (May/June 1985), esp. pp. 118-20.

56. See Edward W. Said, "The Essential Terrorist," *The Nation*, 14 June 1986, 828-33.

57. *Teachers, Writers, Celebrities: The Intellectuals of Modern France*, trans. David Macey (London: New Left Books, 1981), esp. pp. 114ff.

58. See Aronowitz, *The Crisis in Historical Materialism*, and Anthony Giddens, *A Contemporary Critique of Historical Materialism* (Berkeley: University of California Press), 157ff.

59. See Altieri, esp. *Act and Quality* and "A Report to the Provinces," *Profession 82* (New York: The Modern Language Association, 1982), 27f.

60. For some small elaboration of this problem see Bové, *Intellectuals in Power*, 290ff. See also Gayatri Spivak's forthcoming *Master Discourse, Native Informant* (New York: Columbia University Press).

61. This claim would require a much longer analysis to be demonstrative.

62. Jurgen Habermas, "Toward a Reconstruction of Historical Materialism," *Communication and the Evolution of Society*, trans. Thomas McCarthy (Boston: Beacon Press, 1979), 167; hereafter cited in my text as HM.

63. See Habermas, "A Philosophico-Political Profile," esp. pp. 82 and 104.

64. Ibid., 103.

65. On this possibility, Habermas converges momentarily with his strenuous opponent, Jean-Francois Lyotard, *The Postmodern Condition*.

66. For a brilliant analysis of this failure in modern and postmodern literary theory see O'Hara, *The Romance of Interpretation*, esp. pp. 234-35.

67. See Bové, *Intellectuals in Power*, 239-310.

68. Habermas, "Modernity versus Postmodernity," trans. Seyla Ben-Habib, *New German Critique* 22 (Winter 1981): 3-14; see also Habermas, "The French Path to Postmodernity," trans. Frederick Lawrence, *New German Critique* 33 (Fall 1984): 79-102.

69. I realize this is a sweepingly unjustified gesture here. For a thoughtful working out of the problem see Jonathan Arac's "Introduction" to *Postmodernism and Politics*, ed. Jonathan Arac (Minneapolis: University of Minnesota Press, 1986), ix-xliii.

3. De-struction and the Critique of Ideology: A Polemic Meditation on the Margin

WILLIAM V. SPANOS

> The question whether objective truth can be attributed to human thinking is not a question of theory but is a *practical question*. Man must prove the truth, i.e. the reality and power, the this-sidedness of his thinking in practice. The dispute over the reality or non-reality of thinking that is isolated from practice is a purely scholastic question.
>
> Karl Marx, *Theses on Feuerbach*

> Supposing that what is at any rate believed to be the "truth" really is true, and the *meaning of all culture* is the reduction of the beast of prey "man" to a tame and civilized animal, a *domestic animal*, then one would undoubtedly have to regard all those instincts of reaction and *ressentiment* through whose aid the noble races and their ideals were finally confounded and overthrown as the actual *instruments of culture*; which is not to say that the *bearers* of these instincts themselves represent culture. Rather is the reverse not merely probable—no! today it is *palpable*! These bearers of the oppressive instincts that thirst for reprisal, the descendants of every kind of European and non-European slavery, and especially of the entire pre-Aryan populace—they represent the *regression* of mankind! These "instruments of culture" are a disgrace to man and rather an accusation and counterargument against "culture" in general! One may be quite justified in continuing to fear the blond beast at the core of all noble races and in being on one's guard against it: but who would not a hundred times sooner fear where one can also admire than *not* fear but be permanently condemned to the repellent sight of the ill-constituted, dwarfed, atrophied, and poisoned? And is that not *our* fate: What today constitutes *our* antipathy to "man?" for we *suffer* from man, beyond doubt.
>
> Friedrich Nietzsche, *On the Genealogy of Morals*

I

The emergence of "Theory" in recent years as a legitimate site of literary study has, of course, been a salutary development for a marginal criticism committed to the interrogation of the dominant discourse in the Academy. This is not only because it has gone far to disclose the "center elsewhere"—the Transcendental Signified—that, in fact, determines the alleged "disinterestedness" of humanistic inquiry:

> . . . it has always been thought that the center, which is by definition unique, constituted that very thing within a structure which while governing the structure, escapes structurality. This is why classical thought concerning structure could say that the center is, paradoxically, *within* structure and *outside it*. The center is at the center of the totality, and yet, since the center does not belong to the totality (is not part of the totality) *has its center elsewhere*. The center is not the center. The concept of centered structure— although it represents coherence itself, the condition of the *episteme* as philosophy or science—is contradictorily coherent. And as always, coherence in contradiction expresses the force of a desire. The concept of centered structure is in fact the concept of a play based on a fundamental immobility and a reassuring certitude, which itself is beyond the reach of play. And on the basis of this certitude anxiety can be mastered, for anxiety is invariably the result of a certain mode of being implicated in the game, of being caught by the game, of being as it were at stake in the game from the outset.[1]

It is also because, in so doing, Theory has forced the invisible will to power and the policing *praxis* that inform the interested discourse of "disinterestedness" into the worldly arena of the free play of criticism. This double exposure becomes remarkably evident, for example, in Walter Jackson Bate's by now famous essay, "The Crisis in English Studies," published, not incidentally, in the *Harvard* [Alumni] *Magazine*. Circumventing intellectual debate with his adversaries, Bate, in this remarkably candid piece, appeals instead to the executive authority of University administrators to save the literary profession from what he takes to be its headlong suicidal plunge into cultural anarchy consequent on the "forgetting" of "the Renaissance ideal through progressive stages of specialism,"[2] which, though he does not, could as well be understood as the emergence of hitherto repressed discourses that threaten to disrupt the "circle"—and the hegemony—of the humanistic cultural empire. In a rhetoric unmistakably reminiscent, in its appeal to centeredness against "centrifugal heterogeniety" ("CES," 50) and expansiveness, of Irving Babbitt's in *Literature and the American College*

(1908), which prescribes a virulent center-oriented, "New Humanist" agenda that would recuperate the "classics" from the eccentric "Rousseauism" infecting education, this eminent Harvard humanist writes:

> The subject matter—the world's great literature [by which, like Matthew Arnold's "best that has been thought and said in the world," he means the canonized texts of the Western tradition]—is unrivaled. All we need is the chance and the imagination to help it work upon the minds and characters of the millions of students to whom we are responsible. Ask that the people you are now breeding up in departments, and to whom you now give tenure appointments, be capable of this. The number, at first may seem small. But much can be done if one has a really committed and talented nucleus. The very grimness of the job situation has for some years been gradually shaking out of graduate study many who had formerly drifted into it. Small as it is, a larger fraction of it than I can remember consists of gifted young people who really *care*, who are ready to face difficulties and to make sacrifices in order to recapture some understanding of the centrality and larger values of humane letters. At Harvard we have been trying to take advantage of this . . . . But we shall need the help of the administration, in the years ahead, in appointing to the staff models not of trivially specialized expertise, but of a combination of some creative specialism (inevitable in the modern world) with the range and general power of both character and mind that we have been trying to form and develop. With this help we can once again encourage the profession, more actively than we do even now, in the next generation. ("CES," 53)

As Paul de Man, one of the most prominent spokesmen in behalf of the legitimacy of "Theory," puts the critique of Bate's astonishing refusal to debate the issue:

> The crisis in the teaching of literature to which Bate alerts us is genuine enough. This does not mean, however, that his diagnosis or his remedies are valid, even less so since these remedies do not take the form of a reasoned discussion but of an appeal to the administrative officers of the universities to deny tenure to teachers who concentrate on *theory*. The question to Bate's mind is not even in need of discussion. For all people of good will and

good sense, the matter has long since been settled once and for
all. What is left is a matter of law-enforcement rather than a critical
debate. One must be feeling very threatened indeed to become
so aggressively defensive.[3]

One can be generally sympathetic with de Man's indignation
against Bate's refusal to engage the claims of theory in intellectual debate,
but the question he chooses to address in his encounter with "The Crisis
in English Studies" is, I submit, seriously and—because of his enormous
authority—disablingly misplaced. For the question that Bate's synec-
dochal text poses for our historical conjuncture is not, as de Man and
the American deconstructionists he speaks for all too rigorously assert,
merely a matter of a traditional literatary discourse grounded in an outmoded logocentric imperative versus "literary theory," by which de Man
surely means deconstruction. As my epigraph from Marx's *Theses on
Feuerbach* implies, it is, also—at least as I understand it— a question
of the *politics* of Humanism. The law enforcement which, like Don Quixote's necromancers, is Bate's last resort, is not simply a metaphor for
a rhetorical operation designed to forestall another; it is also an act of
political power having its "origin," as does the Harvard Core Curriculum
of 1978, in the privileged principle of "disinterested" inquiry and its
end in the reclaiming of Western cultural hegemony in the face of the
socio-political disruptions occasioned by the "knowledge explosion"
precipitated, in part, by the Vietnam War. This is suggested not only
by the remarkable parallel between Bate's recuperative discourse and
the elitist prescriptions of Irving Babbitt and Paul Elmer More in the
first decades of this century—a continuity, to which I will return, especially focused by his invocation of "a really committed and talented
nucleus" and their tacit appeal to the American Puritans' version of
the Roman/Christian Patristic paradigm of the "saving remnant" and
its providential "errand in the wilderness."[4] It is also suggested by the
coincidence of its Jeremiadic appeal to a principle of ritual consensus
with the "official" educational imperatives more recently formulated
for institutional adoption by William J. Bennett, chairman of the National Endowment for the Humanities and (subsequently) Secretary of
Education in the Reagan administration, in response to the dispersal
of the traditional liberal arts curriculum, which he misleadingly attributes
to "a collective loss of nerve and faith on the part of both faculty and
academic administrators during the late 1960s and early 1970s":

. . . the humanities can contribute to an informed sense of community by enabling us to learn about and become participants in
a common culture, shareholders in our civilization. But our goal
should be more than just a common culture—even television and
the comics can give us that. We should, instead, want all students
to know a common culture rooted in civilization's lasting vision,
its highest shared ideals and aspirations and its heritage.[5]

Bate's appeal to the policing agency of the University in behalf
of recuperating the *litterae humaniores* in the face of the alleged *pro-
liferation* of specialisms and the dispersal of the "Western heritage" is,
in fact, the overt manifestation of the "imperialistic" political *praxis*
necessarily latent, if normally hidden, in the center-determined binary
logic of humanistic discourse at large. To put it provisionally, I mean
by this the logic of re-presentation—of propriety and decorum—the logic
(or ideology) in which the first term (Identity, Universality, Culture,
Disinterestedness, Truth, Sanity, Justice, etc.), which is, in fact, secondary or derivative, is privileged over and thus is empowered to colonize
the second term (difference, temporality, anarchy, error, interestedness,
madness, deviance, etc.), which, in its pre-constituted and pre-named
state, is, in fact, primary, original, and radically different. Or, rather,
the principle of authority and executive power to which Bate, his Harvard predecessor, and his contemporary official counterpart, Bennett,
are driven to invoke by the increasing disruptions occasioned by the
de-territorialization of hitherto repressed discourses informs and is always
already operative in humanistic discourse at large and in the agencies
and institutions of knowledge production and transmission it authorizes
and legitimates. What I want to suggest, at least in part, in the following all too brief remarks, in other words, is that deconstruction as simply
the articulation of the play of rhetorical operations is inadequate to the
critical *praxis* demanded by the exposure of the "center elsewhere"—
and the will to socio-political power informing it—determining the
discourse of Humanism.

II

It is important, for reasons I will articulate later, to foreground
the by now stabilized tendency, especially in departments of literature,
to reduce, as de Man does in his rebuttal to Bate, the emergent "counter-

memory" to rhetorical theory or to theoretical orientations (such as Heidegger's in *Being and Time* and Sartre's in *Being and Nothingness*) seen retrospectively from the vantage point of deconstruction's accomplished translation of the ontological difference into textual *differance*. For this general identification of deconstruction with the oppositional discourse of the counter-memory not only overlooks and obscures other theoretical discourses that resemble its operations, but in so doing neutralizes the adversary political possibilities opened up to thought by the disclosure of the center elsewhere of humanistic discourse. The radical demystification of language by deconstructive reason—the absolute revelation of language as the unsayable (*as language for which there is nothing to reveal*) by its rigorous rationality—becomes a determining and deterministic presupposition that paradoxically, and against its original intention, locks thinking (and the men and women who practice it) into a textual space—the "scene of writing"—without exit, and thereby makes human beings prisoners of the very instrument it invokes to liberate them from the bondage of the ontotheological *logos*. As the Italian Heideggerian Georgio Agamben puts it:

> The fulfilled revelation of language is a word completely aban-
> doned by God. Man is cast into language without having a voice
> or a divine word that guarantees him a possibility of escape from
> the infinite play of signifying propositions. And so, at last, we are
> left alone with our words, alone for the first time with language
> abandoned by any further foundation. This is the Copernican
> revolution that the thought of our time has inherited from nihilism:
> we are the first men who have become completely aware of
> language. What previous generations thought of as Muse, God,
> Being, Spirit, Unconscious, we see clearly for the first time what
> they are: names of language. . . . We restore them to their proper
> place in language, which has dispelled from itself everything divine,
> everything unsayable: entirely revealed absolutely in the begin-
> ning. . . . If at this point, we take up Wittgenstein's image of the
> fly trapped in a glass, we would say that contemporary [French]
> thought in the end has acknowledged the inevitability, for the
> fly, of the glass whose prisoner it is.[6]

To put Agamben's Wittgensteinian metaphor of the fly trapped in the glass of language in my own rhetoric, this absolutely demystified (revealed) mode of inquiry becomes necessarily the agency of the repetition of the *Same*, that is to say, of *in-difference*. As an inclusive perspective that locks or, rather, assimilates different historical discourses and their particular determinations into the a priori one which is "writing in general," such a vision of writing, I submit, betrays the blindness of the insight of the deconstructive problematic. It is, I think, no accident that the assumption of this "absolute premise"—this textualization and reduction of the various historical discursive practices emerging from and accommodating different historical cultural situations, to "signifiers devoid of signification," to free-floating "intertextuality" or "citationality" or "iterability" at the ever-present "scene of writing" or "theaters of trope" (as the title of a recent deconstructive text has it)[7]—defuses deconstructive discourse, especially as it has come to be practiced in American literature departments, of its potential for *praxis*. Under its inclusive ahistorical gaze, all texts are emptied of their concrete worldly content. The particular texts in the philosophical and literary history of the West which have made and continue to make a particular historical difference in the world—Plato's *Phaedrus*, Rousseau's *On the Origin of Languages*, Hegel's *Phenomenology of Spirit*, Nietzsche's *The Birth of Tragedy*, Heidegger's *Being and Time*, Sophocles' *Oedipus Tyrannos*, Shelley's *Triumph of Life*, Melville's *Billy Budd*, Williams' *Paterson*, to name a few that have undergone the rigorous scrutiny of the deconstructive eye—tend, ironically, to become the same text. It is not simply that Rousseau has become "Rousseau" and Melville, "Melville," or that Western philosophy has become "Western Philosophy" and Western Literature, "Western Literature," but also, finally, that Western Philosophy and Western Literature have become "Writing." The socio-political implications of this levelling tendency become historically concrete if, besides such examples from "high culture," we apply the rigorous logic of deconstruction to the texts of Lyndon Johnson in the aftermath of Tonkin Bay or of Ronald Reagan following the invasion of Grenada.

To put this in the specific terms of the historical conjuncture characterizing literary studies in America, and to disclose the reductive implications of deconstructive practice at large at the sites of culture and socio-politics, deconstruction has become, despite its original oppositional purposes, paradoxically the obverse face of the effaced coin it would remint: a negative formalism which mirrors the positive formalism of its ostensible critical adversaries, a new New Criticism that, although it substitutes undecidability for certain meaning, indeterminacy for "ambiguity" or "complexity," structurality for "structure," and the unweaving for the "weaving" of the textual fabric, nevertheless goes on privileging a de-differentiating and finally in-different "pleasure of the text" over its worldly consequences, over the difference, for good or ill, texts make in the world. This reduction, in fact, is what J. Hillis Miller unwittingly accomplishes in the process of making his by now famous (institutionalized) "'Nietzschean" distinction between "canny" and "uncanny" criticism, i.e. between structuralism (including New Criticism) and deconstruction. I quote his text at some length not only to focus the similarity (sameness) of the different rhetorics of these two kinds of criticism, but also to suggest their equally indifferent tonality:

> For the most part these [canny] critics share the Socratic penchant, what Nietzsche defined as the "unshakable faith that thought, using the thread of logic (*an den Leitfaden der Kausalität*), can penetrate the deepest abysses of being, and that thought is capable not only of knowing but even of correcting, (*corrigien*) it.". . . The inheritors today of the Socratic faith would believe in the possibility of a structuralist-inspired criticism as a rational and rationalizable activity, with agreed-upon rules of procedure, given facts, and measurable results. This would be a discipline bringing literature out into the sunlight in a "happy positivism." Such an appropriation of the recent turn in criticism would have the attractive quality of easily leading to institutionalizing in textbooks, courses, curricula, all the paraphernalia of an established academic discipline.
>
> Opposed to these are the critics who might be called 'uncanny,' though they have been inspired by the same climate of thought as the Socratic critics and though their work would also be impossible without modern linguistics, the 'feel' or atmosphere of their writing is quite different. . . .
>
> These critics are not tragic or Dionysian in the sense that their work is wildly orgiastic or irrational. No critic could be more rigorously sane and rational, Apollonian, in his procedure, for example, than Paul de Man. One feature of Derrida's criticism is a patient and minutely philological 'explication de texte.' Nevertheless the thread of logic leads in both cases into regions which are alogical, absurd. . . .
>
> In a different way in each case, the work of the uncanny critics however reasonable or sane their apparent procedure, reaches

a point where it resists the intelligence almost successfully. . . .
Sooner or later there is the encounter with an "aporia" or impasse. The bottom drops out, or there is an "abyssing," an insight
one can almost grasp or recognize as part of the familiar landscape
of the mind, but not quite, as though the mental eye could not
quite bring the material into lucid focus. . . . In fact the moment
when logic fails in their work is the moment of their deepest penetration into the actual nature of literary language, or language
as such. It is also the place where Socratic procedures will ultimately lead, if they are carried far enough.[8]

What Miller "says" about the distinction between canny and uncanny
criticism is in a certain (textual) sense valid. Characteristically, however,
his definition of uncanny criticism entirely generalizes the language of
the canny critics, reduces—levels—their different rhetorics to a "logocentric" weave, thus stripping them of their historically specific discursive
practices. It betrays, that is, the ahistorical nature of deconstructive
criticism. Thus rarified, further, the aporetic abyss—the "uncanny"—
the uncanny critics disclose in their rigorously logical unweaving of the
textual fabric comes to assume the " 'feel' or atmosphere" of, at best,
a mild discomfort in the face of "a labyrinth of words," though more
often, of "a happy negative formalism," of free-floating words—of
"writing in general"—signifying a pleasurable—and disabling—nothing.[9]
Despite its appeal to Nietzsche's "abyss," there is little in Miller's definition of "uncanniness" or anywhere else in his text that suggest the ex-
hilarating disorientation activated by Nietzsche's disclosure of the
"deepest abysses of being." Nor, despite its apparent similarity to Heidegger's existential analysis of *die Unheimlichkeit* (uncanniness) is there
anything in Miller's definition of "uncanniness" that suggests the dread
(*Angst*) that has Nothing (*das Nichts*) for its object, which is fundamental
to Heidegger's understanding of this non-concept.[10] This, it should be
remembered, is the mood (*Stimmung*) of not-at-homeness-in-the-world
that activates not simply the question of being (*die Seinsfrage*), but also,
as the examples of Sartre, Merleau-Ponty, and, I would suggest, Foucault,
Deleuze, and certain neo-Marxists like Marcuse imply, the critique of
historically-constituted and imposed structures on behalf of the retrieval
and exploration of the repressed. Indeed, given its refusal of the ontological status of language (language as the house of being—not *Being*),
Miller's texual definition of uncanniness must annul such a disturbing—

and criticism-provoking—resonance in favor of a negative aestheticism: a mode of "looking at" the play of difference in the "theater of writing" that simply mirrors in reverse the positive aestheticism of the New Criticism and Structuralism. To put this in a way suggested by the etymology of "theater," in disengaging and distancing itself from the historical differences that temporality disseminates, deconstruction becomes *theory*. The word, we recall—for Marx its synonym is "speculative philosophy"—derives from *theoria* ("contemplation, speculation, sight"), which itself derives from *theorós* ("spectator") and, further back, from *théa* ("sight"), and *théasthai* ("to look upon"), all of which have their ultimate focus in *theós* (Latin *Deus*), the omniscient, omnipresent, transtemporal, but always hidden deity beyond the temporal realm of conflict—of crisis, of criticism—who looks down uncritically, which is to say, "indifferently," from that (aesthetic) distance on the totality of things-as-they-are. As a negative aestheticism, it is also a negative theo-logy.

It is this transformation of a potential critical practice (un)grounded in the difference that difference makes in the world into a spectator sport, as it were, that, Miller's protestations to the contrary, renders deconstruction a canny uncanny discourse and explains why, no less than the "canny" discourse of the New Criticism and Structuralism, it has lent itself so unresistingly "to institutionalizing in textbooks, courses, curricula, all the paraphernalia of an established academic discipline." As a theoretical discourse that stages its rigorous speculations at the ever-present "scene of writing," in other words, deconstruction, in turn becomes always already "modern," i.e. fashionable: a commodity drained of historical specificity, serving the hegemonic purposes of the consumer society. We cannot but assent, for example, to the oppositional intent, not to say the characteristically lucid density of Jonathan Culler's *On Deconstruction*. Nevertheless, it is to this level that his "guide" to the deconstructive discourse of Jacques Derrida and Paul de Man finally comes down:

> When even those well read in contemporary theory have difficulty determining what is important or where and how competing theories compete, one is challenged to attempt explanation, especially if explanation can benefit the many students and teachers of literature who have neither the time nor inclination to keep up with theoretical debates, and who, without reliable guides, find

themselves at a modern Bartholomew Fair, contemplating what seems to them a "blank confusion," of "differences/That have no law, no meaning, and no end." This book attempts to dispel confusion to furnish meanings and ends, by discussing what is at stake in today's critical debate, and analyzing the most interesting and valuable projects of recent history.[11]

What is intended as a mode of inquiry committed to calling into question the impulse of traditional logocentric discourses to reduce language, history, culture, society to the certain and useful same, all too easily becomes a technology devoted to the indifferent business of "producing" criticism for institutional consumption. It thus, paradoxically, takes its place alongside all those other "rigorous" scientific discourses in the computerized society that, according to Jean-Francois Lyotard, are legitimated and empowered not by the claims of "truth" imposed by traditional narratives of legitimation, but by the imperatives of "performativity":

> The production of proof, which is in principle only part of an argumentative process designed to win agreement from the addresses of scientific messages, thus falls under the control of another language game, in which the goal is no longer truth, but performativity—that is, the best possible input-output equation. The State and/or Company [in the age of computers] must abandon the idealistic and humanistic narratives of legitimation in order to justify the new goal: in the discourse of today's financial backers of research, the only credible goal is power. Scientists, technicians, and instruments, are purchased not to find truth, but to augment power.[12]

To return to Wittgenstein's metaphor, the most secure prison of all is, of course, a prison that is assumed to be a space of freedom—of difference—a prison in which the incarcerated are unknowingly willing bearers of their own incarceration.

III

In thus thematizing performativity as the principle that legitimates the discourse of deconstruction, my text points to the question posed

by another critique of Bate's "Crisis in English Studies"—one calcu-
latedly very different from Paul de Man's affirmation of "Theory." I
am referring, of course, to Stanley Fish's "Profession Despise Thyself:
Fear and Self-Loathing in Literary Studies," in which he reaffirms "professionalism" as the measure of authentic scholarship and of the authentic dissemination of knowledge against Bate's "antiprofessional" attack
on the rampant "academic specialism" that threatens to destroy the
profession of literary studies. By "professionalism," it is important to
point out, Fish means "the profession of letters itself, with all its attendant machinery, periods, journals, newsletters, articles, monographs,
panels, symposia, conventions, textbooks, bibliographies, departments,
committees, recruiting, placement, promotion, prizes, and the like."[13]

Fish's critique of Bate's authoritarian humanism—and of the university he invokes as its institutional model and recuperative measure—is
persuasive:

> It is this prospect [the "ever expanding horizon of new proj-
> ects, new distinctions, new specializations"] that distresses Bate,
> not only because it will further fragment an enterprise whose co-
> herence he believes to be in danger but because it will disperse
> the power and authority that was once centralized in Harvard and
> its sister institutions. For not only is the horizon lengthening, it
> is also broadening. Not only are there too many practitioners find-
> ing too many things to do, but these practitioners seem unwilling
> to confine themselves to the great tradition of supposedly apolitical
> art ("the best that has been thought and said") and insist, in-
> stead, on bringing into the canon (no longer *the* canon) texts pro-
> duced by hitherto excluded groups. . . .
>
> One begins to see how draconian are the measures that must
> be taken if the enterprise is to be returned to the state Bate
> associates with earlier and happier days; any number of worlds and
> activities will have to be excluded. There shall be no blacks, no
> gays, no Chicanos, no filmmakers, no journalists, no women, no
> businessmen, and even, in some strange sense, no jobs. Bate,
> however, cannot mean this literally. He knows as well as anyone
> else (although it is part of what he laments) that, since the end
> of World War II, men and women of every religious, ethnic, na-
> tional, and sexual persuasion from every possible social class have
> found their way into the world of letters. What he objects to (and

in these circumstances, it is all that he *can* object to) is the tendency of these men and women to comport themselves *as* gays, blacks, Chicanos, and so forth rather than as literary persons who just happen to be of certain race, sex, or color. That is, the social diversity of the members of the literary community would be tolerable if their differences were subordinated to some general project, to some ideal that was not particularized in any way that corresponded to the interests and concerns of this or that group. . . . Bate's real complaint is against specificity (for which, read specialization), and . . . he never quite names (except in the vaguest terms) the positive value to which specificity stands opposed because to name it would be to render it too specific. In order to function as a value at once all-inclusive and yet nonbounded, it must remain undefined, ineffable, operating more or less in the manner of a religious mystery.[14]

This thematization of the will to power—the will to *assimilate* and to pacify interest—informing Bate's project to recuperate the "massive centrality and human relevance" ("CES," 50) of literature is much to the point. But as his definition of professionalism—especially the last few categories of his series—makes abundantly clear, it is the principle of performativity that Fish is finally endorsing in affirming "professionalism" as the measure of scholarship and the means of knowledge dissemination against Bate's attack on the rampant specialism characterizing literary studies at the present conjuncture. Indeed, if anything justifies Bate's Jeremiad against the profession in behalf of the *litterae humaniores*, it is, as I have suggested in pointing to the reducibility of deconstruction to imitable and institutionally useful method, precisely Fish's all too characteristic tendency to interpret the emergence—the de-territorialization—of the historically specific minority discourses Bate would re-colonize by way of the binary logic (and principle of canon formation) of humanism as a product of institutional business. It is to this reduction of their engaged struggle against the humanistic establishment to the performative economy of professional literary production that Edward Said draws our attention in his response to Fish's charge of complicity with Bate's "antiprofessionalism":

> I'm less interested in a kind of jovially affirmed professionalism than I am in critical consciousness, and that . . . cannot exclude the social and historical status of professionals. But until

Fish sets about saying concretely what he defends as "profession-alism" in the very here and now in which he himself is to be found, we can be certain that his arguments will remain as innocent of content as they are at present. Certainly a display of attitudes about professionalism is no substitute for either doing or defining the profession as something worth doing and defining rigorously, and here I am very much in agreement with the gist of Fish's notions about the importance of professionalism. It still isn't true, however, that Fish has actually defended "the profession" from its critics. All he's done is to have defended a pretty amorphous status quo.[15]

This is to say, Fish's professionalism, in so far as it has not been ade-quately defined as worldly *praxis*, lends itself to the ongoing economy of certification by which the emergent, hitherto repressed, voices he invokes against Bate's assimilation project are reduced to so many in-stitutional discourses: a pluralism not only divested of conflict, but also serving a consumer society. It is also this naive affirmation of perfor-mativity as the legitimating principle of professionalism that allows Bate, in his response to Fish, the opportunity of circumventing the socio-political critique of Humanism and, with some degree of justification, of wryly concluding:

About the MLA programs, I can only plead guilty that I said pretty much what he says I did. . . . Fish cannot convert me into feeling that the splintering into so many hundreds of confined subjects—with, at the same time, the abandonment of the earlier, large meetings—was right and that the procedure is justified by label-ing it as "professionalism" (indeed the only true professionalism).[16]

IV

Let me now return to the all too pervasive assumption—exemplified in Paul de Man's response to Bate—that contemporary "theory" or "philology" at large equals deconstruction, or at any rate, is a body of discourses read in the retrospective light of the deconstructionists' grammatological analysis of language. Such an easy acceptance of the privileged status of the deconstructive problematic is unjustifiably pre-cipitous. It overlooks—perhaps intentionally in some degree—other con-temporary discourses analogous to deconstruction in their rejection of a metalanguage and acknowledgment of the "anonymity of the signifying function," which, nevertheless, do not, like deconstruction, "acknowledge the inevitability, for the fly, of the [linguistic] glass whose prisoner it is." I am referring, for example, to the discourses of such posthumanist thinkers as Gramsci, Althusser, Adorno, Benjamin, Foucault, Deleuze, Lyotard, Williams, Macherey, Jameson, Lentricchia, Said, and others, who, however differently, situate language in the world or, more precisely, in the temporal/historical world, in order to undermine its privileged status as an absolute Premise or Origin, whether this premise/origin is that of the mystified foundation or demystified nonfoundation. These discourses are thus enabled to demonstrate that language is without origin and end, that it is always in the midst (*interesse*) and thus interested, a historical construct simultaneously determined by the particular historical/material conjuncture and relatively autonomous, available, that is, for purposes of coercion or liberation.

However different in particulars—and these differences are, of course, substantial—these materialist discourses recognize in common that language operates not simply at the disseminating grammatological site, as the practice of deconstructionists all too naively implies. It also and simultaneously operates at the site of what Foucault calls "discursive practice," where a hidden ideology (an archive or problematic constituted and produced by historical, cultural, and socio-political power) will not tolerate questions which would disrupt its teleological rules of discursive formation and its totalizing end. Thus out of reach of the freeplay of criticism, this dominant ideology colonizes or territorializes the different *Other*, the second—minority—term of the binary logic of metaphysical (including humanist) discourse in behalf of legitimating and sustaining its hegemonic purposes. Accordingly, the "task of philosophy" from this materialistic in-stance, is not, as it tends to be for deconstructive critics, a monophasic operation which, as the following exemplary summary by Jonathan Culler suggests, is intended simply to expose the "double, aporetic logic" of all metaphysical discourses:

> The question that now arises, especially for literary critics who are more concerned with the implications of philosophical theories than with their consistency or affiliations, is what this [the disclosure of "structural inconsistencies in "theories grounded on presence"] has to do with the theory of meaning and the interpretation of texts. The examples we have examined so far [from

Rousseau and Saussure] permit at least a preliminary reply: deconstruction does not elucidate texts in the traditional sense of attempting to grasp a unifying content or theme; it investigates the work of metaphysical oppositions in their arguments and the way in which textual figures and relations, such as the play of the supplement in Rousseau, produce a double, aporetic logic. The examples we have considered give no reason to believe, as is sometimes suggested, that deconstruction makes interpretation a process of free association in which anything goes, though it does concentrate on conceptual and figural implications rather than on authorial intention.[17]

Rather, the task demanded of philosophy (and literary criticism) by the materialistic understanding of language informing the discourses to which I have been referring is a two-phased operation. To radicalize Heidegger's *Destruktion*, it is both de-structive (I emphasize the etymology to suggest its positive moment) and projective. On the other hand, it thinks language to thematize this coercive, this same-making and co-optive (colonialist), ideology in all its historically specific density. In Edward Said's term, it thinks language to bring into explicitness the "affiliations" that a particular historical discourse has (however unevenly developed) with adjacent social classes, political structures, cultural institutions, religious sects or groupings, etc.: "Affiliation," Said writes (with Antonio Gramsci in mind),

is what enables a text to maintain itself as a text and thus is covered by a range of circumstances: status of the author, historical moment, conditions of publication, diffusion and reception, values drawn upon, values and ideas assumed, a framework of consensually held tacit assumptions, presumed background, and so on and on. In the second place to study affiliation is to study and recreate the bonds between texts and world, bonds which specialization and the institutions of literature have all but completely effaced. Every text is an act of will to some extent, but what has not been very much studied is the degree to which—and the specific cultural space by which—texts are made permissable. *To recreate the affiliative network is therefore to make visible, to give materiality back to*, the strands holding the text to the society that produced it. In the third place, affiliation releases a text from its isolation, and imposes upon the scholar or critic the presentational problems of historically recreating or reconstructing the possibilities out of which the text arose. Here is the place for intentional analysis, *and for the effort to place a text in homological, dialogical or antithetical relationships with other texts, classes, institutions, etc.*[18]

This project of thematizing the affiliative network of a historically specific discursive formation, is, of course, ungrounded. Like the project of deconstruction, it understands language as a phenomenon that, despite its willfully assimilative, i.e. structuralist, end, always already deconstructs itself, that can never totalize its structuralist discourse, can never re-present the temporal world to the disciplinary panoptic eye which, in the term bringing Hegel's mode of inquiry to culmination, would *comprehend* (from the Latin *prehendere*: "grasp," or "take hold of") its recalcitrant flux. But unlike the deconstructive project, it understands difference, not as a purely grammatological phenomenon, i.e., as *differance*, which systematically reduces difference to a rationally ordained linguistic premise, a premise that, as I have suggested, de-differentiates historically specific discursive practices and thus overlooks their historically specific power. Rather, it understands difference ontologically, that is, as temporality, which is simultaneous with, if not prior to, language.

The "Fall" of the Word alleged or implied by various metaphysical discourses of the ontotheological tradition from Plato through Hegel and Rousseau to Saussure and Lévi-Strauss is not simply a fall into words—into "writing in general"; it is also and simultaneously a "fall" from eternity or timelessness into temporality, into history. For as Lessing reminded us a long time ago in *Laocoön*, words—writing/reading—are informed by time or, rather, are, unlike the eternal (plastic) Word, a temporal medium. It is, in other words, temporality that disseminates textual difference. This is a truth of which even Derrida (if not those explicators and text-oriented exegetes who, in a scandalous contradiction, interpret his duplicitous discourse for the benighted or who are now applying deconstructive theory to literary texts) is aware when he insists that the text, i.e. writing, always already *defers* the presence, the Word, it would re-present or re-eternalize.

The "second" phase or moment of the task of contemporary philosophy (which is, in reality, simultaneous with the first) is, then, to dis-close the essential decenteredness of language, which ideological uses of language would re-center, spatialize, and accommodate to them

for their hegemonic ends. This also means—and it is a crucial extension of my retrieval of the ontological difference from *differance*—the
equiprimordial de-centeredness of all the sites on the continuum of being, however unevenly developed at any particular historical conjuncture, from being itself to consciousness, language, gender, economic production, morality, law, and civil and political society. Thus language
per se is denied its privileged status as absolute premise, as the base of
superstructural epiphenomena, whether as divine *Logos*, anthropological (or humanistic) *Logos*, or the *differance* of grammatology.

V

Understood as indissolubly equiprimordial with these other sites
on the continuum of being, language is also divested of its status as
abstract discipline—a status bestowed on it by Aristotle when he com-
partmentalized being and inquiry into separate disciplinary categories.
It comes to be understood, rather, as *praxis*: capable of being used "providentially" on behalf of cultural and socio-political hegemony or "im-
providentially," or rather improvisionally, on behalf of freedom. To emphasize the visual metaphor informing these terms, since they are crucial
to the critical purposes of this discourse, language comes to be understood
either as a panoptic instrument of the will to power or a constitutive
horizonal or perspectival agent of negative capability.

The first has been the appropriative way appropriated by Western
philosophy at large, of Plato, for example, in his apotheosis of the *mousiké*
of language to legitimate the ideal, guardian-supervised, *polis*; of Virgil,
in his apotheosis of *fatum* (the destiny inscribed in Jupiter's Book) to
legitimate the Roman Empire; of the Patristic Fathers, in there apotheosis
of language as the Word made Flesh, which is the beginning and end,
to legitimate the eschatological drama of orthodox Christianity and the
Holy Roman Empire; of the American Puritans in their apotheosis of
language as prophecy to legitimate the providential "errand" of the
New England "saints" and the theocratic "City on the Hill" which
is its end; of Bacon in his apotheosis of language as the anthropological
Word of empirical science to legitimate the technocratic state; of Ben-
tham in his apotheosis of language as panoptic geometry to legitimate
the disciplinary society of the "Enlightenment"; of Arnold in his
apotheosis of language as "the best that has been thought and said in

the [Western] world" to legitimate the liberal capitalistic State; of Eliot
in his apotheosis of the imperial "maturity" and "comprehensiveness"
of Virgil's Latin to legitimate the "mind [and socio-political order] of
[a Christian Humanist] Europe"; and even of a certain Lukács in his
apotheosis of language as reflection of objective reality to legitimate
the Stalinist state. It is, to adapt Nietzsche's too restricted terms to my
purposes, the re-actionary way of *ressentiment* of "creative" language
use in which the dominant culture ("we") speaks for, in order to disarm
and domesticate, the always threatening *Other* ("they") or, to put it
another way, in which it miniaturizes the "outside" to the comprehensible and graspable proportions of an *effigy*—a fiction in binary opposition to itself—on which it can take its compensatory revenge against
its unpresentable, i.e. incomprehensible and ungraspable, recalcitrance:

> The slave revolt in morality begins when *ressentiment* itself
> becomes creative and gives birth to values: the *ressentiment* of
> natures that are denied the true reaction, that of deed, and com-
> pensate themselves with an imaginary revenge. While every noble
> morality develops from a triumphant affirmation of itself, slave
> morality from the outset says No to what is "outside," what is
> "different," what is "not itself": and *this* No is its creative deed.
> This inversion of the value-positing eye—this *need* to direct one's
> view outward instead of back to oneself—is of the essence of *ressen-
> timent*: in order to exist, slave morality always first needs a hostile
> external world: it needs, physiologically speaking, external stimuli
> in order to act at all—its action is fundamentally reaction.[19]

This, finally, is the Way informing Walter Jackson Bate's project
to recuperate the *litterae humaniores* and William J. Bennett's to "reclaim
a legacy" in the face of the "shattered humanities."[20] For all their
apostrophes to the "classical, especially Greek, heritage" ("CES," p.
48)—to the potential of the Greek *paideia* for liberating the minds of
men and women—their renewed Humanism (and the society it envi-
sions) is not, as Nietzsche's quite different ("Dionysiac") genealogy of
Greek culture resonantly suggests, Greek at all. Though the issue is too
complex for easy summary and admittedly debatable, I think it is worth
suggesting what would no doubt strike Humanists like Bate and Bennett as a willful violation of scholarship (and a breach of scholarly decorum): that it has been, *mutatis mutandis*, the Roman/Judeo-Christian
or, rather, the Christian Humanist version of Western literary (and socio-

political) history—the narrative of the "saving remnant" espoused in modern times by Sainte-Beuve and T.S. Eliot[21]—that, by and large, has determined the discourse and canon formation of Humanism from the Renaissance through Arnold and Babbitt to Bate and Bennett.

It is true, of course, that modern humanists, especially since the Romantics' revaluation of Greek literature in the early decades of the nineteenth century (by way of Winckelmann, the Schlegels, Schiller, etc.) have apotheosized Homer's Odysseus as the "origin" of the Western literary tradition. Despite their protestations on this point, however, it has been, as it was for, say, Sir Philip Sidney in his *Defense of Poetry*, Virgil's Aeneas, the seed-bearer of and paragon of responsibility (*pietas*) to the "higher cause"—to the logocentric "center elsewhere," as it were—that modern humanists, in the name of the saving remnant, have in fact affirmed as the "standard," the "model," the "measure," for Western Man and for the itinerary of narrative construction. Or, to be more precise, it has been the *Odyssey*—and Greek literature in general—*seen through the corrective eyes of Virgil* (and the Patristic and American Puritan/biblical exegetes), who transformed Homer's errant art into a disciplined Art of Truth in behalf of imperial power. Thus, for example, though Matthew Arnold displaces Saint-Beuve's Virgil as the *classic* poet of the Western tradition in "The Modern Element in Modern Literature," in favor of the "seriously cheerful" poets of Periclean Athens,[22] his displacement does not involve a rejection of the prophetic (teleological) narrative structure of Virgil's *Aeneid*. Nor does it abandon the idea of the classic as the expression of a "comprehensiveness," "maturity," and "adequacy" of *vision*—of "seeing life steadily and seeing it whole"—capable of making intelligible, graspable—and appropriatable—a complex age threatened by intellectual and sociopolitical anarchy. These characteristics, which Sainte-Beuve before and T. S. Eliot after him singled out as the defining terms of Virgil's redemptive art—an art able to give a "shape and significance to the immense panorama of futility and anarchy which is contemporary history"[23]—are according to Arnold precisely those that make Greek literature—and "the small remnant" professing it[24]—the measure for those committed to the "deliverance" of modern man from the disruptive partiality—"the incompleteness"—of a provincial perspective. I quote Arnold at some length to suggest how deeply inscribed the supervisory "Roman" center elsewhere is in his "disinterested" rhetoric:

I propose, in this my first occasion of speaking here [at Oxford], to attempt . . . a general survey of ancient classical literature and history as may afford us the conviction—in presence of the doubts so often expressed of the profitableness, in the present day, of our study of this literature—that, even admitting to their fullest extent the legitimate demands of our age, the literature of ancient Greece is, even for modern times, a mighty agent of intellectual deliverance. . . .

But first let us ask ourselves why the demand for an intellectual deliverance arises in such an age as the present, and in what the deliverance itself consists? The demand arises, because our present age has around it a copious and complex past; it arises, because the present age exhibits to the individual man who contemplates it the spectacle of a vast multitude of facts awaiting and inviting his comprehension. The deliverance consists in man's comprehension of this present and past. It begins when our mind begins to enter into possession of the general ideas which are the law of this vast multitude of facts. It is perfect when we have acquired [as the Greeks did] *that harmonious acquiescence of mind which we feel in contemplating a grand spectacle that is intelligible to us; when we have lost that impatient irritation of mind which we feel in presence of an immense, moving, confused spectacle which,* while it perpetually excites our curiosity, perpetually baffles our comprehension.

This, then, is what distinguished certain epochs in the history of the human race [especially the Age of Pericles] . . . ; on the one hand, the presence of a significant spectacle to contemplate; on the other hand, the desire to find the true point of view from which to contemplate this spectacle. He who has found that point of view, he who *adequately comprehends* this spectacle, *has risen to the comprehension of his age.* . . .[25]

Arnold's displacement of Virgil, in short, does not abandon the panoptic eye—"the true point of view from which to contemplate the spectacle"—that oversees Virgil's world. Nor, to invoke its artistic and sociopolitical allotrope, does it reject the abiding "center" or "capital." It simply relocates the cultural and socio-political Center/Capital from Rome to (a British version of) Athens. The "classic" as such a Center/Capital retains the authority and power that enables it to annul by cultivating and domesticating the "provincialism"—the "doing as one likes"—which, for him as for Sainte-Beuve and Eliot (as well as the exponents of the British Empire), constitutes the most ominous contemporary threat to the law and order of literature, literary history—and the State. This, if we thematize the political implications (something which Arnold himself is exasperatingly reluctant to do), is the conclusion that Frank Kermode draws about Arnold's classical project in *The Classic*:

> Hellenism, rather than a renewed relation with metropolitan Rome, was the English Arnold's cure for "provincialism." He assumed, like the Latin imperialists, that the classic belongs to a privileged order of time and history. But whereas for Sainte-Beuve [and Eliot] this order is continuous, almost genetic, because Latin, and, because French, institutionalized—a quality the Englishman rather envied—for Arnold it is a Victorian version of fifth-century Athens. What the two critics share are a belief in the modernity of the true classic, and the notion of provincialism, which imply a metropolis.[26]

What I am suggesting, in other words, is that, like Matthew Arnold, to whom they insistently appeal, Bate's and Bennett's classical ideal is essentially Roman or, more precisely, a Romanism filtered through the figural lens of Judeo-Christian *ressentiment* and intended to accommodate a disruptive modern or postmodern historical conjuncture to the cultural and socio-political *imperium* of the Occident. Their Humanism is an educational discourse that is not designed to generate originative thinking in behalf of the enhancement of life, a genealogical or destructive thinking always already dialogically engaged in and with its historical occasion—with the ontological, cultural, and socio-political structures that, however unevenly developed, determine and constrain the life of men and women in *this* time and *this* place. It is, rather, as Heidegger suggests in his "Letter on Humanism," a re-presentational discourse, a discourse committed to a model or structure—a master code—assumed to be natural (primary), permanent, universal—and threatened—but which, in fact, is constituted by the dominant culture and is intended to serve as a standard for thought and *praxis*.[27] It is a secondary, derived, and codified discourse, the fundamental imperative of which is the imitation of an authoritative measure—a consensually established archive—and the end of which is not the engendering of negatively capable men and women, but, as Bennett's overdetermined appeal to the Federalist Papers suggests, the training of "good" citizens (*eruditio et institutio in bonas artes*),[28] citizens, to radicalize Heidegger, positively capable of legitimating and extending the hegemonic purposes of the post-industrial West, if not of the advanced capitalist America, they will serve.

This is one of the great ironies of the humanists' iterative invocation of the "Western Heritage." For the "common culture rooted in civilization's lasting vision" to which they appeal is, as Heidegger puts it, an "uprooted" heritage, a free-floating body of fixed doctrine that increasingly assumed priority and privileged status after the Romans codified and standardized the historically rooted ontology of classical Greece:

> The process begins with the appropriation of Greek words by Roman-Latin thought. *Hypokeimenon* becomes *subjectum: hypostasis* becomes *substantia; symbebekos* becomes *accidens*. However, this translation of Greek names into Latin is in no way the innocent process it is considered to this day. Beneath the seemingly literal and faithful translation there is concealed, rather, a *translation of Greek experience into a different way of thinking. Roman thought takes over the Greek experience of what they say, without the Greek word.* The rootlessness of Western thought begins with this translation.[29]

The heritage which the Humanists would reclaim as the Way of Modern Man, that is, which "uproots the historicity of Dasein," renders men and women incapable of understanding "the most elementary conditions which alone make a positive return to the past possible—in the sense of its productive appropriation."[30] But the irony runs deeper than Heidegger suggests. For in inculcating forgetfulness of originative thinking, this cultural heritage also makes men and women the willing subjects and agents of hegemonic authority. It must not be forgotten that it was, percisely at the time when the cultural mystique was in its ascendancy, the appeal to "the white man's burden"—that "thankless" task of cultivating the "barbarians" outside the pale of the Western orbit—that justified the ruthless European conquest of the "Other" world. In short, the Humanism that Bate and Bennett would reclaim is a colonialism.

It is no accident, I think, that the words, "culture," "cultivate," "acculturation"—the privileged Latinate names which have figuratively expressed the generic ideal of humanistic civilization at least since the Renaissance (the names central to Bate's and Bennett's pedagogic programs)—are cognates of "colonize" (from the Latin *colonus*, "tiller," "cultivator," "planter," "settler"; and *colere*, "cultivate," "plant"), all of which have their source in the Roman/Christian translation of the Greek world κύκλος (cycle) or κιρκος ("ring," "circle"), the spatial image of time symbolizing not simply "Beauty" and "Perfection," but also Domination. As the following passage from Plutarch's "Life of Romulus" suggests, it was this codification of the errancy and prodigality of originative Greek thinking—this encircling, cultivation, and colonization of truth as *a-letheia*—which legitimated the Roman political will to power and, in some fundamental sense, enabled the Roman, the Holy Roman, and, as Sacvan Bercovitch persuasively suggests, the American, "*imperium sine fine. . . .*":[31]

> Romulus, having buried his brother Remus, together with his two foster-fathers, on the mount Remonia, set to building his city; and sent for men out of Tuscany, who directed him by sacred usages and written rules in all ceremonies to be observed, as in a religious rite. First, they dug a round trench about that which is now the Comitium, or Court of Assembly, and into it solemnly threw the first-fruits of all things either good by custom or necessary by nature; lastly, every man taking a small piece of earth of the country from whence he came, they all threw them promiscuously together. This trench they call, as they do the heavens, *Mundus*; making which their centre, they described the city in a circle round it. Then the founder fitted to a plough a brazen ploughshare, and, yoking together a bull and a cow, drove himself a deeep line of furrow round the bounds; while the business of those that followed after was to see that whatever earth was thrown up should be turned all inwards towards the city; and not to let any clod lie outside. With this line they described the wall, and called it, by a contraction, Pomoerium, that is, *postmurum*, after or beside the wall; and where they designed to make a gate, there they took out the share, carried the plough over, and left a space; for which reason they consider the whole wall as holy, except where the gates are; for had they adjudged them also sacred, they could not, without offense to religion, have given free ingress and egress for the necessaries of human life, some of which are in themselves unclean.[32]

As I have tried to suggest in pointing to and amplifying on the "reactionary" narrative of the saving remnant invoked by Arnold, Babbitt, Sainte-Beuve, and Eliot, this "Roman/Judeo-Christian" understanding of the symbolic circle—this mystified image of Beauty/Perfection enabling the circumscription and colonization of the difference that temporality disseminates—continues to this day to inform the discourse of liberal Humanism and its appeal to Culture and its Legacy against the threat of anarchy. For the "deliverance" envisioned by the liberal humanists as the consequence of the recuperation of the cultural heritage is not a liberation from constraint, but, as it was for their predecessors, a reactionary agenda of cultural incarceration which, however idealized, has its ultimate source, in the terms of my epigraph from Nietzsche's *Genealogy of Morals*, in the "oppressive instincts that thirst for reprisal" against the claims of life: the claims, that is, of the differences that temporality disseminates.[33] However effaced in their normally benign rhetoric, it is this reactionary socio-political agenda—this strategy for containing and subjugating the disruptive "Other" within the cultural circle—that, as Bate's and Bennett's exemplary appeal to the executive authority of institutional power (the "State") makes clear, constitutes the subtext of the liberal humanists' campaign to recuperate the massive centrality and human relevance of the *"litterae humaniores"* in this post-Vietnam conjuncture of American history.

It is, further, this "reactionary" political agenda—this "regime of Truth," in Foucault's phrase—that Paul de Man must necessarily overlook in reading both Bate's invocation of the small "talented nucleus" (who "really *care*, who are ready to face difficulties and to make sacrifices in order to recapture some understanding of the centrality and larger values of human letters") and his appeal for the instrumental support of the custodians of the university as a question concerning the debate between "theory" or "philology" and traditional literary discourse.

The second way of language understood as *praxis*—historically marginal, if not domesticated, excluded, or altogether repressed in the Western past—is the way of disappropriation appropriated in various modes by the contemporary "philosophy" to which I have been referring. This is the way of what, after Michel Foucault, I call the postmodern counter-memory, which attempts to liberate the appropriated difference that time disseminates from the bondage of the concept, of closure, of the metaphysical circle, at every site on the continuum of being into which it has been forced by the assimilative/speculative and

totalizing spirit of *ressentiment*. It is, in other words, the way that would
"decolonize" or "de-territorialize" the Other subjugated by the Cultural
Memory: the errant text pacified by the representational Canon of
Western literary history; the desire territorialized by the Norm of
enlightened rationality; the de-viant re-formed by the panoptic physics
of power of the disciplinary society; the female enthralled by the phallocentric Father; the laborer reified and alienated by the totalizing economy
of capitalism; the other *ethnos*—the "third" world—subdued and col-
onized by the hegemonic imperialist state, etc. The difference that this
materialist idea of language would retrieve from the concept is not the
"difference" that has its condition of possibility in the ontological priority
of Identity and its end in the extension of knowledge/power. It is, rather,
the difference that is prior to conceptualization and codification, the
difference, as Foucault puts it after Nietzsche and Deleuze, which is "pure
event":

> Consider the handling of difference. It is generally assumed to be
> a difference from or within something; behind difference, beyond
> it—but as its support, its site, its delimitation, and consequently
> as the source of mastery—we pose, through the concept, the unity
> of a group and its breakdown into species in the operation of dif-
> ference (the organic domination of the Aristotelian concept). Dif-
> ference is transformed into that which must be specified within
> a concept, without overstepping its bounds. And yet above the
> species, we encounter the swarming of individualities. What is this
> boundless diversity, which eludes specification and remains out-
> side the concept, if not the resurgence of repetition? Underneath
> the ovine species, we are reduced to counting sheep. This stands
> as the first form of subjection: difference as specification (within
> the concept) and repetition as the indifference of individuals (out-
> side the concept). But subjection to what? To common sense which,
> turning away from the mad flux and anarchical difference, in-
> variably recognizes the identity of things (and this is at all times
> a general capacity). Common sense extracts the generality of an
> object while it simultaneously establishes the universality of the
> knowing subject through a pact of good will. But what if we gave
> free rein to ill will? What if thought freed itself from common sense
> and decided to function only in its extreme singularity? What if
> it adopted the disreputable bias of the paradox, instead of com-

placently accepting its citizenship in the *doxa?* What if it conceived of difference differentially, instead of searching out the common elements underlying difference? Then difference would disappear as a general feature that leads to the generality of the concept and it would become—a different thought, the thought of difference—a pure event. As for repetition, it would cease to function as the dreary succession of the identical, and would become displaced difference.[34]

This understanding of language, conscious of language's awesome power, despite its ultimate "poverty," to comprehend the ungraspable or, what is the same thing, to enframe and transform alterity into standing reserve[35] at every site on the continuum of being, is, I submit, language without presupposition. To adapt Heidegger's reformulation of Nietzsche's "Will to Power" to my purposes, it is informed by *Gelassenheit*: that Negative Capability, that care for or deference to the differential be-*ing* of being, which is unrelenting in its genealogical exposure of the resentful and repressive panoptic Eye—the "center elsewhere"— masquerading as disinterested or objective inquiry, inquiry without presupposition—and which at the same time lets the play of difference be, allows it, that is, to speak for itself. (By defining Heidegger's *Gelassenheit* in terms of Keat's oxymoron, I want, of course, to draw attention to its affinity with the affirmative version of Nietzsche's "Will to Power," to its positive and active connotations [its "capability"] in order to counter the usual understanding of the word as a passive and re-active stance in the face of being. I take *Gelassenheit*, that is, to be a comportment towards the contradictory and pluralistic content of de-centeredness that forcefully resists [does "hermeneutic violence" to] the nihilistic ontological, cultural, and socio-political consequences of a *ressentiment* that would master the differences that time disseminates by an end-oriented strategy of codification in behalf of letting be-*ing* be, of letting "it" become. The difference between Nietzsche's version of the "Will to Power" and this understanding of *Gelassenheit* as Negative Capability is that the former emphasizes the second term of the oxymoron as it were, whereas the latter places its stress on the first. Neither, it must be added, implies a sundering of the oxymoron into a binary opposition.)

Thus the "community" this materialist "idea" of language implies is ultimately a community of difference in dialogical, by which I also mean *improvisational*, relationship. It is a community in which the participants, whether readers of texts, citizens of the *polis*, or dwellers on this earth, always already expose their "tartuffery of words" (Nietzsche),[36] their "everyday language," *Gerede*, (Heidegger),[37] their "prejudices" (Gadamer),[38] their "determining rules of discursive formation," (Foucault),[39] or their "problematic" (Althusser),[40] to the risk of the questions posed by the outside Other, to which their monologic ideological model cannot respond or, perhaps, which it dare not tolerate. It is a community, therefore, that, unlike that "regime of Truth" organized by a transcendental or suprahistorical disciplinary eye, acknowledges its radical historicity—its "this sidedness," in Marx's term—and thus its finite—horizontal or perspectival—vision:

> Henceforth, my dear philosophers, let us be on our guard against the dangerous old conceptual fiction that posited a "pure, will-less, painless, timeless knowing subject"; let us guard against the snares of such contradictory concepts as "pure reason," "absolute spirituality," "knowledge in itself"; these always demand that we should think of an eye that is completely unthinkable, an eye turned in no particular direction in which the active and interpreting forces, through which alone seeing becomes seeing *something*, are supposed to be lacking; these always demand of the eye an absurdity and a nonsense. There is *only* a perspective seeing, only a perspective "knowing"; and the *more* affects we allow to speak about one thing, the more complete will our "concept" of this thing, our "objectivity," be. But to eliminate the will altogether, to suspend each and every affect, supposing we were capable of this—what would that mean but to *castrate* the intellect?[41]

The community in which "there is *only* a perspective seeing, *only* a perspective 'knowing'," is thus always suspicious of such hierarchical antitheses as Eternity/transience, Space/time, Identity/difference, Permanence/change, Totality/fragmentation, Truth/error, Fulfillment/desire, Orthodoxy/heresy, High Seriousness/ludic play, Apollo/Dionysus, etc., all of which, as the discourses of Bate and Bennett testify, inform the still commanding formula of the Father of modern Humanism, Culture/anarchy. It is always suspicious, that is, of metaphysics, which in perceiving *meta-ta-physica*—from after or above things-as-they-are—establishes a binary logic that not only privileges the primary term (Deleuze calls it the "majority" term),[42] but endows it with the absolute right and power of circumscribing/cultivating/colonizing the second ("minority") term.[43]

In short, the community that this materialistic idea of language of the countermemory implies is a de-structive/projective *polis*, always already on the way, open to the dis-closed possibilities enclosed, domesticated, and pacified—made docile and useful—by the imperial majority term, a *polis* the measure of which, as I have said elsewhere, is not the supervisory and providentially ordained rule of equivalence, of assimilation, that has its Origin in one Transcendental Signified or other, and its end in consensus, but the improvisational measure of men's and women's mortal *occasion*.[44] It is not, as it is finally for Walter Jackson Bate and William J. Bennett, a *socius* of Roman or Romanized Christian citizens trained by the forced imitation of normative models—the Classics—in the arts of good conduct, but, as it were, of errant Greeks negatively capable of originative thinking, of thinking critically in the midst: *interesse*.

It is, not incidentally, this de-structive/projective process—this double movement which recollects forwards—that, as I read or, rather, "misread" Heidegger, characterizes the project of retrieving (repeating) *aletheia* from *Veritas* (*adequatio intellectus et rei*) or, what is the same thing, of the hermeneutic circle, at the sites of civil and political society. To get into the hermeneutic circle in the right way is not to assume with a saving remnant—relic or seed-bearers—the recuperative teleological and retro-spective (spatializing) (ad)vantage point of a Virgilian or Augustinian or Matherian or Hegelian or a certain Marxist Re-collection, which would panoptically re-assimilate and circumscribe by force the scatter, the difference, the alterity, the heterogeneity—the dia-spora— that the "fall" into time disseminates. It is, rather, to be *interesse* and to always already undergo a Repetition of the same in behalf of retrieving—of repeating—the difference, the "this-sidedness," which is human being's occasion—the difference that the Recollective "regime of Truth" colonizes, represses, and forgets in fulfilling the nihilistic imperatives of *ressentiment*. Repetition in this always already open-ended sense is, I suggest, something like the dialectic always already at work.

In thus calling for the retrieval of temporality and improvisational or "perspective 'knowing' " from the structure of Being and from the debilitating imperative of imitation and consensus it sanctioned for a belated or historically "mature" people, I do not want to suggest that I am proposing a criticism that willfully forgets the structures of history and historical thinking, a criticism that Nietzsche sometimes appears to espouse—so much so that both commentators on the right and the left have missed his irony in responding to his critique of teleological

versions of historiography. For such an unhistorical thinking, as Nietzsche knew, is not simply impossible; it is finally also conducive to the
arrogance and violence of present and unknowing immediacy, of blind
power. Rather, I am suggesting that criticism undertake the most difficult of all tasks not impossible: the articulation of a mode of inquiry
that is simultaneously *theoria* and *praxis* (ek-sistent in-sistence); that is,
at once fully aware of the coercive structures of history constituted and
imposed by the Western suprahistorical consciousness and at the same
time negatively capable of always already (in the present) operating
futurally, a "youthful" (or originative) thinking, that is, which is simultaneous with, indeed, the consequence of maturity or belatedness: the
awareness of always already being at the end of history. This, I submit,
is what Nietzsche means when, in "On the Uses and Disadvantages
of History for Life," he ironically invokes the "universal history" so
dear to Hegel and his "grey-haired" offspring as the agent of retrieving
the "unhistorical culture" of the Greeks from its codified, sedimented,
and enfeebled old age:

> . . . . for the origin of historical culture—its quite radical conflict
> with the spirit of any 'new age,' any 'modern awareness'—this origin
> *must* itself be known historically, history *must* resolve the problem
> of history, knowledge *must* turn its sting against itself—this threefold
> *must* is the imperative of the 'new age.' . . . Or is it actually the
> case that we . . . must always be no more than 'heirs' in all the
> higher affairs of culture, because that is all we *can* ever be; a prop-
> osition once memorably expressed by Wilhelm Wackernagel. . . .
> And even if we Germans were really no more than heirs [of 'the
> world of antiquity']—to be able to look upon such a culture as
> *that* as our rightful inheritance would make the appellation 'heirs'
> the greatest and proudest possible: yet we would nonetheless be
> obliged to ask whether it really was our eternal destiny to be *pupils
> of declining antiquity*: at some time or other we might be permitted
> gradually to set our goal higher and more distant, some time or
> other we ought to be allowed to claim credit for having developed
> the spirit of Alexandrian-Roman culture so nobly and fruitfully—
> among other means through our universal history—that we now
> as a reward be permitted to set ourselves the even mightier task
> of striving to get behind and beyond this Alexandrian world and
> boldy seek our models in the original ancient Greek world of
> greatness, naturalness, and humanity. *But there we also discover the*

*reality of an essentially unhistorical culture and one which is nonetheless,
or rather on that account, an inexpressibly richer and more vital culture.*
Even if we Germans were in fact nothing but successors—we could
not be anything greater or prouder than successors if we appropriated such a culture and were the heirs and successors of that.

What I mean by this—and it is all I mean—is that the thought
of being epigones, which can often be painful enough, is also
capable of evoking great effects and grand hopes for the future
in both the individual and in a nation, provided we regard ourselves as the heirs and successors of the astonishing powers of an-
tiquity and see in this our honour and our spur. What I do not
mean, therefore, is that we should live as pale and stunted late
descendants of strong races coldly prolonging their life as anti-
quarians and gravediggers.[45]

To shift the focus from the temporal metaphor to its spatial
allotrope suggested by Heidegger in *Being and Time*, criticism in this
"new age"—the postmodern conjuncture—must abandon the Center—
the Capital, as it were—in favor of the margins, the provinces. Or, rather,
it must locate its practice both at the de-centered center and the margins
simultaneously. It must have a "commanding" view of the whole,
however unevenly developed, coercive history of things-as-they-have-
been constituted (construed) in the West and at the same time always
already acknowledge the uncertainty of the "outside," of what *actually*
is and is to come. It is, I suggest, the making of the "outside" (difference) the condition of the possibility of the "inside" (the same) — i.e.
the retrieval (*Wiederholon*) of thinking as Repetition—that makes destructive criticism always already *revolutionary*.

VI

It should now be clear that my appeal to Heidegger's destruction
of the ontotheological tradition against the claims of deconstruction
does not imply, as so many contemporary philosophers and literary
theoreticians who have appropriated his "phenomenological" meditations on Being and Language as the "house of being" overtly suppose,
that Heidegger's project *per se* is adequate to the task of resolving the
crisis of modern European man. For all his commitment to the onto-

logical difference—to the priority of temporality (what I have called "the human occasion")—over a concept of Being determined by metaphysical speculation, Heidegger by and large restricted the task of philosophy, in the last analysis, to the site of ontology, the result, perhaps, of his desire to provide a rigorously philosophical basis for Nietzsche's genealogical insights into the origins of the dominant morality. This theoretical orientation blinded him to the worldly implications of his radically revolutionary hermeneutics, and above all to the decolonizing socio-political imperatives of his disclosure of the temporal be-ing of being. One of the fatal consequences of this delimitation of philosophical inquiry to "fundamental ontology" was his compliance with, if not active complicity with, German National Socialism. Theoreticians who have come under the influence of Heidegger's luminous meditations on the *Seinsfrage* have, then, a special need to remember this unfortunate history. But the question of Heidegger's politics does not have its resolution, as it did for a generation of German intellectuals in the postwar period, including Habermas, in a willed forgetting of his ontological effort to overcome metaphysics, as if that disturbing moment in his practical life never happened. Neither, finally, I think, does it have its resolution in the rejection of the ontological question as both the deconstructors and the genealogists of socio-political power imply. Its resolution, I suggest, lies rather in the thematization of the socio-political implications of the material temporality of being/language he disclosed in his interrogations of the discourse of metaphysics, the teasingly undeveloped implications which his vestigially theoretical problematic inhibited but never, as such a neglected passage as the following suggests, entirely effaced:

> Homelessness is coming to be the destiny of the world. Hence it is necessary to think that destiny in terms of the history of Being. What Marx recognized in an essential and significant sense, though derived from Hegel, as the estrangement of man has its roots in the homelessness of modern man. This homelessness is specifically evoked from the destiny of Being in the form of metaphysics and through metaphysics is simultaneously entrenched and covered up as such. Because Marx by experiencing estrangement attains an essential dimension of history, the Marxist view of history is superior to that of other historical accounts. But since neither Husserl nor—so far as I have seen till now—Sartre recog-

nizes the essential importance of the historical in Being, neither phenomenology nor existentialism enters that dimension within which a productive dialogue with Marxism first becomes possible.[46]

The resonant unsaid in Heidegger's texts makes urgent claims on thinking in our totalized and deracinated time—this Age of the World Picture, as he appropriately called it. It is in response to these claims that I have offered the foregoing all too brief and tentative remarks in behalf of a new—a postmodern—critical *praxis*.

NOTES

1. Jacques Derrida, "Structure, Sign and Play in the Discourses of the Human Sciences," *Writing and Difference*, tr. Alan Bass (Chicago: Univ. of Chicago Press, 1978), 279.

2. Walter Jackson Bate, "The Crisis in English Studies," *Harvard Magazine* Vol 85, no. 1 (September-October, 1982): 52; hereafter cited "CES" in the text.

3. Paul de Man, "The Return of Philology," *Times Literary Supplement*, December 10, 1983. My emphasis. See also Jacques Derrida, "The Principle of Reason: The University in the Eyes of its Pupils," *Diacritics* 13, no. 3 (Fall 1983): 15: "Among many possible examples [of 'great professors or representatives of prestigious institutions,' who, in their belief that 'they are defending philosophy, literature, and the humanities against these new modes of questioning that are also a new relation to language and tradition . . . forget the principles that they claim to defend in their work and suddenly begin to heap insults, to say whatever comes into their heads on the subject of texts that they obviously have never opened or that they have encountered through a mediocre journalism that in other circumstances they would pretend to scorn'], I shall mention only two recent articles. They have at least one trait in common: their authors are highly placed representatives of two institutions whose power and influence hardly need to be recalled. I refer to 'The Crisis in English Studies,' by Walter Jackson Bate, Kingsley Porter University Professor at Harvard . . . and to 'The Shattered Humanities' by Willis [sic] J. Bennett, Chairman of the National Endowment for the Humanities [*Wall Street Journal*, Dec. 31, 1982]. The latter of these articles carries ignorance and irrationality so far as to write the following: 'A popular movement in literary criticism called "Deconstruction" denies that there are any texts at all. If there are no texts, there are no great texts, and no argument for reading.' The former makes remarks about deconstruction—and this is not by chance—that·are, we might say, just as unnerved. As Paul de Man notes in an admirable short essay

['The Return of Philology' . . .], Professor Bate 'has this time confined his sources of information to *Newsweek* magazine . . . . What is left is a matter of law-enforcement rather than critical debate. One must be feeling very threatened indeed to become so aggressively defensive.' "

4. The history of the American uses of the narrative of "the saving remnant," from the Puritan exegetes who accommodated Patristic figural or typological interpretation to their contemporary historical conjuncture (i.e. to their effort to justify their New England theocracy) through the Revolutionary period to the "American Renaissance"—a history in which the initial providential historical perspective of the Puritans became increasingly secularized but never abandoned—is brilliantly traced by Sacvan Bercovitch in *The American Jeremiad* (Madison: Univ. of Wisconsin Press, 1978). According to Bercovitch, the central figure in this "movement from visible saint to American patriot, sacred errand to manifest destiny, colony to republic to imperial power" (p. 92) is Jonathan Edwards. Bercovitch's argument is persuasive. However, I suggest that it tends to obscure, if not to deny, the Federalists' conflation of the imperial Roman with the biblical figural narrative of the saving remnant in their pursuit of a ritual of national consensus—and empire. For the sake of emphasizing the continuity between the Roman hermeneutics—above all, the hermeneutics informing the prophecy/fullfillment structure of the *Aeneid*—that was accommodated by the figural method of the Patristic Fathers to justify the Holy Roman Empire and that figural Puritan/Roman hermeneutics that eventually justified the imperial claims of the post-Revolutionary American Republic, I would like to invoke Cotton Mather's *Magnalia Christi Americana* (1702), in which " 'the mighty deeds of Christ' elevates the pristine New England venture to its highest epic and mythical proportions" (*American Jeremiad*, 87), and to bring to the foreground the following passage buried in a footnote to Bercovitch's text (p. 87): "Mather's millenarianism at this time is worth special emphasis because the *Magnalia* has so often been read as a cry of despair. . . . The significance of those deliverances [which are usually taken to be the expression of despair] are indicated by the title of the last section of this last Book, 'Arma Virosque Cano,' a title that recalls the Virgilian invocation with which Mather opens the History (as well as the numerous echoes from the *Aeneid* thereafter), and so suggests the epic proportions of his narrative. For Mather, of course, New England's story not only parallels but supersedes that of the founding of Rome [by the saving remnant], as his literary 'assistance' from Christ excels the inspiration of Virgil's muse, as the 'exemplary heroes' he celebrates resemble but outshine the men of Aeneas' band— not only as Christians but as seafarers and conquerors of hostile pagan tribes— and, most spectacularly, as the millenium towards which the Reformation is moving provides the far more glorious antitype of the Augustan *Pax Romana*. Undoubtedly, the proper title for Mather's work is the exultant one he gave it: *Magnalia Christi Americana*, 'The Great Acts of Christ in America.' "

However effaced (secularized) in their "Jeremiads," these "imperial" claims and the teleological hermeneutics that legitimate them are, I suggest, implicit in Babbitt's and Bate's texts, especially in their humanistic appeal to the "classical legacy," by which, as I will suggest, they ultimately mean the Roman heritage. For an example of Babbitt's appeal to the narrative of the saving remnant ("which is not subject to mediation or compromise"), see his diatribe against Whitman in *Democracy and Leadership* (Boston: Houghton Mifflin, 1927), 260-61. Babbitt's immediate source is, no doubt, Matthew Arnold's "Numbers; or The Majority and the Remnant," in *Philistinism in England and America, The Complete Prose Works*, Vol. X (Ann Arbor: Univ. of Michigan Press, 1974), 143-64. However, given Babbitt's New England background (his American ancestry goes back to Edward Bobbett, who settled in Plymouth, Massachusetts in 1643), one is justified in speculating that he accommodated Arnold's more or less moral doctrine of the saving remnant to the secularized typological structure inscribed in his discourse by his Puritan heritage. See Edmund Wilson, "Notes on Babbitt and More," *The Shores of Light: A Literary Chronicle of the Twenties and Thirties* (New York: Farrar, Straus and Young, 1952): Commenting on Babbitt's unyielding commitment to the "will to refrain," Wilson observes (p. 459) that it leads to opinions that are "mere unexamined prejudices of a bigoted Puritan heritage which these gentlemen [Babbitt and More]—for all their voyaging through the varied realms of the mind—have never succeeded in sloughing off, and which they persist in mistaking for eternal and universal laws, because—they have put this forward as an overwhelming justification—when they look into their own natures, they find them there."

5. William J. Bennett, "To Reclaim a Legacy: Report on Humanities in Education," rpt. in *The Chronicle of Higher Education* 29, no. 11 (November 28, 1984): 17. For all its lip service to "Mankind" and "human greatness," Bennett's text, both in this passage and many others, makes it clear that by "civilization" he means the "shared ideals" of Western civilization. Indeed, at times even this orbit is selectively reduced to mean the American consensus. Thus, for example, in response to the "respect for diversity" in the curriculum effected by its becoming "more sensitive to the long-overlooked cultural achievements of many groups" (a way of putting it that nullifies the active struggle of minorities in America to gain this "respect"), Bennett writes (p. 21, my emphasis): "We are a part and a product of Western civilization. That our society was founded upon such principles as justice, liberty, government with the consent of the governed, and equality under the law is the result of ideas descended directly from great epochs of Western civilization—Enlightenment England and France, Renaissance Florence, and Periclean Athens. These ideas . . . are the glue that binds together our pluralistic nation. The fact that we as Americans—whether black or white, Asian or Hispanic, rich or poor—share these beliefs aligns us with other cultures of the

Western tradition. It is not ethnocentric or chauvinistic to acknowledge this. *No student citizen of our civilization should be denied access to the best that tradition has to offer."* In this remarkable passage, Bennett 1) reads the past of Western civilization from the selective perspective of the contemporary American socio-political consensus; 2) subordinates learning adjectivally to citizenship; and, most remarkable of all, 3) affirms the coercive imperatives of the American consensus as a natural "right" of freedom and condemns those who would question these—whether racially or economically deprived minorities or educators who perceive a complicity between the kind of education Bennett espouses and a socio-political consensus that deprives minorities—as agents of coercion. Not accidentally, Bennett not only invokes Bate's scholarly authority but also quotes both his ominous diagnosis of the crisis in literary studies and his appeal to the policing agency of the University, though he misleadingly refers (p. 19) to Bate's appeal as an exhortation to "graduate humanities departments to examine their priorities." The prevarications that pervade Bennett's "Report" are epitomized by the euphemism he uses to transform the period of the Vietnam War (and the student protest movement) into the "late 1960s and early 1970s." It is clear that, like Bate's text, Bennett's is addressed not to those who might disagree with him but to the dominant consensus and its magistrates that do.

6. Giorgio Agamben, "The Idea of Language: Some Difficulties in Speaking about Language," unpublished essay presented at the conference entitled "Critique of Ideology and Hermeneutics in Contemporary Italian Thought" at New York University, November 3-5, 1983.

7. Michael Beehler, *Theatres of Tropes: Difference and Representation in Stevens and Eliot* (Baton Rouge: Louisiana State University Press, forthcoming).

8. Hillis Miller, "Stevens' Rock and Criticism as Cure II," *The Georgia Review* 30, no. 3 (Summer 1976): 335-38.

9. For a powerful thematization of the disabling consequences of the logical "rigor" so prized by deconstructive criticism, see Jonathan Arac, "To Regress from the Rigor of Shelley: Figures of History in American Deconstructive Criticism," *boundary 2*, 8, no. 3 (Spring 1980): 249ff. This essay, which plays brilliantly on the etymological ambiguities of "rigor" or, better, which rigorously analyzes its figural play, is a review of Josue V. Harari, ed. *Textual Strategies: Perspectives in Post-Structuralist Criticism* (Ithaca, N.Y., Cornell Univ. Press, 1979); and Harold Bloom, Jacques Derrida, Geoffrey Hartman, and J. Hillis Miller, *Deconstruction and Criticism* (New York: Seabury, 1979).

10. Miller's source appears to be Freud: "Criticism repeats or reformulates again and again 'the same' blind alley, like Freud in 'Das Unheimliche' finding himself repeatedly coming back to the bordello section of the Italian town, however hard he tried to escape it. Any 'Socratic' method in criticism, if carried far enough . . . reaches its limits and subverts itself" ("Stevens' Rock,"

345). Miller invokes Freud probably because Freud's psychological interpretation of *das Unheimliche*, especially after Derrida's textualization of the Freudian unconsciousness (in "Freud and the Scene of Writing," *Writing and Difference*, 196-231) is more amenable to the interpretive exigencies of deconstruction than Heidegger's ontological interpretation. Nevertheless, as Miller's Nietzschean context suggests, Heidegger's *die Unheimlichkeit* is implicated in Miller's definition, if only to suggest for deconstruction, what the uncanny is not.

11. Jonathan Culler, *On Deconstruction: Theory and Criticism after Structuralism* (Ithaca, N.Y.: Cornell Univ. Press, 1982), pp. 17-18. Another set of inaugural terms that pervades Culler's "explanatory" book gathers around the metaphor of the guide or authority, whose function is to lead the bewildered reader through the dark wood of competing theories into the light, i.e. the *truth* of deconstruction. It is ironic that a commentary on a discourse purporting to undermine the truth claims of traditional hermeneutics should present the author and reader in terms of the Virgil/Dante paradigm, that is, precisely the historically powerful paradigm of legitimation that it is the alleged purpose of deconstruction to invalidate.

12. Jean François Lyotard, *The Postmodern Condition: A Report on Knowledge*, tr. Geoff Bennington and Brian Massumi (Minneapolis: Univ. of Minnesota Press, 1984), 46.

13. Stanley Fish, "Profession Despise Thyself: Fear and Self-Loathing in Literary Studies," *Critical Inquiry*, 10, no. 2 (December 1983): 373.

14. Ibid., 355-56.

15. Edward W. Said, "Response to Stanley Fish," *Critical Inquiry* 10, no. 2 (December 1983): 373.

16. Walter Jackson Bate, "To the Editor of Critical Inquiry," *Critical Inquiry* 10, no. 2 (December 1983): 370.

17. Jonathan Culler, *On Deconstruction*, 109-10.

18. Edward W. Said, "Reflections in Recent American 'Left' Literary Criticism," *boundary 2*, 8, no. 1 (Fall 1979): 27. Rpt. in *The Question of Textuality*, ed. William V. Spanos, Paul Bové, and Daniel O'Hara (Bloomington: Indiana Univ. Press, 1982); and Edward W. Said, *The World, the Text, and the Critic* (Cambridge, Mass.: Harvard Univ. Press, 1983).

19. Friedrich Nietzsche, *On the Genealogy of Morals*, tr. Walter Kaufmann and R. J. Hollingdale (New York: Vintage Books, 1969), 36-37. Nietzsche, I suggest, fails to perceive, or perhaps represses his perception of, this crucial continuity between the "master morality" of the Roman Empire and the "slave morality" of the Holy Roman Empire, especially as this continuity is foregrounded by the parallel between the imperative of duty to the "higher cause" in Virgil's *Aeneid* (*pietas*) demanded by the promise/fulfillment structure of his *peregrinatio*, which will legitimate the Roman Empire, and the "responsibility" of the Christian remnant demanded by the promise/fulfill-

ment structure of the Providential narrative, which will legitimate the Holy Roman Empire. Elsewhere, however, in *The Uses and Disadvantages of History for Life*, for example, he makes a distinction between Greece and Rome that suggests, if it does not thematize, this continuity.

20. William J. Bennett, "The Shattered Humanities," *Wall Street Journal*, December 31, 1982.

21. Sainte-Beuve, *Etude sur Virgil* (1891); T. S. Eliot, "What is a Classic?" and "Virgil and the Christian World," in *On Poetry and Poets* (London: Faber and Faber, 1957), 53-71; 121-31.

22. Matthew Arnold, "The Modern Element in Modern Literature," *On the Classical Tradition, The Complete Prose Works*, Vol. 1, ed. R.H. Super (Ann Arbor: Univ. of Michigan Press, 1960), 35.

23. T. S. Eliot, "*Ulysses*, Order, and Myth," rpt. from *Dial* (1923) in William Van O'Connor (ed.), *Forms of Modern Fiction* (Bloomington: Indiana Univ. Press, 1959), 123.

24. Matthew Arnold, "Numbers; or The Majority and the Remnant." In this lecture to an American audience (first published in *Discourses in America* [1885]), which prescribes the remedy for "saving the State" from the stupidities of the "unsound majority," Arnold (p. 147) takes his point of departure from Isaiah: " 'Though thy people Israel be as sand of the sea, only a remnant of them shall return' [X:21]. Even this remnant, a tenth of the whole, if so it may be shall have to come back into the purging fire, and be again cleared and further reduced there. But nevertheless, 'as a terebinth tree, and as an oak, whose substance is in them, though they be cut down, so the stock of that burned tenth shall be a holy seed' [VI: 13]." Not incidentally, T. S. Eliot ("Virgil and the Christian World," p. 122) also invokes Isaiah in his recollective figural effort to establish the continuity between Virgil (in this instance, the fourth *Eclogue*) and the European tradition and to justify the Roman poet's central relevance to the contemporary world: "The mystery of the poem does not seem to have attracted any particular attention until the Christian Fathers got hold of it. The Virgin, the Golden Age, the parallel with the prophecies of Isaiah; the child *cara deum suboles*—'dear offspring of the gods, great scion of Jupiter'—could only be the Christ himself, whose coming was foreseen by Virgil in the year 40 B.C. Lactantius and St. Augustine believed this; so did the entire medieval Church and Dante; and even perhaps, in his own fashion, Victor Hugo." The latter, no doubt, alludes to Hugo's messianic interpretation of Napoleon's historical mission.

25. Matthew Arnold, "The Modern Element," 19-20. My emphasis. Compare T. S. Eliot, "What is a Classic?": "If there is one word on which we can fix, which will suggest the maximum of *what* I mean by the term 'a classic', it is the word *maturity*. I shall distinguish between the universal classic, like Virgil, and the classic which is only such in relation to the other liter-

ature in its own language, or according to the view of life of a particular period. A classic can only occur when a civilization is mature; when a language and a literature are mature; and it must be the work of a mature mind. It is the importance of that *civilization* and of that language, as well as the comprehensiveness of the mind of the individual poet, which gives it universality . . . " (p. 54). "Virgil's maturity of mind, and the maturity of his age are exhibited in this [comprehensive] awareness of history. With maturity of mind I have associated maturity of manners and absence of provinciality" (p. 62).

26. Frank Kermode, *The Classic: Literary Images of Permanence and Change*, (Cambridge, Mass.: Harvard Univ. Press, 1983), 19.

27. See Martin Heidegger, "Letter on Humanism," tr. Frank A. Capuzzi in *Basic Writings*, ed. David Farrel Krell (New York: Harper & Row, 1977), 200-01: "*Humanitas*, explicitly so called, was first considered and striven for in the age of the Roman Republic. *Homo humanus* was opposed to *homo barbarus*. *Homo humanus* here means the Romans, who exalted and honored Roman *virtus* through the 'embodiment' of the *paideia* [Education] taken over from the Greeks. These were the Greeks of the Hellenistic age, whose culture was acquired in the schools of philosophy. It was concerned with *eruditio et institutio in bonas artes* [scholarship and training in good conduct]. *Paideia* thus understood was translated as *humanitas*. The genuine *romanitas* of *homo romanus* consisted in such *humanitas*. We encounter the first humanism in Rome: it therefore remains in essence a specifically Roman phenomenon which emerges from the encounter of Roman civilization with the culture of late Greek civilization."

28. William J. Bennett, "To Reclaim a Legacy," 20: "My own experience attests to the woeful state of the high school curriculum. Recently I met with seventy high school student leaders—all excellent students—from all over the country. When I asked them how many had heard of the Federalist Papers, only seven raised their hands." In his list of core texts that he believes "virtually define the development of the Western mind," his selection from American literature and historical documents are: the Declaration of Independence, the Federalist Papers, the Constitution, the Lincoln-Douglas Debates, Lincoln's Gettysburg Address and Second Inaugural Address, Martin Luther King, Jrs.' "Letter from the Birmingham Jail" and "I have a dream . . ." speech, and such authors as Hawthorne, Melville, and Faulkner (p. 18). The question he chooses to ask the student leaders and, to say nothing about the omissions, the bias in favor of historical documents (emphasized by the rhetoric that trails off into mere literature) point to the civic orientation of Bennett's concept of liberal education.

29. Martin Heidegger, "The Origin of the Work of Art," *Basic Writings*, 153-54. Heidegger's emphasis.

30. Martin Heidegger, "Introduction: the Exploration of the Question of the Meaning of Being," *Being and Time*, in *Basic Writings*, 66.

31. The passage is from Jupiter's reassuring speech to Venus in Book I of Virgil's *Aeneid*, in which he promises the founding of Rome (the New Troy) by Aeneas and the establishment of the Roman Empire (and the *Pax Romana*) in the fullness of time (i.e. the time of Virgil and Augustus): *His ego nec metas tempora pono: imperium sine fine dedi* ("To Romans I set no boundary in space or time. I have granted them dominium and it has no end"). This passage, not incidentally, is quoted by T.S. Eliot in his essay "Virgil and the Christian World," *On Poetry and Poets* (London: Faber & Faber, 1957), 129, in which he affirms Virgil (and the *Aeneid*) over Homer as the *classic* (and cultural model) of Western poetry—and the Western *polis*: "What then does this destiny [the *fatum* that demands and explains Aeneas's *pietas*], which no Homeric hero shares with Aeneas, mean? For Virgil, it means the *imperium romanum*. This in itself, as Virgil saw, was a worthy justification of history . . . . His ego . . ."

32. Plutarch, "The Life of Romulus," *The Lives of the Noble Grecians and Romans*, tr. John Dryden and rev. Arthur Hugh Clough (New York: The Modern Library, n.d.), 31.

33. See also Friedrich Nietzsche, *Thus Spake Zarathustra*, in *The Portable Nietzsche*, ed. Walter Kaufmann (Harmondsworth, England: Penguin Books, 1959), 249ff.

34. Michel Foucault, "Theatrum Philosophicum," *Language, Counter-Memory, Practice: Selected Essays and Interviews*, tr. Donald F. Bouchard and Sherry Simon and ed. Bouchard (Ithaca, N.Y.: Cornell Univ. Press, 1977), 181-82. This essay is a review of Gilles Deleuze's *Différence et répétition* (1969) and *Logique du sens* (1969).

35. See Martin Heidegger, "The Question Concerning Technology," *The Question Concerning Technology*, tr. William Lovitt (New York: Harper Colophon Books, 1977), 26-27.

36. Friedrich Nietzsche, *On the Genealogy of Morals*, 136.

37. Martin Heidegger, *Being and Time*, tr. John Macquarrie and Edward Robinson (New York: Harper & Row, 1962), 211ff.

38. Hans-Georg Gadamer, *Truth and Method*, tr. and ed. by Garrett Barden and John Cumming (New York: Seabury Press, 1974), 244ff.

39. Michel Foucault, *The Archaeology of Knowledge*, tr. A. M. Sheridan Smith (London: Tavistock Publication, 1972), 31-39.

40. Louis Althusser, "On the Young Marx," *For Marx*, trans. Ben Brewster (London: New Left Books, 1977), 66-68.

41. See Friedrich Nietzsche, *On the Genealogy of Morals*, 119.

42. Gilles Deleuze, "Philosophie et minorité," *Critique* (1978), 154-55.

43. For Heidegger's version of this critique of the binary logic of metaphysics, see "Letter on Humanism," 226-27:

Because in all the respects mentioned ["humanism," "logic," "values," the being of man as "being-in-the-world," "the death of god"] we everywhere speak against all that humanity deems high and holy our philosphy teaches an irresponsible and destructive "nihilism." For what is more "logical" than that whoever roundly denies what is truly in being puts himself on the side of nonbeing and thus professes the pure nothing as the meaning of reality?

What is going on here? People hear talk about "humanism," "logic," "values," "world," and "God." They hear something about opposition to these. They recognize and accept these things as positive. But with hearsay—in a way that is not strictly deliberate—they immediately assume that what speaks against something is automatically its negation and that this is "negative" in the sense of destructive. And somewhere in *Being and Time* there is explicit talk of "the phenomenological destruction." With the assistance of logic and *ratio*—so often invoked—people come to believe that whatever is not positive is negative and thus that it seeks to degrade reason—and therefore deserves to be branded as depravity. We are so filled with "logic" that anything that disturbs the habitual somnolence of prevailing opinion is automatically registered as a despicable contradiction. We pitch everything that does not stay close to the familiar and beloved positive into the previously excavated pit of pure negation which negates everything, ends in nothing, and so consummates nihilism. Following this logical course we let everything expire in a nihilism we invented for ourselves with the aid of logic.

But does the "against" which a thinking advances against ordinary opinion necessarily point toward pure negation and the negative? This happens—and then, to be sure, happens inevitably and conclusively, that is, without a clear prospect of anything else—only when one posits in advance what is meant by the "positive" and on this basis makes an absolute and absolutely negative decision about the range of possible opposition to it. Concealed in such a procedure is the refusal to subject to reflection this presupposed "positive" in which one believes himself saved, together with its position and opposition. By continually appealing to the logical one conjures up the illusion that he is entering straightforwardly into thinking when in fact he has disavowed it.

44. See my essay "Postmodern Literature and the Hermeneutic Crisis," *Union Seminary Quarterly Review* 34, no. 2 (Winter 1979): 127-28.

45. Friedrich Nietzsche, "On the Uses and Disadvantages of History for Life," *Untimely Meditations*, tr. R. J. Hollingdale (Cambridge: Cambridge Univ. Press, 1983), 103-04.

46. Martin Heidegger, "Letter on Humanism," 215-16.

4. Critical Communities

DONALD PEASE

I

In a remarkable if relatively obscure review essay of Harold Bloom's groundbreaking study of English Romanticism, Paul de Man deviates rather significantly from his former critical procedures. Recognized, at the time of the publication of this review, more for an influential little book on contemporary criticism entitled *Blindness and Insight* than as a leading practitioner of what would come to be called the Yale School, de Man, we might say, prefigured his role as the leading member of the Yale School by finding Harold Bloom's oedipal model appropriate to his own version of literary history. The review differed sharply from de Man's other critiques. These critiques, organized around an opposition between "critical" insight and the blindness inherent in any linguistic mediation, enabled de Man to expose the blind spots accompanying every critical insight. In this review, however, de Man emphasizes the insights at work in Bloom's poetics of literary history. De Man makes Bloom's *Anxiety of Influence* sound indistinguishable from what de Man would later call an allegory of reading. But he does so only by remaining blind to the specific claims of Bloom's text. "We can forget," de Man writes in splendid indifference to Bloom's equation of forgetting with repression, "about the temporal scheme and about the pathos of the oedipal son; underneath the book deals with the difficulty or, rather, the impossibility of reading, and by inference, with the indeterminancy of literary meanings."[1]

In this review de Man does not deconstruct Bloom; rather, he disarms any deconstructive reading that might later be proposed for Bloom's text. Instead of designating what demands deconstruction in Bloom's oedipal model of literary influence, de Man interprets Bloom's model as a version of his own. De Man does not find in *Anxiety of Influence* an original version of literary history but reads it as a version of what de Man calls the allegorical mode. In de Man's review, Bloom's oedipal model of a poet's psyche gives way to an alternative account that postulates in advance the necessity of its own misreading, and thereby tells the story of its own misunderstanding.

In this rendition de Man differentiates Bloom from virtually every other critic. He does not deconstruct Bloom's theory of misreading but reads his *own* allegory of reading through Bloom's account. By reading Bloom in terms of his version of deconstructive poetics, de Man renders what goes on in Bloom's text indistinguishable from what goes on in the canonical poetic texts Bloom reads; that is, the story, of deconstruction. Through this resourceful reading of Bloom, de Man at once makes the story of deconstruction sound canonical and makes Bloom's project part of de Man's canon.

In subsuming Bloom's story within his own, de Man uses the review format less as a means of violent displacement and more as a way to incorporate a fellow critic's project within his own. Instead of pointing out the differences between his own work and Bloom's, de Man ignores the differences between his story and those within Bloom's text to make their work sound like that of proponents of the same school.

As figures whose work can be read within the same all-pervasive allegory of reading, not just Bloom and de Man but J. Hillis Miller and Geoffrey Hartman, the other proponents of the Yale School, do not have to acknowledge the at times striking differences between their approaches to literature as anything other than what de Man in his review of *Anxiety of Influence* calls intertextual relations. Given de Man's allegorization of anxiety neither do they have to feel anxious over the discrepancy between the positions they held before they became members of the Yale School and their official positions within it. Each member can instead *incorporate* his earlier position within the group project through an *official* deconstruction of it. For example, Hillis Miller can salvage the opposition between distance and desire at work in his earlier phenomenological studies as *effects* of the differing and deferring process, the play of *différance*, deconstruction claims comprises all of literature. And, in marked distinction to what he does when he reads other than Yale critics, de Man's allegory of reading Bloom, or (in the *Partisan Review* essay entitled "Space-critics") J. Hillis Miller, becomes a means of distinguishing those critics who seem to have already decon-

structed their own readings from those who have not. Far from demysti-
fying ideological or mystified positions, de Man's deconstruction here
does the work Louis Althusser identifies as ideological. As a way of
making Bloom and Miller speak the same allegory of reading, de Man's
reviews forge an imaginary relation enabling these critics to identify
their different critical projects with a shared set of assumptions—the
one displayed in de Man's "allegory of reading."

Following the "associative work" de Man's allegory performs for
the different readings of the Yale Critics, Bloom's oedipal model recovers
its value. For while *all* of these critics remain in relation to one another
as members of the same Yale School, that relation turns out to be formal rather than practical. In practice, each member of the school is
in a relationship of anxious rivalry with every other member—as Bloom's
oedipal model predicted. De Man's reviews discriminate the difference
between the members *within* the Yale School from those outside of it.
Bloom's theory of anxious influence designates the relationship bind-
ing the members of the Yale School to one another.

In his review of Bloom, de Man utilizes deconstruction as the
ideological apparatus useful to the formation of a coherent group. In
reading Bloom as an elaboration of a common allegorical discourse,
deconstruction becomes de Man's means of making Bloom's model sound
consistent with his own. But Bloom's discourse also serves a supplementary ideological function. Its oedipal model permits each member of
the Yale School the freedom to claim commitment to the school through
his distinction from all the other members. The group organized by the
dual discourse established by de Man and Bloom rationalizes the alienation of these individual critics from one another. These critics form
their group through a relation between the individual intellectual and
the collective akin to what Sartre in the *Critique of Dialectical Reason*
called *seriality*. According to Sartre, the serial describes a group formation in which the members are in relation with one another only insofar as they are isolated from one another. As a means of organizing
the association called the Yale School, deconstruction constitutes a subject who can function within the school only by working apart from
other members of the school. Placement within the school is affected
by de Man's performative of deconstruction. Once placed within the
school, however, the members depend on Bloom's performative of repression to articulate their relations.

Bloom used repression as a basis for recovering a relation to a group

formation called the tradition through an acknowledgment of his alienation from it. Bloom's theory of repression allows him to remain within
the tradition but through a strange denial, namely that he has been
alienated from his own discourse by the tradition. Repression constitutes
for Bloom a universal form of negation; it is his mode of affirming his
place within the literary tradition by denying its power to place him.
Deconstruction, however, cannot be accommodated by the discourse
of repression. It is what organizes that discourse. As the force of displacement emptied in advance of any positions into which the displaced
can be replaced, deconstruction cannot speak the discourse of repression. As the force of alienation purified of any repressive material it
is what empowers repression to speak. When used conjointly with the
discourse of repression, deconstruction conjures social relations beyond
the control of repression. Repression presupposes a society in which
individuals can be alienated from their desires for the sake of the social
order. Deconstruction denies the social individual the fiction of identity he needs in order to repress another social individual.

De Man exemplifies this social dynamic in his review of Bloom.
In that review de Man does what Bloom would claim no critic should
be able to do; that is, he does not enter into relation with Bloom by
activating the discourse of repression. The discourse of repression implies, however tangentially, that there is a position, a locus of power
(Bloom designates this position "the precursor") which demands repression for its acknowledgment. But de Man denies, in advance, any specific location for power. Consequent to this denial de Man need not
repress Bloom's constructs. He can ignore them in the name of a deconstructive power that need not be located anywhere precisely because
it is in operation everywhere.

Bloom's discourse of repression constitutes a modernist's way of
recovering relations with the literary tradition. It is his way of experiencing a lived relation with the tradition. Bloom's notion of the "anxiety
of influence" enables him to express his alienation *from* and through
the tradition. De Man's deconstruction is not a moment *within* Bloom's
discourse of repression but constitutes a means of reaching consensus
by replacing discussions between persons with divisions at work within
persons and their work. As the mutual disarticulation of two conflicting
discourses, de Man's deconstruction perpetuates the opposing positions
that might otherwise resolve themselves through consensus. Opposed
to any resolution and any consensus, deconstruction turns resolution

and consensus into texts with overlooked tensions, conflicts, and divisions. Then it dismantles these alternative texts.

A more familiar name for a consensus formation that appears as if it were already achieved yet without having undergone the work of consensus formation is *hegemony*. Hegemony occupies a relation to ideology in political discourse analogous to the relation between primary process and secondary elaboration in psychoanalytic discourse. The discourse of repression constitutes the secondary elaboration of primary process. As the proponent of the more pervasive discourse, de Man can ignore Bloom's discourse of repression as a secondary elaboration of his own. As an instance of *hegemony* in praxis, de Man needs Bloom's discourse of repression only in order to localize, however briefly, the otherwise invisible because pervasive power of hegemony. Through his review, de Man treats the hegemonic practice of deconstruction as if it were an effect of regression rather than the reverse.

De Man's deconstructive practice is indistinguishable from the alienating self-divided positions structuring the cultural hegemony. Consequently, after de Man deconstructs Bloom's discourse of repression into an allegory of reading or what he calls an intertextual field of interlocking relations, he simultaneously renders Bloom's *literary tradition* indistinguishable from the pervasive network of dominating power relations organizing cultural hegemony. This is another way of saying that hegemony rather than literary tradition appears as the work of repression.

II

This affiliation between the otherwise merely textual relations of the Yale School and hegemony was pointed out by the founding editor of a journal, *boundary 2*, whose editorial board consists of a school of critics that includes Paul Bové, Daniel O'Hara, Jonathan Arac, and others. William Spanos's remarks on deconstruction as the inheritance from what he calls Modernist critical aesthetes first appeared in "Retrieving Heidegger's Destruction" in *SCE Report* (no. 8, Fall 1980). But the crucial point in this essay was reprinted in Paul Bové's essay critical of the Yale School that appeared in a book entitled *The Yale Critics: Deconstruction in America*.[2] This book was edited by Jonathan Arac and included essays by Bové as well as Arac and O'Hara, two other members of the *boundary 2* school.

Spanos's point:

In thus reducing the signifiers emerging from and addressing *different* historical/cultural situations to a timeless intertextual (ironic) text, deconstructive criticism ironically betrays its affiliation with the disinterested—and indifferent—formalism of the New Criticism . . . which it is one of its avowed purposes to repudiate. The deconstructive reader, like the New Critic . . . becomes a distanced observer of the "scene of textuality," or, in Kierkegaard's term, an aesthete who perceives the text from the infinitely negative distance of the ironic mode. With his levelling gaze, he, too, like his adversaries, refines all writing, in Derrida's own phrase, into "free-floating" texts. All texts thus become the same text.

This critique of deconstruction is written from a critical position informed by Heidegger's theory of ontological destruction and Kierkegaard's distinction between mastered and unmastered irony rather than by the work of Derrida or de Man. As such, it introduces into the arena of American criticism an alternative oppositional discourse to that of deconstruction. And this oppositional discourse—comprised not only of articles appearing within *boundary 2*, but also of special issues of *boundary 2* (on Nietzsche, Heidegger, and Marxist criticism); books such as Spanos's (as yet unpublished) *Icon and Time*, Bové's *Destructive Poetics* and *Intellectuals in Power*, O'Hara's *Tragic Knowledge* and *The Romance of Interpretation*, Arac's *Commissioned Spirits*; the review essays written by each of them; the MLA groups organized by them; the GRIP project they helped found; the conferences in Europe and America in which they participated—matches the critical output of the Yale School. But unlike the members of the Yale School, the *boundary 2* school of critics has received little acknowledgment from the critical establishment. Nor has the work of the *boundary 2* school as a school received acknowledgment in what we could call the reputable journals—*Diacritics, New Literary History*—founded after the migration of deconstruction to America and regularly featuring articles by and on members of the Yale School. When *boundary 2* gets mentioned at all, it is mentioned, as was the case in Josue Harari's collection of essays on the newer criticism, only as a source for articles *by* established newer critics and *not* the source of articles *on* these established newer critics by Spanos, Bové, O'Hara, or Arac. Even the volume on the Yale Critics written and co-edited in part by members of the *boundary 2* school has been ignored rather than reviewed.

There may be a historical rationale for the exclusion of the *boun-*

dary 2 school from consideration by journals that have appropriated, disseminated, and reproduced deconstruction in America. As a historical phenomenon, Derridean deconstruction appeared as a critical reaction against a structuralist methodology that had become a dominant force in European critical practices. In his earlier formulations Derrida directed deconstruction as a critique of structuralism by accommodating the implicit theory of signification in Edmund Husserl's phenomenology and the conception of a logocentric tradition implicit in Martin Heidegger's notion of an ontological destruction, to the binary oppositions that grounded structuralist practice.

In its migration to America, however, deconstruction lost this Heideggerian moment. Instead of appearing as a historically grounded critique of structuralism, post-structuralism appeared in America as what was after or "post" what we were used to calling the New Criticism. Emptied of the Heideggerian moment, post-structuralism did not enter America accompanied by its history. Without the move from structuralism to post-structuralism effected by Derrida's historic turn to Heidegger, post-structuralism entered America instead through a much more *pervasive* binary opposition than the ones at work in the blindness/insight, speech/writing, presence/absence polarities we are used to. Without the prior existence in the American critical establishment of the historicist and hermeneutical claims of Heidegger's ontological destruction, post-structuralism entered America by way of the most pervasive opposition in the modern world, the one opposing the new to the old.

Deconstruction entered America, then, not as a historical phenomenon, or as a modernist strategy, but as a modernization procedure. Instead of placing it in conflictual relation to other modes of interpreting and historicizing a world, such journals as *Diacritics, New Literary History, MLN, Glyph*, and later even *PMLA* generated a frame of acceptance for deconstruction as a newer methodology, one able to make American New Criticism seem outmoded. The cultural acknowledgment, production, and distribution of post-structuralism emptied it of historical content and reduced its context to the opposition between the new and the old.

This mode of assimilating post-structuralism is indistinguishable from the obsolescence procedures constitutive of the logic of commodity capitalism. Post-structuralism translates not only modes of signification but all other aspects of the referential world into effects of a play of *différance*. It reduces temporality to the deferring of "what is not yet" *in* "what has been." Consequent to this reduction, every cultural form turns out to be a negation of "what was" and a promise of "what is about to be." We acknowledge this procedure positively with the over-coming of deadening structures of habit and negatively with the mere passing fancy of *cultural fashion*. As the medium through which "what will be" dismisses everything that "is" as a potential "has been," the post-structuralist's play of *différance* converts every referent as well as the way of signifying referentiality into a formulation indistinguishable from the planned obsolescence of commodity capitalism. But it also permits this double negation of both the positive formation of a past and the positive formation of a future—the conversion of any commodity as well as any conceptual appropriation of the world into the waste heap of potentially outmoded constructs—to be experienced as the freedom from the need for any definitive position. As a result of this dual nega-tion, life in the modern world can be experienced as a "pure passing through" bereft of the need for any definitive or lasting cultural forms at all. Put starkly, deconstruction provides a means of experiencing the pervasive mediations of commodity capitalism (which we could call the production of outmoding) as cultural freedom. And when received, pro-duced, and distributed as a fashion, a making new of what is always already passing, deconstruction permits the *high culture* of literary critics to do precisely what the *mass* culture of alienated producers does: i.e. consume *alienation* as the *passing fashions* they also produce.

Implicit in this description of the way in which deconstruction has been received is a rationale for the rejection of the *boundary 2* school. In focussing on Heidegger's ontological reduction as their sense of the difference between a structuralist and a post-modernist hermeneutics, *boundary 2* as a journal and as a school supplies the historicist context that would invest post-structuralism with a historical value. In supply-ing through a focus on Heidegger the historical moment that would *interrupt* the acceptance of post-structuralism as a fashion as well as the ideological rationale for this mode of acceptance, *boundary 2* introduces a context that can neither be acknowledged by nor accommodated to the cultural appropriation of post-structuralism. And if the history of post-structuralism cannot accommodate *boundary 2* to the cultural fash-ioning of post-structuralism, *boundary 2* can be effectively marginalized and even ignored as unfashionable.

The best way to articulate the difference between the *boundary*

2 project and other post-structuralist practices might be to point out what that project has made possible. By following the way in which the *boundary* 2 school enabled one of its members to effect a transformation from one critical position to another critical position, I hope to discriminate this group from the Yale School. Given the foregoing analysis of modernization, in which a new position simply does not make any difference, this transformation must be unassimilable to the old/new reduction.

This unassimilable critical temporality was actually released through the failure of the critical establishment to acknowledge the *boundary* 2 school. If such acknowledgment is indistinguishable from producing the fashionable, then only that which has not become part of the *fashioning* of contemporary critical practices can participate in a temporality non-synchronous with it. Only those critical practices which have not been subsumed by the modernizing procedures of post-structuralism, and are "out of synch" with it, can be involved in an alternative way of experiencing and representing the temporalization of man in the world.

In "The Ineluctability of Difference," a critical review of Stanley Aronowitz's *The Crisis in Historical Materialism*, Paul Bové signals his transformation from a critic of postmodernism who "wrote too abstractly and ahistorically of the radical flux, disorder, alienation and death which characterize the postmodern world" to the postmodern critic. He managed this transformation by relocating his later critical project "within the context of other oppositional forces and by theorizing the counter-hegemonic in light of their local struggles."[3] What distinguishes these oppositional *forces* from the establishment *figures* we earlier located within Yale School is their resistance to the post-structuralist discourses as constitutive of cultural hegemony. In remaining neither inside nor quite outside the recognition procedures at work in post-structuralism, these oppositional forces cannot be redesignated as the attenuated opposition between the old and the new.

What Bové describes as a relocation of critical practice within a bloc of heterogenous oppositional forces becomes his means of forging a "site," that is, a relation he shares with other oppositional forces yet unassimilable to the hegemonic operations of modernity. Bové's transformation enabled him to experience his project as a historical one, and it was largely effected through his relation to the oppositional positions of the other members of the *boundary* 2 school.

Here a distinction between the *boundary* 2 group and the Yale

School becomes possible. Whereas the Yale School was formed according to the logic of seriality in which the basis for association is the members' sense of their alienation from one another, the members of the *boundary 2* school organize according to the logic of what Sartre called a "group-in-formation," that is, one in which each member is in the position of a mediatory *third* to every other member of the group. A mediatory third turns his own position into a context for reflecting on the common project that draws him in relation to the rest of the group. Consequent to this reflection, the difference between his own work and that of the other members of the group becomes the basis for his further development. The group project thus becomes a means of defining as well as developing the projects of each member.

We earlier noted how the dual functions of de Man's allegory of reading and Bloom's anxiety of influence worked to maintain and justify the seriality at work in the Yale School. For the sake of demonstrating the different relations at work in the *boundary 2* school, I need to show how Bloom's influence theory works together with de Man's allegory of reading to produce the effect of seriality. In converting the relation between a precursor and a belated ephebe into a version of the more universal fear of time passing, Bloom reduces the historical relation between a contemporary poet and one in the historical past into an opposition between old and new. But since, in Bloom's account, the past poet has already fulfilled all the potentials of temporality, the new, through the speech act of repression, can only affirm time's completeness by denying it. By inverting and displacing what we described as the endless obsolescence operations of modernization, Bloom's theory recasts modernization into a conservative structure.

The reduction of time to the opposition between old and new remains constant. Perhaps at this point we might find a more precise historical location for Bloom's anxiety. Bloom developed this theory during the contentious 1960s when the nation's youth generated a counterculture which imported works by Marx, Mao Tse Tung, Marcuse, Reich and others to oppose what was repressive in the dominant culture. But the hegemonic culture reduced the counterculture to the level of a generational conflict setting the youth culture against an older generation. Following this reduction of the counterculture to an old/new opposition, it did not take long for the counterculture to turn into just one more cultural fashion. Bloom's theory made the young feel old in relation to the past by reassessing a term crucial to the youth culture.

In Bloom's theory, "repression" passed over from being a tool for the cultural reproduction of the dominant culture to become a way of fruitfully forgetting one's always belated, because always already mediated, originality.

The counterculture of the '60s then subsisted in at least two quite different cultural realms. In the realm of mass culture, the counterculture provided a framework for the production and consumption of new fashions for the marketplace. It also, however, remained a site for a series of cultural discourses and practices that had never been fully realized. Only the affiliation of the sixties counterculture with youth market permits its representation as a new fashion subject to obsolescence. In the other cultural domain, a wide range of oppositional discourses accumulated a surplus of temporal energies consisting of the not yet realized cultural forms. These oppositional forces could not be outmoded because they never had really become presentable within the dominant culture at all. Here a retinue of discourses, practices, and cultural forces constitute a cultural unconscious for other oppositional discourses like those of the *boundary 2* school, awaiting an opportunity to become realized as cultural forms. The *boundary 2* school, in other words, established its cultural site in a location that remains marginal. While in this site, the *boundary 2* school cannot become outmoded because it remains unrepresentable within appropriate cultural terms.

Again, a comparison with the Yale School is pertinent. After Bloom's theory reduced the temporality of the counterculture into an opposition between old and new, he was able to re-evaluate anxiety about becoming old or belated into the only authentic experience of literary history. Bloom's anxiety, however, was not limited to the encroachment of the youth culture but coincided with a much more pervasive crisis for the humanities. For at the time Bloom wrote *Anxiety of Influence*, humanistic disciplines had ceased to be an adequate response to modernized culture. Mass culture enabled a consumer society to experience the reproduction of needs and desires the market demands to maintain its productivity as pleasing rather than alienating. Mass culture produces a sensibility enabling citizens of the modern world to interpret the non-satisfaction of their desires as the nature of their private lives. By designating *cultural alienation* as a *freedom from the collective*, and the experience of the non-satisfaction of individual desire as describing the authentic collective experience of mass man, the mass culture makes it impossible for the masses to acknowledge their common experience of alienation—from the means of production, wealth, or personal needs. Like the Yale School, mass culture organizes a collective by dispersing its members.

Bloom's anxiety theory was as much a reaction-formation against the modernization procedures of mass culture as it was a reaction against youth culture. It permitted him to remain in touch with the humanistic tradition. Through what we earlier described as a form of "denegation" he remained in relation to a lost tradition but through a repression of a loss of that relation. Paul de Man treated Bloom's always already repressed relation to a literary tradition as if it were another version of cultural hegemony. The hegemonic discourse differs from a literary tradition in that it can neither be localized as an object of interpretation nor become the agency of interpretation. Instead, it supplies a pervasive field for the forces of alienation. In this field interlocking relays of relations distribute displacement, the simultaneous activation and deferral of desire, throughout the field of mass culture. In this field of displacing forces, each individual's sense of private distinction turns into a means of forming an undifferentiated mass. In *reading* these unlocalizable but nonetheless pervasive hegemonic forces through the strong works in the literary tradition, de Man translates the literary tradition into a version of cultural hegemony. By treating the hegemony underwriting mass cultures as if it were a demand coming to them from the humanistic tradition, de Man's allegory of reading thus becomes a perverse way for literary critics to come to terms with the displacement of the humanistic tradition.

Like Bloom, each of the younger *boundary 2* critics—O'Hara, Bové, and Arac—can be divided into an early and a later phase. But unlike Bloom each of these younger critics resists the reduction of their critical turns into an opposition between the old and the new. Like de Man, all of the critics of the *boundary 2* school acknowledge the difference between a metaphysics of presence and an individual instance of signification. Yet, unlike de Man, none of these critics translates this sense of difference into a merely textual operation, a pervasive allegory of reading capable of covering the entire field of existence.

In the passage I quoted earlier, Spanos argued the fundamental difference between his approach and de Man's by insisting on Heidegger's ontological destruction as a means of ensuring a radical sense of interested historically situated temporality. This site is more usually converted into a topos to be contemplated by the disinterested procedures of critical aesthetes who conceive of art works as occasions for the recovery of an infinitely free, because utterly desituated, text. He identifies the displacements of deconstruction with the utterly free play of pure possibility, exercised by what Kierkegaard called unmastered ironists. In place of the unmastered irony of these forever new because forever unsituated critics, Spanos calls for the mastered irony of a critic who always situates possibility in an actual, *worldly relation.*

For Spanos, the so-called American New Criticism as well as the post-structuralist newer criticism reduced the experience of man as a being-in-the-world, whose own most being-towards-death (in Heideggerian phrasing) enabled him to experience the *nothing* at the core of any concrete actualization of temporality. Any analysis that denies the ontological difference releasing Being to *be-ing* freezes or spatializes temporality, thereby converting *Dasein's* be-ing in the world into the disinterested relation of a contemplative subject *overseeing* an aestheticized world.

Heideggerian destruction, for Spanos, is a means of releasing an alternative temporality. In Heidegger, "making time present" always involves a "will be" that reveals itself as a "having been." So ontological destruction involves a strategy of repetition that releases a "what will have been" not yet realized in "what has been." Repetition lets "what has been" become. And everything that covers up this be-ing of what has been—including habit, symbolist poetry, metaphor, disinterested aesthetic attitudes, and deconstruction—becomes an occasion for Spanos's ontological destruction. Two problems attend Spanos's project, however. His anticipation of the joinings together that spatialize the becoming of Being always turns him towards the inauthentic cover-up of be-ing and never towards the genuine revelation of be-ing at work in a worldly situation. His reiterated exposures of these cover-ups verge on becoming a repetition compulsion. Or, put more starkly, his repetition of the same gesture threatens to become his habitual response, and like the ones he demystifies Spanos's response is capable of desituating the authentic temporality of being.

In *Destructive Poetics,* Bové addresses this problem in Spanos's "text" by redirecting the location of repetition.[4] *Destructive Poetics* does not simply use repetition as a means of discovering what prior critics cover up, but becomes Bové's means of moving into history. After beginning with an analysis of the work of two recent critics, Walter Jackson Bate and Harold Bloom, whose new literary histories restored anxiety to the critics' sense of time, Bové proceeds to "destroy" their writing by exposing their notions of the past as versions of what Spanos called a panoptical *idealization* of time. They maintain a privileged temporal site, as a world apart. Their literary history is not in our time but in another time.

Bové discriminates his sense of repetition from their inevitable repetition compulsion in a remarkable reading of de Man. In *Blindness and Insight*, de Man activated Heidegger's analysis of the concealment at work in every revelation; like Heidegger, de Man saw repetition as the cure for false temporality. For his purposes, Bové focuses on the de Man essay that most directly addresses Bové's concerns, "Literary History and Literary Modernity."[5] In this essay de Man brings the claims of literary history and literary modernity together in order to locate the equiprimordial and absolutely irreconcilable claims at work in each. Modernity is a notion of literature as an absolutely free, purely spontaneous act, without a past, while literature, as a representation, or mediation, supplies a past, or a history for that act. And for Paul de Man, the absolute irreconcilability of the two claims releases an aporia, and this aporia marks the void which, for de Man, poetic language names with ever-renewed understanding.

But of course, although de Man does not mention it, there is one way of writing in the present without a sense that what one writes is anything other than a passing experience. Indeed, there is a way of experiencing temporality as an endlessly passing experience that need not be remembered. De Man cites this mode of experiencing existence as *en passant* that marks time passing as such: "*fashion* can sometimes be only what remains of modernity, after the impulse has subsided, as soon—and this can be almost at once—as it has changed from being an incandescent point in time to a reproducible cliché, all that remains of an invention that has lost the deisre that produced it."

Given de Man's notion of an allegory of reading, wherein "allegory undermines and obscures the specific literal meanings," it would seem that what he calls the reproducible cliché of fashion has, in obscuring the specific literal intent of desire, turned *temporality* itself into an allegory of reading. If this is true, however, fashion has also cured that reading of the anxiety de Man finds attending the modern writer, for fashion works to reduce any radically free act to the status of a mark of difference, the negation of what precedes. Fashion also enables one to experience that negation, not as a mediation or a representation but as a process of outmoding that unlike other forms of outmoding does away with either the need to remember or the need to forget. Fashion, that is to say, as the sheer movement of time passing without remainder is the temporality produced by de Man's notion of the allegory of reading. Fashion is what activates the aporetic play of *différance* that turns what has been into what is about to be. It is the temporality of fashion that I earlier suggested had not accommodated the *boundary 2* school.

Paul Bové, in his *Destructive Poetics*, does not acknowledge the relation between fashion and the notion of temporality at work in de Man's allegory of reading. Instead he reads fashion in terms of the difference between habit, which covers over being-towards-death, and an authentic impulse of spontaneity. When so used, "fashion" differentiates Heidegger's notion of habit from de Man's notion of poetic knowledge: "literature, itself," writes Bové, "is capable of such fashion to varying degrees." Bové, in other words, marks his difference from de Man by choosing Heidegger's notion of habit over de Man's fashion. He then proceeds to an elaboration of Heidegger's notion of temporality, forestructure, repetition. And after moving from the *spatialized* temporality of the new literary historians through the authentic temporality of Heideggerian repetition, he moves backward in time to a consideration of the American New Critics who acknowledged neither literary history nor the poem as a temporal event. In moving from the new literary history which spatialized time into an irretrievable past, Bové, like Spanos, uses Heidegger's notion of repetition. For Heidegger repetition provided a means of releasing what has not yet been actualized in any concretization of an event. In his use of Heideggerian repetition, Bové moves back to the New Critics to release from their work a sense of temporality and a sense of history.

What enables this release is not just Heidegger's repetition but the figure from the past from whom Heidegger discovered the notion, i.e. Søren Kierkegaard. Since Kierkegaard exemplified his notion of repetition through a distinction between unmastered irony (the endless possibility of an endlessly free aesthetic subject) and mastered irony (the turning of possibility towards a situation in the world), Bové uses the distinction to separate the New Critics' use of irony, which generates ahistorical texts, from the wish he shares with Spanos to locate an interested and situated text. As it turns out, however, the world in which Bové's texts find themselves situated is the same world Bové has attempted to move them out of. The poems he chooses to interpret repeat

Bové's own critical gestures at work in chapters one and two. And they, too, destroy the *tradition* as a hardened shell of received ideas that never permits Being to become anything but a "has been." What results is a reduction of *repetition* into the position of a habit. Bové's repetition of the same gesture gives the gesture of repetition the palpability of a form capable of being repeated as a practice. In being repeatedly called only to destroy the onto-theological tradition, neither Spanos nor Bové yet feels called to disclose the situation of *being* in the world. If Spanos does not quite acknowledge the need to situate his criticism, Bové clearly does. As we have already seen, in his essay, curiously entitled "The Ineluctability of Difference," Bové marks his turn from a critic of post-modernism to a postmodern critic with both a sense of tentativeness and anxiety.

Of course, Bové could have, in his turn from being a critic of postmodernism to being a postmodern critic, activated what we have called the reduction of temporality to that of the new/old, precursor/belated model. Had he wished to experience the anxiety at work in this turning away, as itself an exemplary struggle, one capable of recuperating all the terms in his own text, *habit, anxiety, care,* he could have turned towards Harold Bloom. Bloom uses anxiety as a means of generating a map of misreading able to designate a precursor's authority over a latecomer. Indeed, Bové could have treated his turn as a turning away from his precursor, William Spanos. But in *Destructive Poetics,* Bové did not affiliate his project with Bloom's anxiety theory. He "destroyed" Bloom's position by affiliating it with the aesthetes, symbolists, and modernists, who in giving Being a disinterested shape find a map for their misreading, an ideal locus masquerading as an anxiety. In this locus, being achieves a definitive form and thereby loses its being. Put differently, as a Bloomsian *plenum,* temporality can only be experienced as if it had been spatialized.

Bové also mounts a second critique: that Bloom's anxiety of influence theory activates a will to power over time passing, but conceals it in terms of a will to power over poetic texts. This second critique puts him in relation not to Spanos but to another member of the *boundary 2* school, Daniel O'Hara who in his first book, *Tragic Knowledge,* had already quite definitely turned away from Spanos.[6] Throughout O'Hara's text, the limitations in Spanos's theory of aesthetic knowledge as always spatialized, of Heideggerian destruction as a release from the will to power over a text, become clear. Through his strategic use

of Ricoeur's hermeneutic phenomenological method, O'Hara places
Heidegger not into a destructive but a dialectical relation with other
members of the literary critical tradition, like M. H. Abrams, whom
Spanos would otherwise have only "destroyed." Using Ricoeur's notion of the rule of metaphor, O'Hara recuperates the need to give shape
to becoming. In O'Hara's reading this need occupies a necessarily dialectical relation with its opposition impulse, the need to let what has been
in a shape become. O'Hara makes Spanos's and Bové's newer relation
with a literary history seem like an old argument. In his reading of it,
Spanos's method does not remain a necessary and sufficient attitude
to a text; once placed in dialectical relation to Abrams, Spanos's destructive reading becomes only one side of a coin. Which is to say that
O'Hara never directly agrees or disagrees (except in footnotes) with either
Spanos or Bové, but lets Ricoeur's method perform his argument, as
an implicit recovery of the need for continued discussion. Theirs become
reasonable positions but open to a conflict of interpretations.

Having contained Spanos within a conflict that really motors an
entire literary tradition, O'Hara then gets on with his business, which
is to disclose, through his ironic relations with Bloom's model, the tragic
knowledge of every work of literature—the release (through the various
identifications with a variety of possible selves) of a creative *self*, and
the accompanying recognition of the void (sometimes sublimely denied
through the projection of a great romantic precursor) that inheres at
the core of the self. In O'Hara's reading of literature and interpretation *through* Bloom, the self is not refurbished as a powerful ego but,
through the play of its antithetical puttings-on and takings-off of identity, comes to an awareness of its own nothingness. Then, O'Hara finds
in the entire present interpretive arena a denial of this tragic acknowledgment through an inflation of the critic grown gigantic over his in-
numerable identifications with the works he interprets, into a sublime
heroic form. Through his use of irony, O'Hara can point to the projections, displacements, denial formations—the tragic knowledge—concealed by the critic's romance of interpretation. To restore the terms
of our earlier discussion, O'Hara redefines the critic's "denegation" and
restores criticism to the nothingness criticism would deny. By suggesting
that O'Hara has performed the turning away through Bloom's anxiety
theory, I am not claiming that he has exhausted the power of anxiety
as a move. In occupying that position to disclose the tragic knowledge—
the "Nietzsche"—Bloom conceals, he exposes the self-inflated claims
of recent critics as well as the limits of his own theory.

Bové does not turn to O'Hara's position but rethinks the limits of his use of Kierkegaard's notion of mastered irony by means of it and *decides*, in not turning to O'Hara's tragic irony, to justify his refusal to make that move by returning to Kierkegaard's notion of mastered irony. Having resurrected that notion, Bové performs the one gesture he did not perform in *Destructive Poetics*—that is, he quite literally turns repetition towards a worldly interpretation, one wherein repetition can become actual without ceasing to be possible. In turning to the specific historical context of an intellectual situated in the world, Bové activates many concerns he shares with Jonathan Arac, who in his book *Commissioned Spirits* also established implicit differences from Spanos in both the question of history as well as the notion of spatialized temporality.[7]

I cannot here begin to do justice to what Arac in this rather remarkable study has achieved. But let me say that in this work he discovered a way to talk about the relation between literature and specific social and historical forces that converted literature into neither a *mere* reflection of the historical nor a *mere* denial of it. Through a complex and subtle interweaving of the "metaphoric" (the gesture towards wholeness) and the "metonymic" (the incompletions resistant to any integration) impulses at work within social as well as linguistic formations, Arac generates a notion of social motive—which is neither quite a cognition nor an action—that allows him to explain the ways in which literature is involved in the social, historical, as well as literary movements of his time.

Movement, the subtle relation between and through powers, becomes his key term. He analyzes and produces movement by following the transformations of such key formations as crowds, careers, story, revolution, and overviews as they appear in textual and social contexts. Since it is this last term—the "overview"—that played such a key role for Spanos, I want to turn to Arac's historical treatment of it to disclose what a historical reading, that is, a reading in which temporality is situated and related to an actual world, can do. As we recall, Spanos opposed *all* overviews as panoptical hoverings above, that led to control, disinterest, and will to power. But Arac, in following Dickens' relations to overview throughout his career, suggests that Dickens, in an overview designed to come to terms with the otherwise sheerly contingent movement of completely unacknowledgable force (the perceptual equivalent of a crowd), discovered an enabling social energy. Dickens only ceased using the overview as a narrative technique *after* it had been translated into the State's means of bureaucratic control.

This historically grounded sense of the way in which a repetition of a key term—*overview*—can unsettle the ground for Spanos's generalized destruction of the overview (that itself tends to become an overview of overviews) enabled Bové to turn from the abstract temporality he was the center of, to the situated critic he was able to become. Which is to say not only that the social formation of the *boundary 2* school constitutes a relation to temporality capable of making a new history possible, but also that the members of this school, through their attention to the implications of their shared developments as postmodern critics, are capable of generating a situation in which this alternative temporality can make a historical difference.

NOTES

1. Paul de Man, Review of Harold Bloom, *The Anxiety of Influence* in *Comparative Literature* 26 (1974): 269-75.

2. Paul A. Bové, "Variations on Authority," *The Yale Critics*, ed. Jonathan Arac et al. (Minneapolis: University of Minnesota Press, 1983), 3-19.

3. Paul A. Bové, "The Ineluctability of Difference: Scientific Pluralism and the Critical Intelligence," *boundary 2*, 11, nos. 1&2 (1982/83): 155-76. Reprinted in *Postmodernism and Politics*, ed. Jonathan Arac (Minneapolis: University of Minnesota Press, 1986), 3-25.

4. Paul A. Bové, *Destructive Poetics* (New York: Columbia University Press, 1980).

5. Paul de Man, "Literary History and Literary Modernity," *Blindness and Insight* (New York: Oxford University Press, 1971), 142-165.

6. Daniel T. O'Hara, *Tragic Knowledge* (New York: Columbia University Press, 1981).

7. Jonathan Arac, *Commissioned Spirits* (New Brunswick: Rutgers University Press, 1979).

5. Heidegger, Hölderlin, and Politics

FRED R. DALLMAYR

The topic of my presentation inserts itself into the broader theme or framework of the Ward-Phillips Lectures this year—the theme of "boundaries" or the lack of them. Not long ago I was privileged to participate in a conference organized in honor of Albert Hirschman, that eminent economist, sociologist, anthropologist, and student of politics; one of Hirschman's challenging books is entitled *Essays in Trespassing.*[1] The following pages also are intended as such an essay in "trespassing." Dealing simultaneously with "Heidegger, Hölderlin, and Politics" means to move across significant academic and intellectual boundaries, chiefly the dividing lines between philosophy, poetry, literary criticism, and political thought; one might also add the demarcation between past and present. The objective of my trespassing effort, I want to emphasize, is not simply to produce an indistinct amalgam of ingredients—which would involve not so much the transgression as the erasure of boundaries; my goal is rather to highlight both the distinctness and the mutual correlation of the respective domains.

Before proceeding I need to qualify my undertaking in several ways. My presentation shall not range broadly over Heidegger's entire opus— which would not only be foolhardy but actually impossible (given the present state of this opus). Nor shall I attempt to comment on all of Heidegger's numerous writings devoted to Hölderlin. My focus is going to be more restricted: I intend to concentrate chiefly on one relevant publication, namely, Heidegger's lecture course entitled *Hölderlins Hymnen "Germanien" und "Der Rhein" (Hölderlin's Hymns "Germania" and "The Rhine")*. Originally presented at the University of Freiburg during the winter semester of 1934/35, the course (or its text) has recently been published as part of the ongoing edition of Heidegger's collected works, the so-called *Gesamtausgabe.*[2]

111

There are several reasons—good reasons, I believe—for focusing on the mentioned lecture course. Heidegger's courses—particularly those offered between 1923 and 1944—were previously, for the most part, unpublished and are only now slowly being made available to the public. Thus, there is the freshness and excitement of a new encounter with Heidegger's thought as one after the other of these volumes appear in print. There is a better reason, however, which has to do with the author himself. Despite the mountain of pages he has written, I think one should realize that Heidegger was first and foremost not a writer of books or treatises but a teacher. The testimony of eyewitnesses fully concurs on this point. All his students—even those who later drifted away from him—are unanimous in extolling the spellbinding character of his lectures and the intense fascination of his oral presentations. In his recently published *Heideggers Wege*, Hans-Georg Gadamer ascribes to his teacher a "nearly dramatic appearance, a power of diction, a concentration of delivery which captivated all his listeners." He also recounts how, in his lectures, Heidegger was able to transform Aristotle (among other classics) from a "scholastic" mummy into a living presence or a speaking "contemporary"—thus providing a dynamic illustration of what Gadamer later was to call *"Horizontverschmelzung"* (fusion of horizons). Hannah Arendt has been no less eloquent on this aspect. In an essay written on the occasion of Heidegger's eightieth birthday she observed: Even before any of his major publications had appeared, his "name traveled all over Germany like the rumor of the hidden king. . . . The rumor about Heidegger put it quite simply: Thinking has come to life again; the cultural treasures of the past, believed to be dead, are being made to speak, in the course of which it turns out that they propose things altogether different from the familiar, worn-out trivialities they had been presumed to say. There exists a teacher; one can perhaps learn to think."[3]

There is another general consideration which, in my view, recommends the lecuture courses to our attention: their discursive and maieutic character. More so than polished texts, the courses offer a glimpse of Heidegger "at work," that is, a glimpse into the laboratory of his thought. Precisely because they were addressed to students rather than a nondescript audience, the courses are more attuned than his books to the need of sustained or progressive learning; they also tend to be more "argumentative," more ready to "unpack" complex notions, and also to confront opposing views in a critical fashion. (These and related ad-

vantages, I feel, completely outweigh certain drawbacks endemic to lecture courses, such as an occasional repetitiveness or a tendency to
recapitulate discussed topics.) Regarding the specific lecture course of
1934 there is an additional motivation for my choice: the fact that it
follows on the heels of a notorious episode or debacle in Heidegger's
life, namely, his service as Rector of the University of Freiburg from
April 1933 to February 1934. As is well known, this episode has placed
a heavy onus, perhaps an indelible stain, on Heidegger's public record—
a stain which some interpreters like to present as evidence of a permanent commitment to fascism. In these pages I shall not enter into a
discussion of this unfortunate interlude and of the dense emotional aura
surrounding it.[4] The issue I want to raise, from a political angle, is
rather whether the Hölderlin-course of 1934 still reflects the sentiments
of 1933 or whether, on the contrary, it manifests a profound disillusionment with, and turning away from, the National-Socialist regime—a
regime which, during the same months, was steadily tightening its grip
on the nation.

Yet, I do not propose to tackle this issue directly or frontally but
in a more roundabout way. Clearly, the chosen lecture course is not
an ordinary political tract or pamphlet, a tract amenable to straightforward political (or ideological) exegesis. The central topic of the course
are two poems or "hymns" by Hölderlin dating back to the year 1801.
Thus, the questions I need to face initially are of a literary character—
and seemingly far removed from politics: Why does Heidegger turn
to poetry, and particularly to Hölderlin's poetry, at this time? Differently and more elaborately put: What is for him the meaning of poetry
(*Dichtung*) and why does he choose Hölderlin to illustrate this meaning?

I

The status of poetry in Heidegger's philosophy is a complex problem which resists brief summary; one way to facilitate access is to stress
the distance from customary aesthetic assumptions (and from modern
"subjectivist" aesthetics in general). Contrary to commonsense beliefs,
poetry for Heidegger is not simply the production of nice-sounding strings
of words, or a purely decorative exercise designed to engender aesthetic
delight. Broadly speaking, poetry in his treatment has "ontological"
status: it is a prominent or eminent mode of the epiphany of "Being"—

where Being does not designate a given object (whose presence could be empirically determined), but rather an ongoing happening, a process of advent and retreat, of disclosure and concealment. Since it is not a fixed entity, Being needs to be continuously recreated and reenacted—although not in the sense of a willful fabrication. Poetry participates in this continuing enactment or "constitution of Being" (*Stiftung des Seins*) by putting it into words—although again not in a direct fashion, but through the medium of poetic language which simultaneously reveals and conceals. In the lecture course of 1934, Heidegger calls poetry also the "original voice or language of a people" (*Ursprache*) because such language permits the constitution of the "being" of a people—namely, by opening up a historical space for its deeds and accomplishments as well as for its failures and catastrophes.[5]

Given this conception of poetry, what is the significance of Hölderlin, and especially of his later hymns? From Heidegger's perspective, Hölderlin's work is exemplary or prototypical precisely with regard to the "constitution of Being." Repeatedly he portrays Hölderlin as the "poet's poet"—not only in the ordinary sense (of distinguished or outstanding poet) but in the deeper sense that his work constitutes the very being or meaning of poetry. To illustrate this meaning the lecture course invokes Hölderlin's poem "As on a Holiday . . . " ('Wie wenn am Feiertage . . . ") which contains these lines: "Yet, it behooves us, poets, to stand bare-headed beneath God's thunderstorms" ("Doch uns gebührt es, unter Gottes Gewittern, Ihr Dichter! mit entblösstem Haupte zu stehen"). As the course comments: "The poet captures God's lightning in his words and inserts these lightning-filled words into the language of a people. Rather than voicing his inner experiences he stands 'beneath God's thunderstorms'."[6]

However, Heidegger ascribes to Hölderlin a further, more specific significance or role: namely, as a "German poet" or as "poet of the Germans"—although, I should add right away, this phrase must not be taken in a restrictive ethnic, or even in a directly referential, sense. Hölderlin is poet of the Germans not merely because he happens to be born among Germans but, more radically, because his poetry "constitutes" the "being" of Germans by opening up a historical possibility for them—albeit a possibility they tend to ignore. The Preface to the lecture course describes Hölderlin as a poet "whom the Germans have yet to face (in the future)." In a later passage Hölderlin is portrayed as "the poet who poetically invents the Germans" or more elaborately as "the poet, that is, the founder (*Stifter*) of German being because he has farthest projected the latter, that is, propelled it ahead and beyond into the most distant future." In which sense or direction has Hölderlin projected this possibility? Heidegger states the answer repeatedly. "He was able," he writes, "to unlock this far-future distance because he retrieved the key out of the experience of the deepest need or agony: the experience of the retreat and (possible) return of the gods." Using a slightly different formulation the Preface notes that—leaving behind our "historicist pretentions"—Hölderlin has "founded the beginning of a different history, a history revolving around the struggle and decision regarding the advent or flight of God."[7]

I intend to return to this issue or struggle later; for the moment I just want to let these phrases linger or resonate. As indicated, the lecture course does not deal with Hölderlin's entire opus but concentrates on two of his later hymns—dating from the period when his mind was slowly beginning to drift toward darkness. Heidegger in his lectures offers a detailed exegesis of the two hymns—which I cannot fully recapitulate here. Nor shall I attempt to give a descriptive account of the "content" of these poems (if such a thing were at all possible). At this point I simply want to pick out a few lines or stanzas to convey the general flavor. In the first hymn, for example, there occur these lines which are addressed by an eagle to a priestess named "Germania": "It is you, chosen, all-loving one who have grown strong to bear a difficult fortune (*ein schweres Glück*)." And the hymn concludes thus: ". . . . on your holidays, Germania, when you are priestess and when defenseless (*wehrlos*) you provide counsel to kings and nations." Finally, some lines from "The Rhine" about half-gods, sons of gods (*Göttersöhne*), poets: "For ordinary man knows his home and the animal knows where to build, but these carry the wound in their inexperienced souls of not knowing where to turn."[8]

While I cannot retrace here Heidegger's entire commentary, I can and need to review some of his major arguments regarding these poems. First, a few words on the reading of poetry or poetic texts. In addition to providing a substantive analysis, the lecture course also offers numerous observations on exegesis or literary interpretation in general—observations which seem directly relevant to contemporary literary criticism. As Heidegger emphasizes, poetry—and Hölderlin's poetry in particular— cannot simply be explained or decoded in terms of historical influences, environmental conditions, and least of all in terms of personal biography. Despite their obvious importance, historical settings in his view cannot be used as a shortcut to interpretation—a shortcut predicated on the assumption that historical periods are more directly accessible to understanding than texts and that the latter can therefore readily be deciphered in terms of the former. Perhaps, he retorts, we may sometimes have to interpret a period or social context in light of its leading texts. Heidegger is more adamant in his critique of psychological or biographical approaches to exegesis. Poetry, he insists, is not the outpouring of inner feelings, the "expression" of personal sentiments or experiences—the teachings of traditional (modern) aesthetics to the contrary notwithstanding. Summarizing the traditional outlook, the course remarks: Inner feelings are here claimed "to find tangible outer expression—for instance, in a lyrical poem. These processes and sentiments in the poet's 'soul' can then be further analyzed with the help of modern 'depth psychology'. Along these lines one can compare writers of different genres as (psychological) types—such as epic, lyrical, or dramatic writers; depth psychology thus turns into typological analysis." As Heidegger bitingly comments: "Expression is also the barking of a dog. . . . This conception places poetry *ab limine* under auspices where even the slightest possibility of real understanding hopelessly disappears."9

Contrary to this subjective-expressive view Heidegger finds the essence of poetry in complete surrender or exposure. Following Hölderlin's suggestion in "As on a Holiday," he writes: Instead of articulating inner feelings the poet "stands 'beneath God's thunderstorms'—'bare-headed', defenselessly surrendered and abandoned." When Hölderlin occasionally speaks of the "soul of the poet," the phrase (he notes) does not designate a "rummaging in inner psychic feelings" or an "experiential core somewhere inside," but rather refers to the "utmost exile of naked exposure." For both Hölderlin and Heidegger, thunderstorm and lightning are the peculiar "language of the gods" which poets are meant to capture "without flinching" and to transplant into the language of a people. As the lecture course elaborates, the "language of the gods" is not a direct mode of speech but rather a set of indirect "winks," cues, or traces. Poetry, from this perspective, is "the transmission of these winks to the people"; seen from the angle of the latter, it is the attempt "to place the being of a people under the aegis of these winks"—an attempt which does not mean their transformation into "observable objects or intentional contents." It is precisely by enduring and transmitting the "winks of the gods," that poetry is said to contribute to the "constitution of being."[10]

Together with the subjective-expressive approach, Heidegger also rejects the definition of exegesis as a reconstruction of the *mens auctoris* (author's intention). In his view, the author's mind—provided it could be uncovered—is not a reliable or "authoritative" guide; actually, it is the poem which constitutes the author as author or poet, rather than the other way around. In reading a poem, he observes, we cannot take refuge in the author's intent as a fixed point; instead, we are drawn into the torrent of the poetic language, into the "cyclone" (*Wirbel*) of the poetic saying. As this observation indicates, Heidegger, in criticizing the subjective or mentalist conception, does not simply opt for a textual objectivism or autonomy, that is, for the timeless, aesthetic essence of a text or opus—such as a "Sophocles in itself, a Kant in itself," or a poem in itself. Rather, interpreting a text requires dynamic participation and involvement on the part of the reader—who, in turn, is not a sovereign master. This means: the reader must be willing to undergo the same surrender that the poet endured; he must himself be ready to enter the cyclone of the poetic word. Thus, Heidegger stresses the need to "participate" in poetry, the need to be drawn into the "power sphere (*Machtbereich*) of poetry" and to let poetry exert its leavening and transforming impact on human life.[11]

II

To be sure, in offering his exegesis of Hölderlin's poems, Heidegger does not himself speak as a poet but as a thinker or philosopher; his interpretation is a distinctly philosophical endeavor or labor. Repeatedly the lecture course portrays the relation between thinking and poetry (*Dichten und Denken*) as a relationship marked by both distance and proximity—that is, as a relationship of two enterprises whose "boundary" is both a connecting link and a line of demarcation. In Heidegger's view, thinking and poetry are neither synonymous nor are they worlds apart; as he notes (in another context), they "dwell close together on high mountain tops separated by an abyss." The lecture course, in any event, is not merely a poetic paraphrase or a "literary" exercise; instead, it deliberately pursues the task of philosophical penetration, an effort guided by the need for "lucid sobriety" (*heller Ernst*) as distinguished from calculating wit or academic pedantry. "If any poet," Heidegger writes, "demands for his work a philosophical approach, it is Hölderlin; and this not only because as poet he happened to be 'also a philosopher'—and even one whom we confidently can place next to Schelling and Hegel. Rather: Hölderlin is one of our greatest, that is, most impending *thinkers* because he is our greatest *poet*. The poetic understanding of his poetry is possible only as a philosophical confrontation with the manifestation of Being achieved in his work."[12]

Judged in strictly philosophical terms, the lecture course is significant not only because of its analysis of Hölderlin's poems but also—in equal measure—because of the light it throws on Heidegger's own perspective and on the development of his thought. The course, I would claim, offers numerous clues regarding the so-called *"Kehre"* (or reversal) in his thinking, that is, the move from a *Dasein*-focused to a more Being-focused outlook—although the transition was extremely nuanced and subtle. I have to be very brief on this topic (since the entire text may, of course, be read as a set of philosophical clues). The reader acquainted with *Being and Time* will encounter many themes familiar from that work—especially the theme of the ontological status of *Dasein*, of man as the "witness of Being" whose *Dasein* is lodged in the existential tension of "thrownness" and "project" (*Geworfenheit* and *Entwurf*). There are also comments on "being-toward-death" as well as on *Mitsein* and authentic "co-being." As the lecture course states: "Being directly touches and concerns us—we cannot even exist without being entangled in Being. But this being or existence of ours is not that of an isolated subject but rather a historical co-being or togetherness as being-in-a-world." In line with the earlier work, the course also contains significant passages on the meaning of "time"—particularly the distinction between ordinary time seen as the "mere flux of successive nows" and genuine time as the advent or manifestation of Being.[13]

In addition to these more familiar topics the course at various points moves beyond the perimeters of *Being and Time* in the direction of Heidegger's subsequent works. Thus, the portrayal of *Dasein* as a "linguistic event" (*Sprachgeschehnis*) and as "dialogue" (*Gespräch*) foreshadows arguments more fully developed in *On the Way to Language*. "Only where language happens," the lectures state, "can being and non-being disclose themselves; this disclosure and concealment, however, is who we are." Similarly, the description of genuine time as a "waiting for the *Ereignis*" may be said to adumbrate later discussions of this mode of ontological happening (sometimes translated as "appropriation" or "appropriating event"). A prominent feature of the lecture course is also the recurrent reference to "creators" or "creative agents" (*die Schaffenden*)—a topic which, as we know, became crucial in some of Heidegger's writings during the immediately following years. In particular, the subdivision of "creators" into poets, thinkers, and "founders of states" (*Staatsschöpfer*) is a striking anticipation of an argument familiar from "The Origin of the Work of Art" (of 1935-36); the same could be said about passages dealing with the role of conflict or "agon" (*Streit*) as precondition of ontological "harmony" (*Innigkeit*).[14]

III

I shall not prolong this review of philosophical themes; instead, I want to turn to another "boundary": that connecting poetry and thinking with politics. I intend to approach this boundary on two levels: a more overt and a more latent or subterranean level. First, let me draw your attention to some overtly political passages in the lecture course. There are a great number of these—some quite forthright and brazen if placed in the context of 1934. The opening pages of the course refer to a fragment from Hölderlin's late opus which reads: "About the highest I shall be silent. Forbidden fruit, like the laurel, however, is most of all the fatherland. This (fruit) everyone should taste last." And Heidegger comments: "The fatherland, our fatherland Germany—forbidden most of all, removed from everyday haste and busy noise. . . . With this we already indicate what our focus on 'Gemania' does not mean. We do not wish to offer something usable, trendy or up-to-date and thereby advertise our lecture course—which would convey the pernicious impression as if we wanted to garner for Hölderlin a cheap timely relevance. We do not seek to adapt Hölderlin to our time, but on the contrary: we want to bring us and those after us under the yardstick of the poet." Our fatherland, forbidden most of all—surely strange words at a time of patriotic and chauvinistic frenzy.[15]

But there is more to come. Commenting on Hölderlin's portrayal of "Germania"—as a priestess or else as a dreamy maid "hidden in the woods"—Heidegger compares this image with a famous national monument: the statue of Germania in the Niederwald forest. This monument, he notes, depicts "a massive woman (*ein Mordsweib*) with flowing hair and a giant sword. By contrast, Hölderlin's Germania is by today's standards 'unheroic'." What makes things worse is the reference to a "defenseless" Germania offering counsel to nations. Thus, Heidegger adds mockingly, Hölderlin "is apparently a 'pacifist', one who advocates the defenselessness of Germany and perhaps even unilateral disarmament. This borders on high treason." A little later, during a discussion of the expressive view of poetry, the course directly attacks one of the regime's most representative poets or literary figures: Erwin G. Kolbenheyer. In a speech given at various German universities the latter had claimed that "poetry is a necessary biological function of a people." Heidegger retorts: "It does not take much brain to realize: this [description] applies also to digestion—which likewise is a biologically necessary function of a people, especially a healthy one." The same discussion contains a "dig" at Alfred Rosenberg, the regime's star ideologist, and at the doctrine of racial biologism or biological racism. The expressive view, Heidegger insists, is mistaken regardless of whose sentiments are involved: whether these sentiments are those of a single individual or a "collective soul," whether (with Spengler) they reflect the "soul of a culture" or (with Rosenberg) they express a "racial soul" or the "soul of a people." Regarding fascist biologism another passage should also be mentioned. In light of his stress on "earth" and "homeland" Heidegger has sometimes been assailed as harboring a sympathy for the ideology of "blood and soil" (*Blut und Boden*). Alluding to the practice of literary criticism of his time—to the "dubious arsenal of the contemporary science of literature"—the lecture course states: "Until recently everyone was looking for the psychoanalytic underpinnings of poetry; now everything is saturated (*trieft*) with folkdom and with 'blood and soil'—but nothing has really changed."[16]

Here, for good measure, are a few more stabs at pet fascist conceptions or slogans. Advocating a view of philosophy as perpetual questioning, Heidegger writes, in mock self-criticism: "Questioning? But no: the decisive thing is clearly the answer. That much every pedestrian or man on the street understands, and since he understands it, it must be right and the whole outlook is then called 'folkish science' or 'folk-related science' " (*volksverbundene Wissenschaft*, the official aim of every discipline at the time). Or again, a little later, Heidegger finds a linkage between the fascist view of culture and the bourgeois "culture industry." "Only small times," he observes, "when the whole *Dasein* decays into fabrication—only such times officially cultivate the 'true, good, and

beautiful' and establish appropriate state ministries for this cultivation."
This confusion is compounded by the mistaken assumption that folk
culture could be enhanced "through the expanded institution of pro-
fessorships for folk science and primeval history." Elsewhere, Heidegger displays his chagrin over ongoing developments in academia and
education in general. His turn to Hölderlin, he insists, does not reflect
an attempt to salvage a national heritage or to "utilize [the poet] in
a direct political manner"—things "which no doubt we shall encounter
abundantly in the coming years, following the completed political integration (*Gleichschaltung*) of the humanities." In a sardonic vein—
pondering future prospects of philosophy—the lecture course notes at
one point that "it now appears as if thinking will soon be entirely
abolished."[17]

While criticizing the political winds of the time (I should add)
Heidegger does not depict his own preoccupation with Hölderlin as a
simple retreat from politics or as an abandonment of the political arena
as such. On the contrary, the lectures explicitly present this concern
as a kind of counter-politics or as signaling a radical change of political
course. "Since Hölderlin has this hidden and difficult meaning to be
the poet's poet and the poet of the Germans," we read, "therefore he
has not yet become a guiding force in the history of our people. And
since he is not yet this force, he should become it. To contribute to
this task is 'politics' in the highest and most genuine sense—so much
so that whoever makes headway along this line has no need to talk
about 'politics'."[18]

IV

What alternative course or direction does this counter-politics suggest? We approach here, I believe, the deeper or less overt significance
of Hölderlin in the context of 1934—and, more broadly, in the context of our age. Heidegger delineates this significance by elaborating
on the "basic mood" (*Grundstimmung*) of the two poems "Germania"
and "The Rhine," a mood which underlies and permeates the poetic
saying in these hymns as a whole. By "mood," one needs to emphasize
right away, Heidegger does not mean an inner-subjective feeling or
psychological sentiment. Readers of *Being and Time* cannot be misled
on this point, which is reiterated in the lecture course: "mood" in

Heidegger's usage is a kind of ontological "tuning" or "attunement"—
the attunement of *Dasein* and Being, or the mode in which Being is
revealed/concealed in a *Dasein* or (as here) in poetry. As he says, "mood"
(*Stimmung*) denotes "least of all the merely subjective or the so-called
interior of man"; rather, it means "the original exposure into the vastness
of beings and the depth of Being."[19]

Turning first to "Germania," what—in Heidegger's exegesis—is
the basic mood or tuning pervading the poem? According to the lecture course, this tuning derives from a fundamental, though subterranean event of our age: the flight or disappearance of the gods. Hölderlin's
hymn begins with these lines: "Not them, the blessed ones who once
appeared, the images of gods of old, them I may no longer call. . . ."
However, this non-calling is not simply an act of resignation, least of
all a sign of abandonment or indifference; rather, non-calling is a
synonym for the patient endurance of a loss, for a longstanding and
profound suffering. This means: the tuning or mood of "Germania"
is essentially one of "mourning" (*Trauer*). Yet, in the treatment of both
Hölderlin and Heidegger, mourning is not identical with mere emotional sadness or melancholy, and certainly not with a plaintive anxiety or distress. Rather, as a mode of attunement, mourning has a sober
and almost serene quality; in Heidegger's words, it is not a psychological
but a "spiritual" (or ontological) category. Occasioned by the loss of
gods, the mourning pervading "Germania" is in fact a "hallowed" or
"sacred mourning" (*heilige Trauer*). Moreover, mourning here does not
signify a breach or simple farewell. As in the case of a loved one, the
experience of the loss of gods actually nurtures and strengthens the bond
of love and the desire for reunion. As Heidegger notes: "Where the
most beloved is gone, love remains—for else the other could not at all
have gone (as the beloved)." Thus, mourning here is both acceptance
of the loss—a refusal to cling—and a determined waiting for reconciliation, an expectant readiness for the return of the gods.[20]

The theme of mourning is further elaborated in the second hymn,
"The Rhine," whose focus is on the role of half-gods or demigods—
namely, as exemplary mourners. In Hölderlin's presentation these
demigods are directly guided by a divine mission or destiny (*Schicksal*)
and thus are able to chart a course for human life; they include the
great streams or rivers (like the Rhine) which create a path for human
habitation, and also the poets who carry the gods' lightning to men.
In Heidegger's commentary, half-gods are basically "over-men and under-

gods" (*Übermenschen und Untergötter*). When thinking about the being of man, he observes, we necessarily point beyond man toward a higher region; in thinking about gods, on the other hand, we inevitably fall short and remain at their threshold. Hence the importance of half-gods as mediators and place-keepers of the "in-between" realm. Standing directly under divine mandates, half-gods are particularly vulnerable and exposed; being specially attuned to the withdrawal (and possible return) of the gods, their existence is marked by intense suffering and endurance. In effect, their suffering is the emblem of their mediating and creative role. Thus, as in the case of "Germania," the basic mood or tuning of "The Rhine" is one of hallowed mourning, occasioned by the flight of the gods. In Heidegger's words: "The manner in which the being of half-gods—the mid-point of Being as a whole—is disclosed is suffering. This great and alone decisive kind of suffering, however, can pervade *Dasein* only in the form of that mood which manifests simultaneously the fugitive and approaching power of God and the exposed plight of human life: the mood of sacred mourning and expectant readiness."[21]

V

One should mark this well: mourning—sacred mourning—as the central mood of Hölderlin's hymns and also of Heidegger's entire lecture course. How incongruous—in 1934, and still today. How much disillusionment and personal agony must have preceded and nurtured this mood in the case of both Hölderlin and Heidegger. How far removed, how radically distant is this outlook from the ebullient self-confidence of the fascist regime in 1934, from the mood of national "resurgence" (*Aufbruch*) at the inception of the "Thousand-year *Reich*."[22] (Nineteen thirty-four, one may recall, was the year of the mammoth Party Congress in Nuremberg which, in a celebrated film, has been glorified as "triumph of the will.") How distant is this outlook also from our own contemporary life—from our own ebullient self-confidence in the unlimited blessings of technological progress.

Mourning, sacred mourning—about what? About the god-lessness of our age, about the withdrawal and absence of the gods. I should add right away that mourning of this kind is not simply a call for moral or spiritual renewal or for a mobilization of religious faith; least of all is it a call for a strengthening of church institutions or confessional ties.

Godlessness here is not a question of the vitality of established churches
or of inner-personal belief. Instead: it has to do with the absence of
gods from our civilization and our existence as a people, that is, from
our way of life or way of being. It has to do with our relegation of the
divine to a decorative status on holidays, to the status of folklore at
religious festivals. As Heidegger emphasizes: "The issue is not how an
empirically given people handles its traditional religion or denomina-
tional faith. Rather, at stake is the genuine advent or non-advent of
God in the life of a people out of the agony of its being."[23]

The stress on a common "way of life" (or ontological condition)
highlights another dimension of the key mood of the two hymns: the
reference to a "homeland" or "fatherland." For Hölderlin and Heidegger, mourning is not an isolated-individual experience or subjective state
of mind; rather, it is a mourning "in" and "with the homeland" (Heimat)
or "with the native earth" (heimatliche Erde). However, homeland here
does not simply denote a natural habitat or an empirical-ecological setting; nor is it a mere abstraction or speculative-metaphysical idea. As
interpreted in the lecture course, homeland is rather the site of an ontological mediation—the name for a concrete promise, namely, for a potential dwelling place of the gods.[24] Properly speaking, mourning is possible only on the basis of such a promise. For, how could one talk of their
withdrawal or advent if gods lived in an immutable realm separated
from humans by an unbridgeable gulf? And how could one sense or experience their loss if human life were invariably wretched? Mourning
thus necessarily involves a transgression of traditional metaphysics (predicated on the juxtaposition of two separate "worlds").

VI

Let me slowly come to a close. I have explored Heidegger's exegesis of Hölderlin's hymns and also some of their—overt and covert—
political implications. I do not wish to leave the impression that I find
all of Heidegger's arguments equally persuasive. Some passages still carry
overtones of a youthful exuberance ("Sturm und Drang") which required
further seasoning; some details also are not entirely congruent, in my
view, with the overall direction of his thought. Thus, I find dubious
Heidegger's persistent reference to "the people" (Volk) in the sense of
a homogeneous entity or totality. Precisely his non-objectivist ontology

and his stress on "ontological difference" should have suggested to him a greater differentiation or heterogeneity among people (perhaps along the lines of Arendt's notion of "plurality"). Appeals to "the people" or a bland populism are particularly problematic if the people—here the German people—are assigned an eminently poetic or historically creative role; surely subsequent years and decades must have disabused Heidegger of such hopes. Together with the concept of "the people" I would also question the notion of "the state" as used in the lecture course, especially in the portrayal of "founders of states" as exemplary historical agents; too heavily burdened with modern metaphysical weight, "the state" does not seem an adequate vehicle for Heidegger's thoughts.[25] Finally, I find disconcerting the excessive emphasis on conflict and "agon" (*Streit, Feindseligkeit*)—an emphasis which renders "harmony" (*Innigkeit*) extremely precarious if not impossible. In the exegesis of "The Rhine," this emphasis is actually so strong and pervasive that Heidegger almost omits to comment on a crucial theme in Hölderlin's poem: the impending "wedding feast of gods and men." In this instance the experience of subsequent years and the outbreak of the war seemed to have a remarkable effect. When Heidegger again offers a lecture course on Hölderlin (in the winter of 1941-42), his focus and the basic tuning of his course is precisely this "wedding feast" (*Brautfest*).[26]

Yet, I wish to end on a different note: by returning to 1934. In the midst of fascist triumphalism Heidegger's lecture course is pervaded by overwhelming grief. What is the significance then of Hölderlin in Heidegger's perception? Who is this poet as reflected in the two hymns and in the lectures? He is, simply put, a caller in the desert, a voice in the wilderness of our age—or, as Heidegger says, a "first fruit" or "first born" (*Erstling*) liable to be sacrificed. What does the voice proclaim? Mostly this: prepare the ground, make straight the paths—for a possible return of the fugitive gods, and thus for a possible reconciliation or "wedding feast."[27] Not that through our attitude or activity we could somehow halt their flight or force or fabricate their reappearance; but our grief and expectation may at least serve as an invitation or solicitation encouraging their return. Mourning thus is preparatory for a different age: for a way of life which would again be suffused with lightning and poetic imagination, a life in which young men could again "see visions and old men dream dreams." This is also the meaning of the fatherland as a hallowed or promised land. Heidegger concludes the lecture course by once again invoking the fragment with which he began: "About the highest I shall be silent. Forbidden fruit, like the laurel, however, is most of all the fatherland. This (fruit) everyone should taste last."

NOTES

1. Albert O. Hirschman, *Essays in Trespassing: Economics to Politics and Beyond* (Cambridge: Cambridge University Press, 1981).

2. Martin Heidegger, *Hölderlins Hymnen "Germanien" und "Der Rhein"*, ed. Susanne Ziegler (*Gesamtausgabe*, vol. 39; Frankfurt-Main: Klostermann, 1980); hereafter abbreviated *Hölderlins Hymnen*.

3. Hans-Georg Gadamer, *Heidegger Wege* (Tübingen: Mohr, 1983), 14, 118; Hannah Arendt, "Martin Heidegger at Eighty," in Michael Murray, ed., *Heidegger and Modern Philosophy: Critical Essays* (New Haven: Yale University Press, 1978), 294-95.

4. I have addressed some aspects of this episode in my "Ontology of Freedom: Heidegger and Political Philosophy," *Political Theory* 12 (May 1984): 204-34. The text of Heidegger's "Rektoratsrede" of May 1933 has recently been republished, together with a retrospective epilogue written by Heidegger in 1945; see Hermann Heidegger, ed., *Die Selbstbehauptung der deutschen Universität* (Frankfurt-Main: Klostermann, 1983).

5. *Hölderlins Hymnen*, 20, 33, 64, 216-217.

6. Ibid., 30. For the English version see *Friedrich Hölderlin: Poems and Fragments*, trans. Michael Hamburger (Ann Arbor: University of Michigan Press, 1967), 375 (translation slightly altered). For a more general assessment of Hölderlin's poetry by Heidegger see "Hölderlin und das Wesen der Dichtung," in Heidegger, *Erläuterungen zu Hölderlins Dichtung*, ed. Friedrich-Wilhelm von Herrmann (*Gesamtausgabe*, vol. 4; Frankfurt-Main: Klostermann, 1981), 33-48.

7. *Hölderlins Hymnen*, 1, 220.

8. *Friedrich Hölderlin: Poems and Fragments*, 405, 407, 410 (translation slightly altered).

9. *Hölderlins Hymnen*, 6-7, 26-28. With a clear political edge Heidegger adds (p. 28): "If anything deserves the much abused label 'liberal', it is this conception. For, on principle and from the outset, this conception distances itself from its own thoughts and beliefs, reducing them to mere objects or targets of opinion. Poetry in this manner becomes an immediately given phenomenon among other phenomena—a phenomenon which is further characterized by the equally non-committal designation as 'expressive manifestation' of an inner soul."

10. Ibid., 30-33.

11. Ibid., 19, 45, 58-59, 145. Repeatedly the lecture course also comments on the status of metaphors in poetry—a theme which is important because of the connection between "meta-phors" and "meta-physics." Thus, referring to the first stanza of "As on a Holiday," Heidegger states (pp. 254-55) that these lines do not offer a "poetic comparison such as an 'image' or a 'metaphor'." For, in a poetic comparison, "what is compared with what? Typically a process in nature with a spiritual-mental experience. But what do we mean by 'nature' and by 'spirit'? . . . . No matter how we construe these terms, what is the point of a comparison if the poet insists that nature itself educates the poet?"

12. *Hölderlins Hymnen*, 5-6, 8. See also Heidegger, *What is Philosophy?*, trans. William Kluback and Jean T. Wilde (New Haven: College University Press, 1956), 95.

13. *Hölderlins Hymnen*, 55, 61, 173-75. As Heidegger insists (pp. 73, 174) the "ownness" (*Jemeinigkeit*) of *Dasein* and of individual death does not nullify the ontological character of co-being. Accentuating the aspect of "thrownness" in every project, the course establishes a close linkage between "Being" and "suffering," associating genuine human existence with the need continuously to "undergo" its own calling (*Leiden seiner selbst*, 175).

14. *Hölderlins Hymnen*, 51, 56, 69-71, 117-18, 123-28, 144, 275.

15. Ibid., 4; see also *Friedrich Hölderlin: Poems and Fragments*, 537 (translation slightly altered).

16. *Hölderlins Hymnen*, 17, 26-27, 254. Regarding Heidegger's invocation of "blood and soil" in his so-called "Rektoratsrede" of May 1933 compare the sensible comments of Graeme Nicholson in his "The Politics of Heidegger's Rectoral Address," in *Proceedings: Heidegger Conference* (18th Annual Meeting, University of Wisconsin-Stevens Point, May 1984), 212-13.

17. *Hölderlins Hymnen*, 5, 41, 99, 221. In another context (p. 210), Heidegger attacks the portrayal of Christ as "*Führer*"—a portrayal, he says, which is"not only an untruth but also, what is worse, a blasphemy vis-à-vis Christ."

18. Ibid., 214.

19. Ibid., 142.

20. Ibid., 80-82, 95. As Heidegger adds (p. 95): "Sacred mourning is ready to renounce the old gods; yet—what else does the mourning heart desire but this: in relinquishing the gods to preserve immaculate their divinity and thus, through a preserving renunciation of the distant gods, to remain in the proximity of their divinity. The not-being-able-to-call the old gods, the acceptance of the loss, what else is it—it is nothing else—but the only possible, resolute readiness to wait for the divine." Together with Hölderlin, incidentally, Heidegger (p. 84) interprets the term "sacred" or holy in the sense of "unselfish"—something which radically transcends the domains of both individual or general interest (or utility).

21. Ibid., 165-66, 182. For an attempt to find a more overt political meaning in "The Rhine" see Johannes Mahr, *Mythos und Politik in Hölderlins Rheinhymne* (Munich: Fink Verlag, 1972).

22. Heidegger was well aware of the mentioned incongruence or contrast. As he writes (*Hölderlins Hymnen*, 80): "The flight of the gods must first become an experience and this experience must push *Dasein* into a basic mood in which a historical people as a whole endures the plight of its godlessness and brokenness. It is this basic mood which the poet seeks to implant in the life of our people. Whether this happened in 1801, and whether in 1934 it has not yet been perceived and grasped—this is not the issue since dates are immaterial at such a watershed."

23. Ibid., 147.

24. Ibid., 88, 90, 104, 122-23.

25. In this respect some of Heidegger's later works contain an important self-correction. Thus, a lecture course held in summer of 1942 contrasts the "polis" construed as an ontological site to the modern conception of "the state." See Heidegger, *Hölderlins Hymne "Der Ister"*, ed. Walter Biemel (*Gesamtausgabe*, vol. 53; Frankfurt-Main: Klostermann, 1984), 100-01.

26. See Heidegger, *Hölderlins Hymne "Andenken"*, ed. Curd Ochwadt (*Gesamtausgabe*, vol. 52; Frankfurt-Main: Klostermann, 1982), 76-78, 188.

27. In Heidegger's words: "The task is to take seriously the long-standing flight of the gods and in and through this seriousness to anticipate their return—which means: to participate in the preparation of their renewed advent and thus to refashion the earth and the land anew." See *Hölderlins Hymnen*, 146, 220-221.

A version of this essay appeared in *Heidegger Studies* 1 (1986).

6. Contemporary Issues in Feminist Theory

DONNA PRZYBYLOWICZ

One of the essential and controversial issues confronting feminist critics today is the necessity for theory—should we utilize the patriarchal discourses we have inherited or should we develop our own language and mode of expression? Many women feel that the language of theory, as a powerful tool of domination, represents a reality experienced by the oppressors: "Ultimately a revolutionary movement has to break the hold of the dominant group over theory, it has to structure its own connections. Language is part of the political and ideological power of rulers. . . . We have to change the meanings of words even before we take them over."[1] According to the latter view, such a patriarchal discourse propagates certain historical norms and social forms of power, thus becoming an instrument of political and ideological domination: this authoritarianism of theoretical language makes the reader a passive recipient of a privileged message or knowledge of another person or group. Thus we see that one of the most serious problems facing feminist critics today has to do with the division between theory and practice, the former usually associated with the hegemony and valorization of male-inspired methodological structures and abstract systems of thought and the latter with the materialist thrust and political activism underlying and motivating female discourse.

In the following pages we will observe many ways in which women resist patriarchal linguistic models. In positing the possibility of an emancipatory feminist speech, responses have been: "revisionary" in that they have sought to demystify, decode, modify, and supplement male critical theories by adding a feminist perspective or point of reference to these "androcentric" models;[2] "gynocritical" in that they deal with women as producers of textual meaning and instead of adopting male values and paradigms they construct new modes of expression based on the authority of their own experience;[3] "revolutionary and linguistic" in that they attempt to discover and utilize an appropriate female language, a nonoppressive and nonalien practice of writing that would articulate the body and woman's unconscious; or "marxist" in that they re-read male theoretical texts (particularly by Marx and Freud) through an Althusserian "symptomatic" analysis. These will be the main areas of exploration in this article, areas so large that I will only be able to cover them in a cursory way.

Many women critics feel that feminist scholarship is weakened by the lack of a firm theoretical perspective and that our first task is to examine the inadequacies of male structures—a task which in turn will promote the development of the foundations of feminist theory: "Women cannot simply ignore the history of thought because it is, among other things, misogynist. We have to understand why men have created the abstraction woman."[4] This fits in with the concept of comparativism: in analyzing "the territorial approach to feminist criticism"[5] of Spacks, Showalter, Moers, and Gilbert and Gubar,[6] who describe the circumscribed world of women writers and their milieu, Jehlen argues that an understanding about the entire culture and women's sphere within it must be based in a universal context. Thus one must analyze the contradictions between pure appreciation and a political analysis of a work: in other words, one must detach one's subjective and moral judgments of a text from a more objective and distanced examination of the overt and covert, the conscious and unconscious ideological and political messages discovered in the work, messages which may be personally distasteful or repulsive to a particular reader—"the problem, if we as feminists want to address our whole culture, is to deal with what we do not like but recognize as none the less valuable, serious, good."[7] Jehlen feels feminists are in conflict with their culture and its literary traditions, and thus need to analyze texts in terms that the author may have repressed, may have detested, or may have not used. So it is necessary, from Jehlen's viewpoint, to do what Millett does in Sexual Politics:[8] adopt a comparative stance that can reveal the abyss between the male/female, subject/object oppositions imposed by society. She therefore advocates an ideological and deconstructive analysis of the dominant literary culture, canons, methods, and ideas: it is only in scrutinizing the "universal" values of a humanistic tradition that the embedded contradictions of an ideological criticism become obvious and acute. Finally, Jehlen feels Nina Baym's defense of women novelists is unnecessary,[9] for "if history has treated women badly, it is entirely expected that a reduced or distorted female culture . . . will show it."[10] Therefore, rather than looking to past accomplishments or claiming more than exists, she suggests women should and can rightfully look to the future as potentially fulfilling the promise inherent in the present. Thus Jehlen's method of comparativism can give the critic the necessary distance for re-vision, for apprehending the contradictions within a text or society that reveal the crucial ideological issues.

Alice Jardine also deals with these issues posed by Jehlen's comparativism and Showalter's gynocriticism. She suggests that the attempt to purify writing of "male *topoi*" is "a return to the worst of our tradition. . . . The elaboration of a feminist strategy of reading/writing reaching *beyond* while in dialogue with that tradition is what is difficult, but is a more promising approach. First, by continuing to explore fictions, whether coded as literature or theory, we might establish a topology of textual strategies—or any modalities of foreclosure—which threaten the symbolic."[11] One must necessarily observe the historical totality: in order to do so one must be aware of the strategies of containment, those structures of a patriarchal society that have successfully silenced women. However, Jardine also acknowledges the need to concentrate on women's writing (gynocriticism), those so-called "marginal" texts that have been ignored and suppressed by a male standard of what is "good" or valuable, for, although sympathetic to the French feminist critics, she notes that their work is "derivative, caught in an erotic and didactic network of male theoretical fictions," which "is perhaps not unrelated to the fact that very rarely does any one there work on women's writing."[12] As we shall see, the focus of the French feminist critics has been the literature of the male avant-garde writers.

American feminist theory has been criticized for being empirical, antispeculative, based on the concepts of a unified ego, an integrated self, sexual identity, and Husserlian intentionality. In focusing on a description of the social, psychological, and material situation of women, American feminists are pragmatic and interested in proposing ways to alleviate it. They are also involved in reconstructing and reevaluating the past accomplishments of women in order to reveal the repressed discourse, the silence imposed by *"history"* on this displaced and oppressed group. "The assumption is that women have been present but invisible and that if they look they will find themselves," will discover a "her-story."[13] American feminists have been resistant to structuralist, poststructuralist, and deconstructionist theories, which they feel are emblematic of a supposedly objective, yet deadly masculine discourse. Instead, they want to extol the subjective authority of experience, of female expression. They reject psychoanalysis and Marxism, for the most part, as being male-defined and sexist, and are in favor of praxis, of activism and practical application rather than theory and intellectual abstractions: situating the locus of patriarchal power in intersubjective relations, they want to restructure drastically the family unit. However, there has also been a concern among American feminists to remove or lessen their sense of isolation and distance from the increasingly theoretical community around them that has been, for so long, oblivious to the importance of women's writing.

The whole conflict between theory and praxis has sparked considerable debate among feminists on both sides of the Atlantic. Even though American feminists see their French counterparts as elitist (since their discourse requires a knowledge of several disciplines—linguistics, psychoanalysis, philosophy, semiotics, Marxism), as "involved in a kind of word play," and as immersing themselves in a "theory detached from what we have to struggle with,"[14] they are fascinated by and often compelled to master this difficult approach that is based in a transdisciplinary perspective, which is obviously important to the success of women's studies. Cheri Register warns about the dangers involved in a hostility toward *écriture féminine*: such antagonism could result in what she calls "prescriptive criticism" involving the

> 'erection' of a feminist critical imperialism that mouths dogma and prescribes *the* right way to package a feminist product. If we do not preserve openness and diversity through continued, dynamic debate of our differences, if we cease to be receptive to new tools and concepts which may illuminate aspects of female oppression or repression, then American feminist scholars will fall prey to the sameness and repetition we condemn in masculinist critics, and it will lose its revolutionary impulse.[15]

Such a plea for tolerance and an understanding of other approaches to feminist issues, rather than a response of exclusion which dictates further isolation from the world, is certainly necessary for the success of the women's movement. The accusation of "elitism" directed at such theoretical feminists can also be the grounds for a parallel attack on "prescriptive" critics. Although disagreement and argument are essential for the progress of any cause, such contradiction must be transcended by a more basic level of unity in purpose (i.e., to undermine a patriarchal culture and its values), or the old adage "divide and conquer" may become a crude reality.

A re-reading and a synthesis of marxist and psychoanalytic theory through a "symptomatic" analysis should be the initial step in the development of a feminist methodology since such an approach would deal with both public and private spheres of human development. Most interesting, in this respect, are the British and French varieties of feminism, which have attempted such a combination of approaches. At this point, therefore, I will examine the latter syncretic experiments and show some of the challenges and dangers in these positions. For example, in England Marxist feminists have been using male French theorists, Althusser and Lacan, to explain how the subject is ideologically and sexually constructed in order to yield a feminist critique of Marx's ideas on production and reproduction. Annette Kuhn and Ann Marie Wolpe call for a theory, based on a materialist problematic, which conceives human society as defined by its productivity and which conceptualizes history as the locus of the transformation of the social relations of production and reproduction. The latter situation, in terms of the position of women, would involve the concern with the nature and characteristics of the sexual division of labor and its relationship to the historical context as well as the social relations peculiar to the modes of production, that is, relations between classes.[16] Thus masculinity and femininity imply class and sex designations.

Feminists have consistently accused Marxism of being male-defined in theory and praxis and of failing to address the subordination of women and to analyze this historically in terms of the relation of women to the modes of production and reproduction. Therefore, Marxism must come to terms with the sexual division of labor and the family, for in dealing with women only in terms of class, the labor process, and the state, it is unable to address the actuality of their oppression and struggle which cuts across class, nationality, and modes of production. With a materialist analysis of this problematic, one can construct a Marxist feminism. "While Marx's historical model gives great significance to the dialectical structure of the productive labor process . . . male-dominated culture has not given a high value to the creative power of reproductive labor and the act of giving birth: . . . men have obscured the fact that the material base of human history is human reproduction."[17] Production and reproduction are necessary to the survival of the human race, and women must therefore be integrated on equal terms in the productive world and men must participate as well in the relations of reproduction, of sharing equally in the raising of the next generation.

Marxist feminists would like to "reappropriate patriarchy for materialism, for an approach to women's situation in its historicial specificity."[18] Patriarchal relations take their particular configuration from the dominant modes of production. Within capitalism, for example, patriarchy functions through class relations: while questions of human reproduction are crucial to the subordination of women, different contradictions evolve for women from varying class positions. (Although patriarchy is often used as a central concept in explicating women's oppression, it must be comprehended historically in relation to other forms of economic and political domination.) Thus the goal is to establish the interaction between modes of production and structures of patriarchy at particular historical moments.

Partriarchy as an ideology should be examined in Althusser's terms: he defines ideology in *Lenin and Philosophy* as a representation of an "imaginary" relationship of individuals to their real condition of existence—it interpellates them as subjects. This construction of the latter by and within ideology should be read "symptomatically," that is, in a psychoanalytic framework, in order to render a genuinely materialist theory of the constitution of subjectivity. "Where Marxist theory explains the historical and economic development of society, psychoanalysis in conjunction with dialectical materialism is the way to understanding ideology and sexuality,"[19] both of which are rooted not only in our consciousness but in our unconscious as well.

Unlike Mitchell's espousal of a separatist socialist-economic and cultural-feminist revolution, McDonough and Harrison feel that the relationship between class and sex must not be severed but dealt with dialectically.[20] Thus the concept of patriarchy must be discovered in the interaction between the relations of production and human reproduction, that is, must reveal how the patriarchal suppression of women in the family is intertwined with the desire to control their sexuality and fertility. "Marx provides no conceptual tools for theorizing the subordination of women in terms of the social relations of human reproduction,"[21] for propagation is considered as "natural" and thus outside the historical process. However, women do exist concurrently in both class and patriarchal relations. Just as the labor process is located within a certain mode of production and its social relations, so is the procreative activity. Women's class situation controls the type of patriarchy to which they will be subjected: the offspring of the upper and lower classes function to reinforce the power of the male capitalist and his need for legitimate heirs and new laborers. Thus McDonough and Harrison conclude that "any adequate analysis of relations in the family must take into account the specific political and ideological oppression of women, as it relates both to their sexual subordination in the family and to their economic subordination in wage labour."[22] The public sphere of production must be considered along with the private sphere of the family and reproduction, and the sexual division of labor and patriarchal relations must be examined in terms of class position.

Much French feminism is split between an espousal of a rigorous theoretical stance and a rejection of male intellectual structures as destructive. Monique Wittig, for example, claims, as do many American feminists, that the emphasis on language has made French women writers neglect the material reality, that is, deny the possibility of praxis outside the symbolic.[23] In this respect, such theorizing and concentration on the revolutionary potential of language and the subversion of received logocentric values has become a substitute for political activism. There is the fear that this subordination of and detachment from the "real" can only render further mystification of the "feminine" and will only yield a new "rhetoric." On the other hand, with a strong background in Marxist-dialectical thought and recent deconstructive criticism that questions the structures of Western philosophy, its logocentric metaphysics and principles of identity, feminists like Cixous, Kristeva, Clement, and Irigaray, concentrating on the subversive apsects of writing and reading, feel that there should be a reconsideration of heterogeneity, alterity, plurality, and difference. They have been critical of their more pragmatic American counterparts who, they feel, attempt to fit into the patriarchal system as equal to men and in the process reinforce the logo-, phallo-centric order. Strongly theoretical in their writings, they employ Marxist dialectics and psychoanalysis in order to study in depth the relationship between women's oppression and other aspects of their culture; to discover the significance of the unconscious, the divided self, and displaced desire in their questioning of the stability of the supposedly integrated ego; to posit the language of the two sexes as different; to explore, as a result, women's texts, fantasies, and libidinal drives so as to discover the relationship between their bodies and their syntax; to recognize their antagonism to an alien language imposed upon them; and to represent the ways in which women have become objects of exchange in the economy of their societies. They conclude that only masculine libidinal structures have been represented in society, for women have been absent and silent, debarred from history.

Thus the most important issue these critics deal with is that of a female discourse (*écriture féminine*). Since women have been objectified and commodified, they can only become subjects if they learn to "speak 'otherwise' ": "perhaps, we can *make audible* that which agitates within us, suffers silently in the *holes of discourse*, in the unsaid, or in the non-sense."[24] For these feminists "the female" speaks through the gaps and blanks in the "symbolic" chain of signifiers, that is, through the silences and holes in the syntactical and semantic logic of the male discourse. Change and revolution in society can only come about through a dismantling of the "symbolic" order, of bourgeois and humanistic languages, of the belief in the unified subject; and supposedly this can be accomplished through a subversion of conventional syntax, a problem that will be considered in length later. *Écriture féminine* combines theory with a kind of subjectivism, resulting in a kind of writing that is very different from traditional academic discourse: the reason for this is the need to obliterate the boundaries that divide fiction, poetry, and criticism, in this way also destroying the tendency to assign the intellectual capability for abstraction, speculation, and analysis to the male and the capacity for emotional, sensual, and intuitive responses to the female. Thus for Cixous, Kristeva, and Irigaray writing represents a procreative desire that will bring about the death of the patriarchal order—its economic, social, political, and linguistic systems. Instead of advocating identity and equality, they want women to stress their own difference, their otherness as the repressed, as the gap in the signifying chain, and in this way obliterate the privileging of one term of the binary opposition, a logocentric approach that sets up the conflict between male and female, mind and body, reason and emotion. So French feminist groups are also divided between theory and praxis. A group like "politique et psychanalyse," although employing male theoretical models (Freud, Lacan, Marx), has adopted *écriture féminine* as an approach to radical social change, whereas a group like "feministes revolutionnaires" has advocated the destruction of the patriarchal order, has utilized consciousness-raising groups as a way for accomplishing this on a practical level, and has dismissed psychoanalysis as disruptive and harmful to feminist aims.[25]

Josette Féral points out that difference is not to be perceived simply in reference to a masculine standard or norm, "whose negative side it would be while remaining inscribed within the realm of identity."[26] It involves a negation of phallocentrism and cannot be circumscribed within any system or structure of authority. As alterity, heterogeneity, multiplicity, a woman is no longer a marginal being, an inverted image or repressed double of man; she is an absolute difference. Therefore, in subverting and questioning the existing discourse and order, one is rejecting the foundations of a phallocentric patriarchal society and its whole notion of the "Truth," the idea of identity and of the unity of the subject as the possessor of knowledge (as contrasted, for example, to Chodorow's positing of a strong core of self, which fits in with American psychology and its goal of establishing a stable, healthy ego).[27] Women will have to create new languages and values, and reconstitute society by destroying the dominant structures and stressing the necessity of difference and heterogeneity for the individual. As Kristeva states: "A woman is a perpetual dissident as regards the social and political consensus; she is an exile from power and thus always singular, divided, devilish, a witch. . . . Woman is here to shake up, to disturb, to deflate masculine values, and not to espouse them. Her role is to maintain differences by pointing to them, by giving them life, by putting them into play against one another."[28]

Women are perceived as the negative portion of the following dichotomies—self/other, master/slave, dominant/marginal, subject/object. The hegemonic enforcement of these binary oppositions present no possibility for any genuine difference external to the existing systems of authority: "The Oneness of the master confronts the slave's duplicity, fullness confronts the void, and presence confronts absence."[29] As man's "other," as his unconscious and repressed side, she reflects and reproduces his denied and hidden desires; without her, his being is partially or completely obliterated, yet he needs to free himself overtly from this dependency by dominating and possessing the other, by denying woman's subjectivity and objectifying her as the embodiment of his projected desires.[30] Society is predicated on the oppression of woman, the denial of her difference, her exclusion from knowledge, and her alienation from herself and the world.

The French feminists also discuss the repression of the female unconscious, which must not be granted any specificity by a patriarchal culture, for the latter instinctively senses its subversive qualities and therefore wishes to relegate women's responses to the realm of iden-

tity, to the male paradigm and norm. Cixous, Irigaray, Leclerc, and
Kristeva see that recognition of the female unconscious represents access to a specific female discourse. So for these critics, women's oppres-
sion/repression is not only discovered in the economic, political, and
social order but in the very Logos, in the language through which
signification is produced. What we comprehend as the "real" is but
a representation of the "symbolic" as it has been constructed by men,
the latter of which simply perpetuates the alienating identifications set
up in the "imaginary" order during the mirror stage. As we will see,
Kristeva counters the latter problem with her conception of the "semiotic." In deconstructing and exposing the phallocentrism of societal
structures, these French critics mentioned above feel the world can be
transformed, specifically through *écriture féminine* and its revolutionary
power. Such writing is fluid, fragmented, explosive, nonlinear, polysemic,
and dialogic and attempts to "speak the body" (the unconscious) rather
than utilize the logical, monologic, ambiguous functional language of
men. Such expression of women's difference includes this realm of the
unconscious and must do so if the dominant discourse is to be decon-
structed and revolutionalized. Cixous stresses that our culture's ideology
is predicated on the repression of the female unconscious in particular.
But as Domna C. Stanton points out, Cixous's description of the unconscious seems little like Freud's: "When it speaks to you . . . it tells
you the old stories which you have always heard, since it has been constituted by the repressed of the culture. But that [level of the unconscious]
is always reshaped by the forceful return of a libido, which is not so
easily controlled, and by the singular, by the noncultural, by a language
which is savage and which can certainly be heard."[31] This unconscious,
freed of social and cultural restrictions and taboos, must be the basis
of a future politically informed female text.

   Écriture féminine is visualized as a way of discussing women's writing
that emphasizes the value of "the female" and postulates the theoretical
problematic of feminist criticism as a project of "difference." Such an
approach is identified as revolutionary and subversive, as the instrumental
basis instigating the social, political, and cultural transformation of existing structures. Woman is called upon to "write her self": it is the
act by which she can signify "her shattering entry into history which
has always been based on *her suppression*. To write and thus to forge
for herself the anti-logos weapon. To become *at will* the taker and the
initiator, for her own right, in every symbolic system, in every political

process." Writing becomes the most powerful way of expressing the resources of the unconscious, of repossessing the female body, which man has claimed as his property: ". . . it will give her back her goods, her pleasures, her organs, her immense bodily territories which have been kept under seal."[32] In these statements Cixous shows the necessity of verbalizing the long repressed and tabooed aspects of female sexuality and pleasure (*sa jouissance*), and thereby dephallocentrizing the body. Women will not be silenced nor marginalized in society.

Cixous, of all the French feminists we shall discuss, seems to be the most clearly influenced by Derrida's deconstructive theories—his criticism of phono-, logo-, phallo-centrism. In "The Laugh of the Medusa" and "Sorties" she employs his method of dismantling binary oppositions: "Thought has always worked by opposition, Speech/Writing, High/Low. By dual, *hierarchized* oppositions. Superior/Inferior. . . . And all the couples of oppositions are couples. Does this mean something? Is the fact that logocentrism subjects thought—all of the concepts, the codes, the values—to a two-term system, related to 'the' couple man/woman? . . . The hierarchization subjects the entire conceptual organization to man. A male privilege, which can be seen in the opposition by which it sustains itself, between activity and passivity. Traditionally, the question of sexual difference is coupled with the same opposition: activity/passivity."[33] Rejecting the biological inferiority of women, she criticizes Freud and Jones in reinforcing the thesis of a 'natural', anatomical determination of sexual difference-opposition. . . . both implicitly support phallocentrism's position of power."[34] For Cixous this refers man to "*his* torment, his desire to be (at) the origin."[35] She sees phallocentrism as the enemy of both men and women, as the only structure produced and recorded through the ages; therefore "it is time to transform. To invent the other history."[36]

In her discussion of sexual difference and its ideological and sociopolitical determination, Cixous vehemently argues that "we can no more talk about 'woman' than about 'man' without getting caught up in an ideological theater where the multiplication of representations, images, reflections, myths, identifications constantly transforms, deforms, alters each person's imaginary order and in advance, renders all conceptualization null and void."[37] Women's identity is dispersed and differential, nonexistent, just as the term "man" is socially construed as the dominant, hegemonic force: "The belief that 'one is a woman' is almost as absurd and obscurantist as the belief that 'one is a man'. . . . In 'woman' I see something that cannot be represented, something that is not said, something above and beyond nomenclatures and ideologies."[38] Thus woman cannot and should not be defined since the term itself is a social and not a natural construction. One must not search for her identity (which cannot be pinned down), but must hypothesize about her discourse by deconstructing the male models that reveal the desire for an origin and plenitude and man's insistence on his own identity.

Cixous situates the conception of this overdetermined ideological circumstance in the heterogeneity of each individual's "imaginary" order. She is here dealing with Lacan's notion of the latter, which describes the subject's narcissistic relationship to his ego and involves a relationship to others as counterparts, as projections or reflections of inner compulsions and repressed desires, a relationship to the world and signification in terms of set ideological reactions and in terms of similarity or unity. To transform this store of "imaginary" identifications, which supplies the material for accession into the "symbolic" order, is an essential part of the search for a woman's discourse. Cixous realizes that the re-inscription of the "imaginary" cannot be conducted by the centered subject, for in attempting to revise the political situation of a phallic masculine economy, the "otherness" of the unconscious cannot be ignored or repressed. In this respect, feminists must go beyond attacking patriarchy on an ideological level but must make a transformation in the "symbolic" dimension, which necessitates a change in the "imaginary" order. Because of woman's awareness of difference, plurality, and polymorphous bodily pleasures, "It is impossible to *define* a female practice or writing, and this is an impossibility that will remain, for this practice can never be theorized, enclosed, coded—which doesn't mean that it doesn't exist. But it will always surpass the discourse that regulates the phallocentric system; it does and will take place in areas other than those subordinated to philosophical-theoretical domination."[39] This surplus of signification or supplementary zone of feminine discourse refers to that space outside the dominant patriarchal structure, the place for a revolutionary women's language, of all that has been repressed in history, a realm of liberated desire. Women's writing is thus dialogic: it exists within and embodies the cultural, social, and political heritages of the hegemonic and nonhegemonic forces. So it must concern itself with the influence of past patriarchal values and forms as well as with the suppressed messages of female precursors. Because of this multiplicity, for women the "imaginary" is subservient to constant fluctuation, and the concept's grasp on it is always deferred. Cixous questions Lacan's way of interpreting every code as referring to the Name-of-the-Father, or the mother-who-has-the-phallus, and warns of such centrism, "Beware, my friend, of the signifier that would take you back to the authority of a signified!", suggesting that the Lacanian notion of the phallus as the "transcendental signifier" is dangerous—one should "Break out of the circles; don't remain within the psycho-analytic closure."[40] "Woman un-thinks the unifying, regulating history that homogenizes and channels forces, herding contradictions into a single battlefield."[41]

Cixous therefore argues for a "bisexuality" "on which every subject not enclosed in the false theater of phallocentric representationalism has founded his/her erotic universe": in one's self there is the presence of both sexes, and at present "it is women who are opening up to and benefiting from this vatic bisexuality which doesn't annul differences but stirs them, pursues them, increases their number. In a certain way, 'woman is bisexual'; man—it's a secret to no one—being poised to keep glorious phallic monosexuality in view."[42] However, the problem of the political, historical, and ideological difference that irremediably divides the male from the female critic of phallocentrism is not clearly delineated by Cixous. How does bisexuality solve this?

For Cixous the unconscious is where the repressed (and woman) manage to survive. Women's territory is dark, black, for they have been "confined to the narrow room in which they've been given a deadly brainwashing"—victims of Apartheid—because they are made to believe, "you are Africa, you are black. Your continent is dark. Dark is dangerous." Cixous claims that men have been allowed to write about their sexuality, but what they have stated thus far is derived from the binary opposition of activity/passivity, "from the power relation between a fantasized obligatory virility meant to invade, to colonize, and the consequential phantasm of woman as a 'dark continent' to penetrate and to 'pacify'."[43] But she states that "The Dark Continent is neither dark nor unexplorable. It is still unexplored only because we've been made to believe that it was too dark to be explorable. And because they want to make us believe that what interests us is the white continent, with its monuments to Lack."[44] Since women have been denied access to their physicality and have been told to ignore it, they must learn to write through their bodies and invent a language that fractures codes, rhetorics, classes, institutions, history, knowledge, and accepted laws and regulations. However, the main problem with this identification of woman with the unconscious, the Dark Continent, is, as we shall see later, that it places her once again in the stereotyped role imposed by a masculine libidinal economy—she is the repository of repressed desire, sensuality, irrationality, etc.

Kristeva's "semanalysis" and "semiotic" realm are radical and innovative concepts. In redefining the whole idea of text, she questions linguistic, semiotic, and literary codes and attempts to set up a new conceptual approach to language yet without ignoring the restrictive and transferential forces in social and political reality that produce discursive practice. Her description of the speaking subject in a particular ideological situation is developed in association with Freud's and Lacan's theory of the unconscious. In order to understand more clearly this latter influence, one has to remember that Lacan's interpretation of Freud stresses not the ideal of a centered ego but the positing of the decentered self and the subversiveness of the unpredictable id, the unconscious which destroys the subject's sense of completeness and coherence within the structures of society. Lacan perceives language as the paradigm for the functioning of the unconscious, for it constructs the individual, who in using it internalizes the powerful patriarchal laws of the culture (the "symbolic," the Name-of-the-Father, the Law, social order—all of which operate on the basis of the repression and control of women's bodies). The individual is thus split between the subject created by its position in language (in this view one's identity is linguistically based) and the alienating forces within the self.

The patriarchal law is external to the mother/child relationship until the moment of the Oedipal complex, which brings about the beginning of the triadic familial interaction; the Name-of-the-Father is the third term and links the infant to the social and "symbolic" order. The child thus proceeds from a relationship of identity and unity to one of difference and heterogeneity: she is thus initiated into the patriarchal culture. Meaning is dictated by the logocentric law of the Father. In abandoning these principles of the integrated, centered self and of social adaptation into the system, the French feminists concentrate on the revolutionary potential of the unconscious, on woman's relationship to the maternal, and on the "female" presence in language. These are things that Lacan does not explore and that must be examined both in terms of their present and future function within and beyond the strategies of containment of a patriarchal culture. "In 'woman' I see something that cannot be represented, something that is not said, something above and beyond nomenclatures and ideologies."[45]

In extending and modifying psychoanalytic theory Kristeva proposes her idea of the "semiotic" stage, which is antecedent to cognitive awareness of self as different from the other.[46] She states that the "symbolic" is initiated in the mirror phase in which the infant learns to deal with absence and representation (the "fort-da" game), with the uses of language. In other words, she perceives all social phenomena as "symbolic" (formulating the dominant discourse), while the "semiotic" is that originary space before the sign, that pre-Oedipal phase in which the infant experiences a unity, a privileged oneness with the mother's body, a realm of unmediated primary narcissism. Kristeva notes the difference between the "symbolic" (paternal) and "semiotic" (maternal) realms. The former defines language that expresses the speaker's conscious control: in learning syntactical structures the individual internalizes a predelineated concept of identity, a process that involves stipulating as a given the subject and its objects. However, the "semiotic" works closely with the unconscious, and designates the differentiating and stratifying practices in language that precede the subject's positing of a grammatically coherent, structured signifying chain:

> It [the semiotic] is chronologically anterior and synchronically transversal to the sign, syntax, denotation, and signification. Made up of facilitations and their traces, it is a provisional articulation, a non-expressive rhythm. Plato (*Thaetetus*) speaks of a chora, anterior to the One, maternal, having borrowed the term from Democritus' and Leucippes' "rhythm". . . The semiotic is a distinction, non-expressive articulation; neither amorphous substance nor meaningful numbering. We imagine it in the cries, the vocalizing, the gestures of infants; it functions, in fact, in adult discourse as rhythm, prosody, plays on words, the non-sense of sense, laughter.[47]

The "symbolic" order does not entirely displace the "semiotic" but simply comes to dominate in writing and speech. In other words, there is the constant dialectical interaction of both modes in the process of signification. As Kristeva mentions in the above quote, this alternation of modalities is revealed in the syntactical incongruities, the silences, the breaks in meaning, the subversion of the patriarchal language of power, and the influx of the instinctual drive for sexual pleasure or

jouissance. All of these characteristics of the "semiotic" destroy the notion of the unified consciousness and reveal the unconscious as an other,
as a suppressed locus of meaning concurrently existing, yet running in
opposition to the "symbolic" and its uses of language.

Kristeva does not see the maternal and pre-Oedipal stage of the
"semiotic" as somehow representing the model for the specificity of
women's writing. Instead, it is proposed as the basis of a theoretical
bisexuality that is modeled on that of the unconscious. It is "not an-
drogyny but a metaphor designating the possibility of exploring all aspects
of signification,"[48] and thus it allows for the recognition of sexual difference and multiplicity within the process of signification, which is
not the case with the existing phallocentric patriarchal cultures. The
dialogical or polyphonic discourse that reveals the irrupting "semiotic"
forces depicts the decentering and questioning of the subject. The female
writer based in the "semiotic" is constantly involved in the process of
producing or engendering a text ("genotext" as opposed to a "pheno-
text" that follows the conventional rules of communication). This dialogism or multiplicity is inherent in language; the atemporality, repetition, disturbances in the syntactic chain, rhythmic character show
evidence of the revolt against paternalistic strictures, "*history*," the
logocentric ideal of identity and unity, and a striving for the nonverbal
as opposed to a language that manifests the sedimented layers of a masculine economy and ideology:

> All of these modifications in the linguistic fabric are the sign of
> a force that has not been grasped by the linguistic or ideological
> system. This signification renewed, 'infinitized' by the rhythm in
> a text, this precisely is (sexual) pleasure [*la jouissance*]. . . . The
> fragmentation of language in a text calls into question the very
> posture of this mastery [of speech, a 'phallic' position]. The writing
> that we have been discussing confronts this phallic position either
> to traverse it or to deny it. The word 'traverse' implies that the
> subject experiences sexual difference, not as a fixed opposition
> ('man/woman'), but as a process of differentiation. The word 'deny'
> means that the subject constitutes a fetishistic shelter in order to
> avoid castration. Only the truly great 'literary' achievements bear
> witness to a traversal, and therefore, to sexual differentiation. In
> this way, the subject of writing speaks a *truth* proper to any speak-
> ing subject, a truth that the needs of production and reproduc-

tion censure. All speaking subjects have within themselves a certain bisexuality which is precisely the possibility to explore all the sources of signification, that which posits a meaning as well as that which multiplies, pulverizes, and finally revives it.[49]

However, Kristeva is not concerned with whether women express themselves in different ways than men; she proposes the dialectical functioning of both the "symbolic" and the "semiotic" modalities within texts written by either sex. Thus this shows her attraction for and valorization of literary and philosophical[50] avant-garde writers such as Artaud, Proust, Joyce, Mallarmé, Beckett, Derrida, and Althusser, in whose works she sees the "semiotic" as threatening to irrupt into the "symbolic" and to expand indefinitely the horizon of possible meaning. She therefore connects her conception of *écriture féminine* to this revolutionary potential she perceives in the avant-garde movement. Women's writing fits into this bursting of the limits of signification in terms of its being involved in a "body-to-body" discourse with the maternal,[51] creating gaps in meaning, silences in the text, ruptures and breaks within language, thus representing what has been repressed, what is subversive and destructive to the Logos and antagonistic to the notion of a unified consciousness. Such a potentially revolutionary text, through its expression of the language of the "semiotic," destroys and deconstructs patriarchal power-structures and liberates the traces of the unconscious, the suppressed meaning, the language of women's difference.

Kristeva proposes that women should incorporate within their discourse these avant-gardist principles (and she includes here male writers who speak as women do). Her analysis of the sign "woman" is paralleled by her deconstruction of the sign "man" as it persists in a logocentric culture:

> On a deeper level, however, a woman cannot 'be'; it is something which does not even belong in the order of *being*. It follows that a feminist practice can only be negative, at odds with what already exists so that we may say 'that's not it' and 'that's still not it.' In 'woman' I see something that cannot be represented, something that is not said, something above and beyond nomenclatures and ideologies. There are certain 'men' who are familiar with this phenomenon; it is what some modern texts never stop signifying: testing the limits of language and sociality—the law and its trans-

gression, mastery and (sexual) pleasure—without reserving one for males and the other for females, on the condition that it is never mentioned. From this point of view, it seems that certain feminist demands revive a kind of naive romanticism, a belief in identity (the reverse of phallocentrism), if we compare them to the experience of both poles of sexual difference as is found in the economy of Joycean or Artaudian prose or in modern music—Cage, Stockhausen. I pay close attention to the particular aspect of the work of the avant-garde which dissolves identity, even sexual identities; and in my theoretical formulations I try to go against metaphysical theories that censure what I just labeled 'a woman'—this is what, I think, makes my research that of a woman.[52]

Kristeva advocates a feminist struggle that cannot be separated from a revolutionary, class, or anti-imperialist struggle. The issues she finds so crucial are the fragmentation of the subject and the inscription of heterogeneity and difference. She claims that feminism avoids these problems and instead postulates that "women are 'separate' complete 'individuals' with their 'own identity'. . . . We run the risk of creating within feminism an enclosed ideology parallel to the ideology of the dominant class. . . . Call it 'woman' or 'the oppressed social class': it's the same struggle, and you never have one without the other."[53] She does not divorce the feminist, class, or race struggles from one another and sees them as the same form of oppression, of social and cultural atavism.

Thus Kristeva, in her debate about the political potential of the avant-garde, privileges the revolutionary and schizophrenic nature of the latter just as Lukács valorizes the realistic over the expressionistic novel. One can only question how such a deconstructive practice will function—will it not in its anarchic course negate all attempts at social organization? And after the irruption of the "semiotic," will the nature of the "symbolic" be changed in any substantial or revolutionary way? How does one deal with the "symbolic" projections of the individual's instincts and drives in terms of a mediation with an external world that is contradictory and opposed to the expression of such drives?

Kristeva's emphasis on the literary and philosophical avant-garde and its revolutionary and political potential as the model for women writers is questionable. It is true that women in the past have been less willing to experiment radically with existing conventions; their sub-

ject matter has reflected such innovation and daring but not their techniques. However, even if one deconstructs identities and releases the
avant-garde energies of heterogeneity, discontinuity, dialogism, disturbances, displacements, and distortions in the traditional syntactic and
semantic structures, one does not necessarily escape from the historically
determined aspects of sexism nor subvert the existing order. Like Cixous,
Kristeva is a deconstructor of logocentric systems of identity, of rationalistic discourses, yet she too remains trapped within masculine systems
of thought. Both valorize texts of male avant-garde writers and thinkers
and disregard female poets, novelists, and essayists. But women must
move beyond this kind of criticism and consider other discourses that
also expose the power and domination of the hegemonic patriarchal
forces in society.

Also problematic, as Jardine has pointed out, is Kristeva's inclina-
tion to pose the "semiotic" as a kind of panacea for women's supposed
exclusion from the "symbolic": "If the 'feminine' exists, it does so only
within the order of the symbolic. How individuals—both male and
female—exist in the Symbolic as well as in sexual difference, is determined by the real; that is, by the political in the form of artistic and
cathartic, economic and power, class and sexual systems at any given
historical moment."[54] Therefore, if we examine the premises of *écriture
féminine* we must ask whether a subversion of the existing order can
be attained through language and whether there is a space external to
the "symbolic" from which women can express their difference. The
"feminine" in writing, as Jardine suggests, remains a question in the
future. At the present, the only way the "feminine" can be explored
is through the ways in which women have been exploited by, excluded
from, or coopted by the logocentric institutions of their societies. So
we must emphasize, as I mentioned earlier, the importance of examining, through a "symptomatic" reading, the strategies of containment,
the ideological limits, of a patriarchal and monologic system in order
to go beyond and develop a new awareness of the contradictions, the
dialogism in the existing order and the ruling discourse and thereby
render new solutions and directions.

Irigaray claims that psychoanalysis excludes a consideration of
women's plural sexuality because of its commitment to phallocentric
theory—otherness is suppressed in order to sustain this unity. But French
psychoanalysis questions such assertions that reject multiplicity and ex-
amines the inherent contradictions within this theory and its compulsive

need for mastery. Irigaray feels that woman's "sexuality, always at least double, is in fact *plural . . . woman has sex organs just about everywhere . . .* the geography of her pleasure is much more diversified, more multiple in its differences, more complex, more subtle, than is imagined—in an imaginary centred a bit too much on one and the same."[55] Masculine systems of representation are specular; that is, their self-reflexivity makes woman simply an inverted image of the hegemonic subject—she is a lack whereas the male is plenitude. Her difference becomes hierarchy, part of the binary opposition upon which theories of sexual superiority are based. Femininity comes to mean a stereotyped role or image superimposed upon woman by the narcissism of a patriarchal culture. Irigaray sees "the exclusion of a female imaginary" as placing woman in a situation where "she can experience herself only fragmentarily as waste or as excess in the little structured margins of a dominant ideology, this mirror entrusted by the (masculine) 'subject' with the task of reflecting and redoubling himself. The role of 'femininity' is prescribed moreover by this masculine specula(riza)tion and corresponds only slightly to woman's desire, which is recuperated only secretly, in hiding, and in a disturbing and unpardonable manner."[56] *Écriture féminine*, as we have seen, endeavors to undo such repression whereby woman simply becomes the mirror, the duplication of man's desire. This need to deconstruct the dominant ideology is shown through the emphasis on women's writing which exposes the difference that has been suppressed and ignored by the hegemonic forces in society that dictate historical values.

Thus Irigaray wants to avoid the ideal of a unified meaning or the hierarchy imposed by binary oppositions, and instead sees woman as signifying everything in language that is plural, as pointing beyond the monopoly of an appropriating and denigrating masculine economy. " 'She' is indefinitely other in herself. . . . One must listen to her differently in order to hear an *'other meaning' which is constantly in the process of weaving itself, at the same time ceaselessly embracing words and yet casting them off to avoid becoming fixed, immobilized."*[57] "Woman would always remain multiple, but she would be protected from dispersion because the other is a part of her, and is autoerotically familiar to her. That does not mean that she would appropriate the other for herself, that she would make it her property. Property and propriety are undoubtedly rather foreign to all that is female."[58] Woman is not only perceived as bisexual, but as possessing a multiplicity of sexual organs and pleasures.

However, Irigaray asserts that before woman can enjoy these pleasures "the analysis of the various systems of oppression which affect her is certainly necessary," for by resorting to "pleasure alone as the solution to her problem, she runs the risk of missing the reconsideration of a social practice upon which *her* pleasure depends."[59] She calls for more than an isolated movement, a "woman's evolution," or a more general Marxist solution in terms of a resolution of the class conflict (since women are dispersed in many classes with conflicting demands) and suggests that "if women are to preserve their auto-eroticism, their homo-sexuality, and let it flourish" they should not renounce "heterosexual pleasure" or communication because this would be "another form of this amputation of power that is traditionally associated with women."[60] As a first step, she seems to propose her version of a "symptomatic" reading of masculine texts since women only have access to language through such types of representation. In order for women to go beyond such discourse and develop their own voice and power, Irigaray proposes that they must try "mimetism," in other words reproducing yet exposing and attaining knowledge of the repressive systems.

> To play with mimesis, is, therefore, for a woman, to attempt to recover the place of her exploitation by discourse, without letting herself be simply reduced to it. It is to resubmit herself . . . to 'ideas,' notably about her, elaborated in/by a masculine logic, but in order to make 'visible', by an effect of playful repetition, what should have remained hidden: the recovery of a possible operation of the feminine in language. It is also to 'unveil' the fact that, if women mime so well, they do not simply reabsorb themselves in this function. *They also remain elsewhere.*[61]

A woman may use the male structures of language and syntactical expression, but she does not simply become reduced to them, for in questioning the underlying premises of such systems she then utilizes them in order to reveal the nature of her exploitation and suppression. So Irigaray, in her deconstructive attack on logocentrism, is exposing the myths about women that have been articulated and circulated by a male ideology. Her idea of a "symptomatic" reading of masculine texts is the first step beyond which woman can free herself, can transgress the boundaries set up by her society, and thus express herself through a recuperation of the female desire and sexuality in discourse, a discourse that is fluid rather than fixed.

For Irigaray, then, a woman must avoid inscribing herself within a prescribed male order and must disengage herself from masculine concepts and an alien language that threatens to disappropriate her and to destroy her identity: "If we continue to speak the same language to each other, we will reproduce the same story."

> On the outside, you attempt to conform to an order which is alien to you. Exiled from yourself, you fuse with everything that you encounter. You mime whatever comes near you. You become whatever you touch. In your hunger to find yourself, you move indefinitely far from yourself, from me. Assuming one model after another, one master after another, changing your face, form, and language according to the power that dominates you. Sundered. By letting yourself be abused, you become an impassive travesty.[62]

"If we continue to speak this sameness, if we speak to each other as men have spoken for centuries . . . we will fail each other. . . . This wearisome labor of doubling and miming" is not enough.[63] Therefore, Irigaray wants to expose the phallocentric and logocentric systems, to subvert the ideal of identity and of a single signification, to reveal the ideological determinants that enclose and imprison the woman writer, and finally to liberate her from these oppressive structures by pointing to the suppressed message, the palimpsest that contains the plurality of female desire and *jouissance*.

We have examined a range of feminist responses (in varying degrees) surrounding the dialectic of theory/praxis. Many feminists want to demystify existing male models and systems that have repressed feminine discourse (i.e., logo-, phallo-centrism); some object to the anti-theoretical, anti-male positions that could lead to further isolation and marginality for women; others attempt to link up the examination of women's unconscious and her language with the specificity of her body and experience of *jouissance*. Several problems arise out of these various approaches. I would first like to look briefly at these approaches and then extrapolate some sort of alternative that would utilize several of these views.

Madeleine Vincent describes the "new feminists" involved with the Communist Party in France as identifying the problem of inequality as one affecting both men and women: "For a large number of women it is becoming clearer that their fate is linked to that of workers as a whole. . . . Isn't it better, to arrive at a real emancipation of women, to unite all men and women who suffer from the same political situation, a situation managed for the exclusive profit of the rich and the powerful?" Such an approach concentrates on the problem of class as the crucial factor in determining an individual's situation in society—the oppressed are all categorized under one heading, and the varying causes for such oppression are the same and are to be solved in the same fashion:

> If we direct against men the action necessary for women's progress, we condemn the great hopes of women to a dead end. At the same time, if we consider that the two struggles (one against exploitation of the classes, the other against men) are to be led independent of each other, we deprive the democratic fight of forces necessary to its victory. And we resolve none of the problems of women.[64]

Such an approach of the Marxist variety can be detrimental to the women's movement since it obfuscates the issues of class and sexism.

Other radical groups seem to be intent on forging a feminist materialism. They manifest a "refusal to probe, to elaborate, to project any concept of 'woman' that would be unrelated to a social context" and "an effort to deconstruct the notion of 'sex differences' which gives a shape and a base to the concept of 'woman' and is an integral part of naturalist ideology. The social mode of being of men and women is in no way linked with their nature as males and females nor with the shape of their sex organs."[65] For such groups, the need to destroy the differences between the sexes and the hierarchy that evolves from the privileging of the male is essential to bring about a change in the status quo. They insist that "*all women belong to the same social class*" and also propose a "breaking away from naturalist ideology" by creating a French feminist movement that relies on "adhesion to this concept which diverged from the reigning Marxist orthodoxy."[66] However valid some of these criticisms and goals may initially appear, there can also be some problems in attempting to categorize women as belonging to the same social class and, as a corollary to this, as having the same dilemmas to confront in their diverse societal milieus. To obliterate the concept of a "natural" difference between men and women is necessary, but this does not solve the problems arising from the environmental, historical, and political differences that confront women in their societies.

There are also those feminists who try to show the gaps within a Marxist theoretical framework, that is, its inability to deal coherently with the oppression of women and its desire to deal with everything in terms of class rather than sex and race as well. "One must study the connections between sexist mentality, institutions, laws and the socio-economic structures that support them. These structures are part of a specific system different from the capitalist system, and we call this system 'patriarchy'."[67] The latter involves a special relation of production between the sexes. Marxist feminists of this type are attempting, through a "symptomatic" reading of Marx and Freud, to come to terms with the gaps in male discourse (to read the political unconscious) and to perceive the relationship between class and sex, yet to see them as distinct and different modes of oppression.

Thus women's language is seen as a search for a female identity, but the question arises as to whether such a discourse does express a real rejection of the masculine system and ideology and whether such a rejection is possible or desirable. As mentioned earlier, there are many feminists who advocate destroying male language by developing another that would be "closer to woman's lived experience, a lived experience in the center of which the Body is frequently placed."[68] Chantal Chawaf proposes a woman's writing and speech that would articulate the body: "In order to reconnect the book with the body and with pleasure, we must dis-intellectualize writing. . . . And this language, as it develops, will not degenerate and dry up, will not go back to the fleshless academicism, the stereotypical and servile discourses that we reject. . . . Feminine language must, by its very nature, work on life passionately, scientifically, poetically, politically in order to make it invulnerable."[69] However, it is perhaps too dangerous to place such emphasis on the body as the basis for a search for female identity, even if it is metaphorical and dealing with the issue of biological difference as revealed in writing. This type of essentialism can be so reductive as to place women in the situation from which they tried to escape. For example, this concentration on the body can lead into the problem of otherness, of the hierarchical privileging of one term of the binary opposition: the positing of the "natural" biological inferiority of women (as emotional, sensual) versus the "natural" superiority of men (as intellectual, rational). As the editorial collective of *Questions féministes* points out: "This difference has been used as a pretext to 'justify' full power of one sex over the other. . . . For the oppressor, it is safer to speak of natural differences that are invariable by definition. That is the basis of racist and sexist ideologies. And thus a status of inferiority bound to a status of difference."[70] By claiming such a "status of difference" women are succumbing to the stereotypes imposed by men—we are perceived as marginal, as outsiders, as the inferior part of the binary opposition of Nature/Woman vs. Man/Culture: this simply reinforces woman's relation to nature and sexual pleasure and reverses the established masculine hierarchy, yet does not destroy or deconstruct the whole system of binary oppositions. Woman's object-status is clearly identified with her reproductive function; she is both the passive sex-object (victim of denigration, violence, or lust) and agent of procreation (victim of economic, social, and political expediency). In order to transform such deeply embedded ideological reactions, one must emphasize the point that "nature had programmed female sexual pleasure independently from the needs of production."[71] A woman must not look to pleasure as the isolated solution to her problem, but can only enjoy such pleasure after an analysis of the systems of oppression that affect and obstruct her actions. Thus she must not privilege the body, for this would mean subscribing to binary models and would imply consent to the logocentric system rather than resistance to its dictates.

The advocacy of a female means of expression is also problematic since much of the language praised by French feminists is connected in style if not in content to male models. And the idea that female language is subversive because it is closer to the body, pleasure (*jouissance*), sensation, and nature is debatable, since this is equivalent to rejecting the reality and the power of social mediations, those that are responsible for repressing women physically and intellectually. One must set women's struggle within a socio-historical context, within that patriarchal system of sexual and class conflicts, and not within a mystical relationship to the body or to nature. In other words, social and historical differences cannot be replaced by metaphysical categories that imply innate and generic differences. The desire to develop a revolutionary mode of expression that is female and subversive and that can change the existing structures of society is certainly an admirable goal, but language must first name and analyze oppression, and in order to do so women have to utilize the knowledge and concepts they have inherited, whether male or female.

It would be necessary for women to examine their position in society in terms of Gramscian "consent" and its relationship to either a dominant or hegemonic culture. Consent can be passive and indirect (dominant culture) and can be instrumentalized by those in control— in other words, it is coercive since force creates consent by laws, norms, ideological values, and forms of legitimation of power, which lead to a devaluation of rights and liberties. Or consent can be active and direct (hegemonic culture): isolated and atomized individuals willfully give their consent within the mystifying relations of exploitation and power in capitalist societies. The latter requires a real exchange between those who rule and those who are ruled, and the "expansiveness of consent" in such situations excludes any repressive relationship between them. Hegemony is mainly a strategy for attaining the active consent of an oppressed group, thus creating a collective political will that is capable of unifying the base- and super-structure: Gramsci says that "the State is the active complex of practical and theoretical activities with which the ruling class not only justifies and maintains its domination, but manages to win the *active support of those over whom it rules*."[72] The hegemonic class (or sex) universalizes its own interests and ensures that the latter become the basis of the value systems of the subordinate groups. This unity of political and economic objectives and of intellectual and moral intentions is what characterizes a hegemonic class. The question arises as to whether women have been part of a dominant or hegemonic culture—in other words, has their consent been achieved through force and direct coercion or has it been accomplished through their assent to and complicity with the hegemonic patriarchal structures? Women have been subjugated and controlled in both ways, but perhaps the most effective method operative in Western culture is to get their coopera- tion voluntarily, get them to support the system that has been oppress- ing them. At the present moment, they are now rebelling against these hegemonic structures and combating those who have advocated a sex- ist set of values and have saturated the entire culture with them in such an insidious way that the issues of domination, exploitation, and manipulation are repressed and displaced. These are the debilitating, historical realities women must face in their desire to reconstruct society.

Women must therefore go beyond simply declaring their difference, which in some ways works against attaining equality. The main battle is to destroy the hegemonic phallocentric system. The demand should not be for an exclusively female society but for a society where men and women share the same anti-logocentric, anti-hierarchical values. Women's history and accomplishments must be acknowledged and not subordinated to a marginal status or relegated to silence. And finally one must remember that women's contributions to society exist because of a division of labor based on sex *and* class, which reflects the attitudes of a patriarchal order. However, the denial of female identity by the members of *Questions féministes* is also self-defeating: they state, " 'I will be neither a woman nor a man in the present historical meaning: I shall be some Person in the body of a woman' "; "The word 'woman', I can't and never could bear it. It is with this word that men insulted me. It is a word from their language, a corpse filled with *their* fantasms against us. . . . The reality 'woman' is sociological (political), the product of a relation between two groups, and of an oppressive relation."[73] It is true that one's gender is socially determined, which has produced ideologies of sexual inferiority and superiority, yet as the French feminists Cixous, Kristeva, and Irigaray have stressed, it is important for women to maintain their difference, to develop their own voice in order to counteract the stultifying and sterile male order. It is thus important to work within the dominant system in order to deconstruct and change it, but it is also necessary to maintain one's position outside it in building an alternate vision that could displace the hegemonic one.

Therefore, to posit a metaphorical biological difference in language (i.e., bodily basis of women's intelligence) that excludes mediation by linguistic, social, political, and artistic structures is dangerous. Women should develop their own language to question the dominant masculine ideology and discourse, for the need for a revolutionary mode of expression that would initiate changes is an important one, but the ways suggested to accomplish this are not quite clear. Women's writing must inevitably operate to some extent within male discourse, but it must attempt to deconstruct it and reveal the repressed or hidden message—to write what cannot or was not written. McConnell-Ginet feels there is no biological "evidence that would suggest the sexes are preprogrammed to develop structurally different linguistic systems."[74] Language is not innate or instinctual, but is produced by cultural, historical, ideological, ethnic, economic, class, and familial factors. Because of these various patternings, women have been unable to express themselves. Therefore, there is the possibility that they could invent a language that destroys existing structures but that also has a utopian thrust in that it also speaks outside phallocentric systems and attempts to establish its own discourse, which as Felman suggests "would no longer be defined by the phallacy of masculine meaning."[75] Many things must be examined in determining the nature of women's past, present, and future relationship to language and her society—how the female psyche is shaped by sex-role socialization, by its relation to the "symbolic" and to the patriarchal culture from which women have been excluded. Therefore, feminist criticism must both operate within and beyond the system: through a symptomatic reading one can discern the repressed, submerged content and in this way consider the multiple strata of the text, the dialogic messages that embody the social, political, literary, and cultural heritages of the hegemonic and nonhegemonic forces in history, which explain women's writing in terms of the male intellectual models and modes of influence, in terms of why women have consistently been excluded from the traditional canons set up by male critics, and in terms of pointing to ways of reading, writing, and speaking which frees her from the values of such a system. One must establish a "her-story," a consideration of women's accomplishments through the ages and a projection of future possibilities for her development and emancipation, but one cannot ignore the hegemonic discourse, the "his-tory" that has determined women's oppression.

NOTES

1. Sheila Rowbotham, *Woman's Consciousness, Man's World* (Baltimore: Penguin Books, 1973), 32-33.

2. Elaine Showalter, "Feminist Criticism in the Wilderness," in Elizabeth Abel, ed., *Writing and Sexual Difference* (Chicago: University of Chicago Press, 1982), 13.

3. Elaine Showalter, "Towards a Feminist Poetics," in Mary Jacobus, ed., *Women Writing and Writing About Women* (London: Croom Helm, 1979), 25, 28.

4. Mary O'Brien, "Feminist Theory and Dialectical Logic," in Nannerl O. Keohane, Michelle Z. Rosaldo, and Barbara C. Gelpi, eds., *Feminist Theory: A Critique of Ideology* (Chicago: University of Chicago Press, 1982), 99-101.

5. Myra Jehlen, "Archimedes and the Paradox of Feminist Criticism," in *Feminist Theory*, 197.

6. Patricia Meyer Spacks, *The Female Imagination* (New York: Avon Books, 1976); Elaine Showalter, *A Literature of their Own: British Women Novelists from Bronte to Lessing* (Princeton, N.J.: Princeton University Press, 1977); Ellen Moers, *Literary Women: The Great Writers* (Garden City, N.Y.: Doubleday and Co., 1976); Sandra Gilbert and Susan Gubar, *The Madwoman*

in the Attic: The Woman Writer and the Nineteenth-Century Literary Imagination (New Haven: Yale University Press, 1979).

7. Jehlen, in *Feminist Theory*, 192.

8. Kate Millett, *Sexual Politics* (Garden City, N.Y.: Doubleday and Co., 1970).

9. Nina Baym, *Women's Fiction: A Guide to Novels by and about Women, 1820-1870*, (Ithaca: Cornell University Press, 1978).

10. Jehlen, in *Feminist Theory*, 208.

11. Alice Jardine, "Pre-texts for the Transatlantic Feminist," *Feminist Readings: French Texts/American Contexts, Yale French Studies* 62 (1981): 226-27.

12. Ibid., p. 225.

13. "Why This Book?", *New French Feminisms: An Anthology*, ed. Elaine Marks and Isabelle de Courtivron (Amherst: University of Massachusetts Press, 1980), xi.

14. Sandra Gilbert, "Introduction," YFS 62, p. 10.

15. Cheri Register, "American Feminist Literary Criticism: A Bibliographical Introduction," in Josephine Donavan, ed., *Feminist Literary Criticism: Explorations in Theory* (Kentucky: University of Kentucky Press, 1975), 18-24.

16. Annette Kuhn and Ann Marie Wolpe, "Feminism and Materialism," in Kuhn and Wolpe, eds., *Feminism and Materialism: Women and Modes of Production* (London: Routledge, & Kegan Paul, 1978), 7.

17. O'Brien, in *Feminist Theory*, 104, 107; see 111 as well.

18. Roisin McDonough and Rachel Harrison, "Patriarchy and Relations of Production," in *Feminism and Materialism*, 11.

19. Ibid., 18.

20. Juliet Mitchell, *Psychoanalysis and Feminism* (London: Penguin, 1975).

21. McDonough and Harrison, in *Feminism and Materialism*, 32.

22. Ibid., 39.

23. Monique Wittig, *Les Guérillères*, trans, David Le Vay (London: Owen, 1971) 134.

24. Xavière Gauthier, "Creations," in *New French Feminisms*, 163.

25. See "Introduction III, Contexts of the New French Feminisms," in *New French Feminisms*, 31.

26. Josette Féral, "The Powers of Difference," in Hester Eisenstein and Alice Jardine, eds., *The Future of Difference* (Boston: G.K. Hall and Co., 1980), 88-91.

27. Nancy Chodorow, *The Reproduction of Mothering: Psychoanalysis and the Sociology of Gender* (Berkeley: University of California Press, 1978).

28. Kristeva quoted by Féral, in *The Future of Difference*, 92-93.

29. Féral, 89.

30. For other descriptions of this process of objectification see Simone de Beauvoir in *New French Feminisms*, 41-56, and Catherine MacKinnon,

"Feminism, Marxism, Method, and the State: An Agenda for Theory," in *Feminist Theory*, 1-30.

31. Cixous quoted by Domna C. Stanton, "Language and Revolution: The Franco-American Dis-Connection," in *The Future of Difference*, 78.

32. Hélène Cixous, "The Laugh of the Medusa," in *New French Feminisms*, 250. See also Hélène Cixous, "Le Sexe ou la tête?" *Les Cahiers du GRIF* 13 (October 1976), issue called *Elles con-sonnent, Femmes et langages* II; Hélène Cixous and Catherine Clément, *La Jeune Née* (Paris: Union Generale d'Editions, 1975).

33. Cixous, "Sorties," in *New French Feminisms*, 90-91.

34. Ibid., 93.

35. Ibid., 96.

36. Ibid., 93.

37. Ibid., 96.

38. Julia Kristeva, "Woman Can Never Be Defined," in *New French Feminisms*, 137.

39. Cixous, "The Laugh of the Medusa," 253.

40. Ibid., 262-63.

41. Ibid., 252.

42. Ibid., 254.

43. Ibid., 247.

44. Ibid., 255.

45. Kristeva, "Woman Can Never Be Defined," 137.

46. Naomi Schor, "Female Paranoia: The Case for Psychoanalytic Feminist Criticism," *Yale French Studies* 62, 211.

47. Kristeva quoted by Schor, 211.

48. Jardine quoted by Carolyn Burke, "Psychoanalysis and Feminism in France," in *The Future of Difference*, 112. See Julia Kristeva, *Polylogues* (Paris: Editions du Seuil, 1977); "The Subject in Signifying Practice," *Semiotexte* 1:3 (1975): 19-26; *About Chinese Women* (New York: Urizen Books, 1977); *Desire in Language: A Semiotic Approach to Literature and Art*, ed., Leon Roudiez, trans. Tom Gora, Alice Jardine, and Leon Roudiez (New York: Columbia Univ. Press, 1980); *La Révolution du langage poétique* (Paris: Editions du Seuil, 1974). See also Philip E. Lewis, "Revolutionary Semiotics," *Diacritics* 4:3 (Fall 1974): 28-32; Carolyn Burke and Jane Gallop, "Psychoanalysis and Feminism in France," in *The Future of Difference*, 106-121.

49. Kristeva, "Oscillation Between Power and Denial," in *New French Feminisms*, 165.

50. Gayatri C. Spivak, "French Feminism in an International Frame," *Yale French Studies* 62, suggests that Kristeva's and Cixous's consideration of the avant-garde includes literary and philosophical writers.

51. Kristeva quoted by Burke, in *The Future of Difference*, 112.

52. Kristeva, "Woman Can Never Be Defined," in *New French Feminisms*, 137-38.

53. Ibid., 141.

54. Jardine, "Pre-texts for the Transatlantic Feminist," YFS, 235.

55. Luce Irigaray, "When the Gods Get Together," in *New French Feminisms*, 102, 103. See also Luce Irigaray, *Ce Sexe qui n'en est pas un* (Paris: Editions de Minuit, 1977); *Speculum de l'autre femme* (Paris: Editions de Minuit, 1974).

56. Irigaray, "When the Gods Get Together," 104.

57. Ibid., 103.

58. Ibid., 104.

59. Ibid., 105.

60. Ibid., 106.

61. Irigaray quoted by Mary Jacobus, "The Question of Language: Men of Maxims and *The Mill on the Floss*," in *Writing and Sexual Difference*, 40.

62. Luce Irigaray, "When Our Lips Speak Together," trans. Carolyn Burke, *Signs* 6 (Autumn 1980): 69, 73-4.

63. Ibid., 69, 71.

64. Madeleine Vincent, "A Basic Fact of Our Time," *New French Feminisms*, 126, 127, 128-29.

65. "Variations on Common Themes," Editorial Collective of *Questions féministes*, in *New French Feminisms*, 214-5.

66. Ibid., 216.

67. Ibid., 217.

68. Ibid., 218.

69. Chantal Chawaf, "Linguistic Flesh," in *New French Feminisms*, 177-78.

70. "Variations on Common Themes," in *New French Feminisms*, 218, 219.

71. Evelyne Sullerot, "The Feminine (Matter of) Fact," in *New French Feminisms*, 155.

72. Antonio Gramsci, *Selections From the Prison Notebooks*, trans. Quintin Hoare and Geoffrey Nowell Smith (London, 1971), 244.

73. "Variations on Common Themes," in *New French Feminisms*, 226, 224.

74. Sally McConnell-Ginet, "Linguistics and the Feminist Challenge," in Sally McConnell-Ginet, Ruther Borker, and Nelly Furman, eds., *Women and Language in Literature and Society* (New York: Praeger, 1980), 13.

75. Shoshana Felman, "Women and Madness: The Critical Phallacy," *Diacritics* 5 (Winter 1975): 10.

7. Rhetoric and Realism;
or Marxism, Deconstruction, and the Novel

JONATHAN ARAC

I

The terms of my title suggest certain kinds of questions that are asked nowadays by serious critics of novels. These questions were not asked, or considered serious, in America as recently as some twenty years ago, when the premises of New Criticism still dominated the agenda, not even by critics like Harry Levin or Lionel Trilling who resisted the most extreme claims of literary autonomy.[1] For these questions detract from the formal integrity of individual works. They threaten both to disarticulate works internally and to open works to external relations, and they thus participate in that active "unbounding" to which this volume is devoted.

Such questions might ask about instances, single or recurrent, of language that is not clearly under aesthetic control, that does not conduce to greater beauty or intelligibility when it is focused upon. Such inquiry, indissociable from the work of Paul de Man, may be related to further interrogations of the ways in which a work may be seen *not* to fit together, such as the "generic discontinuity" that Fredric Jameson has made a special focus for his thinking about the novel. Whether for Jameson or de Man, such unsettling of formal integrity will then be related to comparable cases in the worlds of thought or action; they turn from literature in itself to its relations with philosophy and history.[2]

For my present purposes, I am taking "deconstruction," for which de Man is exemplary, in relation to questions of "rhetoric." By rhetoric I mean here a system of relations within language that tampers with meaning in ways that have at least since Plato been considered antagonistic to the goals and procedures of philosophy. At the same time that it is deviant, however, rhetoric is not idiosyncratic, for as a systematic repertory it pre-exists the individual shaping of a single writer or work. That is to say, rhetoric appears "literary" compared to philosophy but "mechanical" compared to literature. For my second set of terms, I am relating "Marxism" to questions of "realism," by which I mean broadly inquiries that relate literary works to history, society, politics, the economy. One advantage I find in the terms of rhetoric and realism is that in ordinary usage they form a pair whose relative evaluation is unstable. Realism is the stuff of life that saves literature from the mere artifice of rhetoric; rhetoric is the fictionality that saves literature from the quotidian banality of realism.

Under the sway of New Criticism, following a process that had run through the whole nineteenth century, "rhetoric" was reduced to the vagueness of "paradox" and the catch-all of "metaphor." Such elements were understood as necessarily present in any successful work and thus became merely defining features of the "literary," rather than allowing for the differentiation of one work or corpus or genre or period from another. For New Criticism, "realism" was simply banished in favor of autonomy. However disingenuously, the "themes" and "imagery" of literary works were understood to inhere uniquely within them, unrelated to other forms of knowledge or action.

The "realism" that by twenty years ago was less opposed than considered beyond the pale of discussion was taken as a servile, transparent copying of the world. The fate of the notion of "representation" in European theoretical debates of the twentieth century is too complex to address here, but it is worth noting that also in the United States a complex genealogy overdetermines the New Critical dismissal of realism. In the early decades of this century, the question of realism arose polemically as part of a generational conflict within bourgeois high culture, with those we now call "modernists" opposing realism as part of a rejected "Victorianism." Beginning at about the same time but coming to a head somewhat later, in the 1920s, and 1930s, the question of realism functioned in a larger class conflict within American society: the agrarian conservatism of the New Critics stood against the populist democracy that Parrington's *Main Currents in American Thought* served intellectually to legitimize. In the 1930s and 1940s, the question of realism was contested within the American left: the so-called Trotskyites of the *Partisan Review* furthered modernism against the so-called Stalinist culture of socialist realism and the Popular Front.[3]

Thus the "Truants," as William Barrett has named the group around the *Partisan Review*, joined the "Fugitives" along with the British "Bloomsbury" group in supporting what Ortega y Gasset had described as "the dehumanization of art." For the question of realism, I find especially telling Ortega's optical metaphor: writers had ceased to look through the window, choosing instead to focus on the faint internal reflections that play over the pane's surface. In Anglo-American literary culture, this dehumanization could be seen in Joyce's dissolution of the everyday into myth, in Eliot's fragmenting of the lyric subject into myth, in Yeats's stirring turn to the barbaric violence of myth.

Myth, however, provided the ground from which arose the intellectual breakthrough that displaced New Criticism. Through attention to myth the native structuralism of Northrop Frye turned New Criticism into Poetics, and his *Anatomy of Criticism* (1957) stimulated a lively interest in literary theory. More important for the story I am telling, however, is the work of Claude Lévi-Strauss, and I can understand the eager attention to the work of Lévi-Strauss in American literary culture—far more than among professional anthropologists—only by the apparent congruity of his concerns with theirs. That is, New Criticism had taught students of literature to value the study of myth, and Frye had whetted the appetite for theory. Thus the enthusiasm for Lévi-Strauss and for structuralism generally. Meanwhile in France, structuralism spread quickly from the study of myth to the broader study of collective representations in modern cultures. Just twenty years ago appeared pathbreaking exemplars of structuralist studies of popular culture (Roland Barthes on James Bond), of ideology (by Louis Althusser), of literature (by Gérard Genette and Tzvetan Todorov). These works along with the more epistemological inquiry of Michel Foucault all made clear that the relations between cultural products and the world were neither immediate nor transparent nor reduplicative. Literature related to the world through the relations it held to other systematic means of coding, or organizing.[4]

To leave this somewhat breathtakingly high road of rapid summary, let me offer a moment of reading from *Don Quixote*, the novel that continues to stand as the founding instance of the genre, to illustrate what I mean by starting to think of realism—the relation of literature to other sectors of life—in terms of the relations between different systems or codes.

Recall the encounter between Don Quixote and the barber (part one, chapter 45). Quixote insists that the barber has the famed golden helmet of Mambrino; the barber retorts that it's just his brass shaving basin. But all the other "honorable gentlemen"—to humor Quixote— take a vote, and the barber finds his basin "turned into Mambrino's helmet before his eyes." The barber can only grant that "might makes right." Against this conspiracy of gentlemen, however, a servant speaks his opinion that the basin is a basin and nothing else, and a trooper of the Inquisition insists likewise—"as sure as my father's my father"— provoking a brawl. Here the question of "black" and "white," of "truth" and "lie," the nature of reality as designated by words, is contested. It remains comic in the *Quixote*, but Nietzsche would argue that "the lordly right of bestowing names is such that one would almost be justified in seeing the origin of language itself as an expression of the rulers' power." And Virginia Woolf posed the fundamental questions of the novel as a form: "What is reality?" and "who are the judges of reality?"[5]

In this passage from the *Quixote* it takes the authority and power of the class structure, the church, and patriarchy to fix words to things in a way that makes them stick. Yet for Cervantes the novel itself is a "stepchild," a deviant from the paths of these authoritative transmissions. The novel thus takes a distance from the powers that ground our ordinary life. They all claim authority from the way things naturally are, and the novel opposes them by showing that things may be otherwise. This is a fundamental criticism of life, achieved through a criticism of linguistically modeled codes of culture and literature.

We face then a double revision, both in our understanding of the works we have considered realistic and in our understanding of the critical practice that we might consider realistic. Works are no longer to be treated as mirrors; the task of criticism is no longer to "replace" the work, substituting for it a past author's intention or social origin. Rather a contemporary "realist" criticism will strive to *place* the work in action, to elucidate what it did and does. Such criticism will therefore ally itself with studying the "effective history" of works in their reception and institutionalization.[6]

I would like to conclude the framework I have been offering with a typological sketch and a bemused warning. I have been characterizing four types of criticism which may be compared with regard to the critical actions and objects that make them up, critical action as a matter of both tone and gesture, critical object as both internally and externally construed. The tone of New Criticism is admiration and its gesture is to individualize, taking its object internally through its formal integrity and externally through its uniqueness. If New Criticism admiringly individualizes, structuralism carefully socializes: while it grants the formal integrity of works considered internally, its major concern is the intelligibility that only becomes possible through establishing the systematic relation of a work to other cultural forms. Deconstruction quizzically fractures, exposing a formal heterogeneity that cannot be separated from intertextuality, and thus renders unworkable the distinction of internal and external. Marxism militantly remolds: recognizing a formal heterogeneity that cannot be contained as a philosophical contradiction but must be related to social conflict, it strives to establish lines of struggle where deconstruction had left only permeable membranes. My bemusement comes from a sense that the single critic whose work bears the fullest—necessarily complex—relation to all these issues is Mikhail Bakhtin,[7] but he did his work several decades before the period I have been attending to, and therefore my warning: there is more to the story than I have been able to tell here.

II

I would like to turn now to some critical reading from the project of mine that has spurred these initial reflections. Here I take *Madame Bovary*, a work no less essential than the *Quixote* to understanding realism, rhetoric, and the novel as they have figured in our culture. I begin from a matter of textual spacing, go on to consider a related rhetorical figure, and move toward matters of historical judgment that engage the crucial grounds of debate in contemporary cultural politics.

One of the most striking aspects of *Madame Bovary* is Flaubert's extraordinary economy in the use of direct speech. Recall that, between the first meeting of Charles and Emma, and the time some twenty pages and twenty months later that they go to the fancy ball at Vaubyessard, there is no dialogue between Charles and Emma. When dialogue does occur, one of the striking stylistic features is the frequent use of ellipses. At such crucial points in the book as Emma's last night with Rodolphe before their planned elopement, or her last, desperate appeal to him for money to save her from financial ruin, there stand prominently on the page the three dots (. . .) that mark the incompletion, the fragmentation of their sentences, their inability to proceed, to get anywhere. We sense within this device not only the characters' inadequacy, but also the writer's impatience with them. Our participation in the illusion of character and story makes us feel that even if the characters lack the fluency of the heroes and heroines of romance and melodrama, they nonetheless would be saying something more than they do if the writer were not cutting them off, giving us only the minimum necessary to make the book comprehensible. The narration of the famous Agricultural Fair scene exemplifies this aspect most fully. There the ellipses that truncate the speech of the councillor precisely mark the will of the author who shifts from this stream of fatuity to the no less fatuous love-talk by which Rodolphe is seducing Emma, and as we readers can be trusted to get the point, the fragments become shorter and shorter.

By his ellipses Flaubert not only exposes but also plays with other forms, such as melodramatic romance. After they have ridden off into the woods, and he has started to urge her on to love, Rodolphe pleads with Emma not to return, but to "Stay a minute longer! Please stay!"[8]

> "I shouldn't, I shouldn't!" she said. "I am out of my mind listening to you!"
> "Why? . . . Emma! Emma!"
> "Oh, Rodolphe! . . . " she said slowly, and she pressed against his shoulder. (11, 9; 438.)

If we know what's happening now, it's not from the actors' words but because we recognize the convention that passion strikes mute, that love is beyond words, a convention that Flaubert here simultaneously mocks and employs.

Rodolphe's later reflections upon Emma's attempts at romantic eloquence, which the narrator spares us from having to read, lead to one of the most famous passages in all of Flaubert's writing:

> He had so often heard these things said that they did not strike him as original. Emma was like all mistresses; and the charm of novelty, gradually falling away like a garment, laid bare the eternal monotony of passion, that has always the same shape and the same language. He was unable to see, this man so full of experience, the variety of feelings hidden within the same expressions. Since libertine or venal lips had murmured similar phrases, he only faintly believed in the candor of Emma's; he thought one should beware

of exaggerated declarations which only serve to cloak a tepid love;
as though the abundance of one's heart did not sometimes over-
flow with empty metaphors, since no one has ever been able to
give the exact measure of his needs, his concepts, or his sorrows.
The human tongue is like a cracked cauldron on which we beat
out tunes to set a bear dancing when we would make the stars
weep with our melodies. (II, 12; 466).

In defining a sense of incommensurability between needs and words,
Flaubert emphasizes deficiency. In George Puttenham's terms, Flaubert
favors the "figure of default," "ellipsis."[9] If ellipsis is most literally the
mark used in writing or printing to indicate the omission of a word or
words, it is also the rhetorical figure by which words are omitted which
would be needed to complete the grammatical construction or fully to
express the sense. Thus even when the marks of ellipsis are not physically
present and when grammar is observed, we still may find Flaubert's
language regularly elliptical, missing something that would be needed
fully to express the sense. One strains to hear celestial music behind
the clattering of kitchenware.

Characters within the novel sometimes find themselves in this
position. During his first acquaintance with Emma, as he went home
at night, "Charles went over her words one by one, trying to recall
them, trying to fill out their sense, that he might piece out the life she
had lived" (I, 3; 312). But more often, as in the passage cited above
the metaphor of cloak or garment suggests the concealment that language throws over feeling, so elsewhere too speech is characterized as
"a rolling-wheel that always stretches the sentiment it expresses" (III,
1; 505). This drastic literalization of the etymological sense of "express"
seems thoroughly to doom any hope for truth in expression. If Emma
was the victim of Rodolphe's unbelief in her love, similar metaphors
describe the advantage that she later takes of Charles through her use
of language. Her existence becomes "one long tissue of lies, in which
she wrapped her love as under a veil in order to hide it" (III, 5; 538).

Thus expression is if sincere doomed to failure and is otherwise
merely a tool of deceit, as when Rodolphe in his conversation with
Charles "fills with banalities all the gaps where an allusion [to Emma]
might slip in" (III, 11; 610). The writer, therefore, must try another
strategy, not that of expression but of implication. If the Greek elleípo
comes to mean to "fall short" and to "leave out," its original meaning
is to "leave in." The *OED* quotes Cowley on ellipsis as "leaving some-

thing to be understood by the reader." This procedure has many variations. We may have a simple ellipsis of time, as after Emma has fainted
we read:

> "I'll run to my laboratory for some aromatic vinegar," said
> the pharmacist.
>   Then as she opened her eyes on smelling the bottle: (II, 13,
> 481.)

This passage omits the time and action of getting the bottle, but no
reader fails to follow, even though the continuity of the scene has been
thus subtly disrupted.

The same technique marks the scene in which Emma and
Rodolphe first make love. After "she abandoned herself to him," a new
paragraph begins "The shades of night were falling." All description
of their physical love has been passed over, but the suffusive interanima-
tion of Emma and nature in the paragraph suggests clearly enough that
it has been very satisfying to her, even though all direct description
of her emotional response is also omitted:

> The shades of night were falling; the horizontal sun passing be-
> tween the branches dazzled the eyes. Here and there around her,
> in the leaves or on the ground, trembled luminous patches, as if
> hummingbirds flying about had scattered their feathers. Silence
> was everywhere; something sweet seemed to come forth from the
> trees. She felt her heartbeat return, and the blood coursing through
> her flesh like a river of milk. Then far away, beyond the wood,
> on the other hills, she heard a vague prolonged cry, a voice which
> lingered, and in silence she heard it mingling like music with the
> last pulsations of her throbbing nerves. Rodolphe, a cigar between
> his lips, was mending with his penknife one of the two broken
> bridles. (II, 9; 438.)

This passage may stand for the way in which expression yields to implication in two senses; first in the way that Emma's emotional state
emerges through language of perception and through analogies worked
upon that, so that nature rather than Emma receives the direct description; second in that we know from Flaubert's correspondence that this
scene was one in which he felt himself directly participating, but only
in Emma's sense of oneness with the scene do we find traces of Flaubert's
experience.

The last sentence of the passage poses a further question about the implications of ellipses in the book. It puzzles me at least; I've never been at all sure how to take it, and my reading in criticism suggests that disagreement persists. Most simply we are offered the choice of taking the last sentence as the deflation of the reverie into the hum-drum world of the everday, through such contrasts as that of the far-off and the near, the ecstatic woman and the practical man, the world of nature and the world of man bridling nature; or else we may feel that here this everyday sight and activity are transfigured through the con-text, that for Emma the halo of the scene surrounds Rodolphe. We may take the difference between these two interpretations as the difference between understanding the last sentence as part of Emma's perception and understanding it as the narrator's withdrawal from Emma to a blank registration of the scene, freed from the veils of her ecstasy.

The book's whole technique of juxtaposition without any explicit clues as to why the juxtaposition has been made leaves us often at a loss, and no less puzzling are the disconnections that are typographically introduced between items that we might ordinarily expect to be part of a continuous series. After Emma and Rodolphe have made love, we read:

> She was charming on horseback—upright, with her slender waist, her knee bent on the mane of her horse, her face some-what flushed by the fresh air in the red of the evening.
>
> On entering Yonville she made her horse prance in the road. People looked at her from the windows. (11, 9, 438-9.)

If the sentence of entry into Yonville takes a paragraph of its own to emphasize that it is a new phase of the trip between the woods and the town, we still must scratch our heads to come up with an explana-tion for why the next sentence is a new paragraph. Of course we can always find some reason—say the disjunction between the censorious community and the individual striving for a freedom beyond its con-fines, the outdoors vs. the indoors—but it will always seem arbitrary. Such paratactic sequences seem rich and precise in the obvious willful care that has gone into their construction, yet they are also curiously uncontrolled, for there is no narrator whose reassuring presence we can refer all these moments back to. It is for this reason that it was necessary in making so many of my points along this argument to say "we read" and that my initial observations began from a matter of typography. With Flaubert we are in the realm of the textual. His elliptical style creates the default of any constant narrative presence and leaves us warily by ourselves in making the necessary interpretations to tease out the implications and thereby show our understanding.

The contrast between the bumbling incapacity in his characters' ellipses and the magisterial authority in Flaubert's elliptical procedure begins from the first use of ellipsis in the book, in the account of Charles Bovary's first day in school. As a newcomer with a grotesquely elaborate headgear and a shy inarticulacy, Charles has provoked the ridicule of his classmates:

> "What are you looking for?" asked the master.
> "My ca . . ." Charles replied.[10]
> "Five hundred verses for all the class!" shouted in a furious voice, stopped, like the *Quos ego*, a fresh outburst. (I, 1: 295)

Flaubert sets against Charles's helplessness the master's power, likened to that of Neptune calming the winds in the *Aeneid* (I, 135). The master's power, however, is neither divine nor natural; it is strictly literary and disciplinary—a task of book Latin.[11] The Virgilian model to which it is referred long served as a textbook instance (e.g. in Quintilian) of a rare and impressive figure of speech—itself an instance of literal default—Aposiopesis, "silencing." "*Quos ego*," Neptune's threat, is not a full sentence but might be translated best by Elmer Fudd, "Why, you, I'll . . ." But in this case divine or literary power makes the words wholly effective at calming the "outburst."

We may conclude the examination of ellipsis in *Madame Bovary* by invoking the geometrical figure of the ellipse, a regular oval, smooth and continuous and enclosed, that nevertheless "falls short" of the harmony of a circle because it is not determined by one unique center but by two foci, the sum of the distances from which is a constant for any point on the curve. Much in the book relates to the failure of centering in Emma, and we may now emphasize the duality within her. If her attempt to make a center of her love for Leon failed to establish a center of spiritual value in the midst of the surrounding bleakness of small town domesticity, it is perhaps, in the logic of the book, because there is a simultaneous yet different attempt at centering within her, one that values the concreteness of her surroundings over any supposedly higher values. Her "nature" is also "positive in the midst of its enthusiasms" and "loved the church for the sake of the flowers, and music for the words of the songs" (I, 6; 327). Thus she can believe not in the possibility of creating a place of happiness within herself but rather "that certain places on earth must bring happiness, as a plant peculiar to the soil, and that cannot thrive elsewhere" (I, 7; 328). Thus she materialistically confuses "the sensuous pleasures of luxury with the delights of the heart" (I, 9; 345). There is no center from which she lives, and the oscillation between foci deforms her life.

The sentence that best emblematizes this elliptical pattern is the famous, "She wanted at the same time to die and to live in Paris" (I, 9: 346). The sentence establishes no opposition between the two points; different as they are, together they work to define the limits of her aspiration. They also mark the two foci from which interpretations of the book have worked. The absolute of death marks the perspective from which the worldly desires of the book must seem vanity, whether in the framework of traditional Christian morality, for which Emma is, as for Homais, "a lesson, an example, a solemn picture" (III, 8; 587), or from the modernistic, neo-romantic perspective of absolute irony, which equally sees her life as blind, self-mystifying delusion. At the same time the sense of a full life in a specific place recalls the work of such critics as Poulet and Richard, in their analyses of the rich interplay of consciousness and materiality in the language of the book, in the experience of Emma and Flaubert both.[12]

The book itself defines these terms of response within Emma as she watches *Lucia di Lammermoor* and feels both the life within the work and the death within the work, its relation to human experience and to inhuman form. At first she "recognized all the intoxication and the anguish" of her affair with Rodolphe: "The voice of the prima donna seemed to echo her own conscience, and the whole fictional story seemed to capture something of her own life." But from this participation she begins to slip away, or to rise, into the distance: "But no one on earth had loved her with such love. . . . Such happiness, she realized was a lie, a mockery to taunt desire. She knew how small the passions were that art magnified." In her attempts at "detachment" she achieves a perspective that corresponds closely to the defenses of much modern criticism, and sees "this reproduction of her sorrows" instead as "a mere formal fiction." Thus she is freed to "smile . . . inwardly in scornful pity, when from behind the velvet curtains at the back of the stage a man appeared in a black cloak." Her attention is on the literal details of the theatre, the "stage," the "curtains," not Edgar but only "a man in a black cloak." This superior position, however, proves no more stable than had the previous one, and "swept away by the poetic power of the acting, and drawn to the man by the illusion of the part," Emma returns to projection and "tried to imagine his life" (II, 15; 496-98).

Our presumption of superiority to Emma, the "scornful pity" that we may feel for her, and that Flaubert may have also felt at moments in composition, should not blind us to the fact that as readers we are involved in the same difficulties as she is. Without some participation and feeling on our part, the work will remain a "mere formal fiction."

This sequence may remind us that Flaubert's distrust of speech, as rolled fabric, is also related to a distrust of narrative, considered equally inadequate to the complexities of reality. In his writing narrative tends to behave like the guests at Emma's wedding: "The procession, first united like one long colored scarf that undulated across the field, along the narrow path winding among the green wheat, soon lengthened out, and broke up into different groups that loitered" (I, 4; 316). The attempt at what we now call "spatial" composition is suggested in Flaubert's own metaphor of composition that refuses both passion and the linear time of organic continuity: "Books are not made like babies but like pyramids, with a premeditated plan, by placing huge blocks one above the other."[13] This observation, reflecting the tension between "quest for origins" and "discovery of the mausoleum" that Edward Said has elucidated for the nineteenth-century novel in general, may be supplemented by one of the most teasing moments in the book, the short paragraph that forms the hinge between the introductory description of Yonville and the narration of the Bovarys' arrival within this prepared scene: "Since the events about to be narrated, nothing in fact has changed at Yonville. The tin tricolour flag still swings at the top of the church-steeple; the two streamers at the novelty store still flutter in the wind; the spongy white lumps, the pharmacist's foetuses, rot more and more in their cloudy alcohol, and above the big door of the inn the old golden lion, faded by rain, still shows passers-by it poodle mane" (II, 1; 357). No history has intervened to change the visual relation of church and state (and thus the Revolution of 1848 and *coup d'etat* of 1851 are denied); the forces of nature have not been able to tear away the streamers; preservatives have slowed the organic to a virtual standstill, and the discrepancy between the splendid name of "Golden Lion" and the poodle-like image that absurdly fails to represent it stands as a static emblem of what Emma is to experience in narrative. But that narrative changes "nothing in fact."[14]

This remark, one of the very few places in the book that draws explicit attention to the act of narration, is puzzling, for at the end of the book not only is Emma dead, and also Charles, but Lheureux and Homais have achieved new triumphs. We may take it that these deaths and triumphs mark no change but only the continuation of the "moeurs de province" to which the book's subtitle devotes it. Nonetheless, it seems better to take the statement very literally, rather than trying to claim that some changes are really no changes, and to recognize in "the events about to be narrated" a definition of the whole rest of the book. The unconscious processes of linguistic change that have transformed "in fact" (it works the same for French *en effet*) from an assertion about the world to a mere introductory turn of phrase—making it, in Roman Jakobson's terms, more a matter of code than of context[15]—are here brought to consciousness by the pressure of Flaubert's writing as it asserts the systematic self-reference of the book. "In fact" nothing he describes will ever change after "the events about to be narrated" because they exist only in the fiction of the book. Every word of it to the end is one of those events, and when the book has ended nothing changes within it.

III

Having called on the resources of rhetorical analysis made possible by deconstructive criticism, a realist criticism must now question the Flaubertian positions that we have succeeded in specifying. If in this literature the "*Quos ego*" of Flaubert's ellipsis silences history's outbursts, there may yet be more to the story. We may share Flaubert's scorn for narrative eventfulness, and we therefore laugh at a satirical description of *Madame Bovary* as a moralistic antiromance, "the history of a wicked woman who goes from one abomination to another, until at last the judgment of Heaven descends upon her, and, blighted and blasted, she perishes miserably."[16] Yet when the book was prosecuted upon publication, essentially this view of it was offered by the defense attorney (to whom Flaubert subsequently dedicated the book). *Madame Bovary* was rescued and legitimated by the vestigial narrative structure that it wishes to mock. The critic who emphasized the book's disconnections, its refusals to reach full, satisfactory, conventional expression, was the Prosecutor. He charged Flaubert with presenting "the poetry of adultery" and insisted that tacking on a bad ending could not redeem such initial excess.[17]

Both attorneys seem rather clownish to us, yet the issue between them is one of the oldest and most complex in cultural theory: the relations of part and whole. Both Longinus, who approved, and Plato, who disapproved, agreed with the Prosecutor's premise that literature moves us most powerfully at *moments*, which are fragments separate from any totality. On the other hand, from Aristotle's *catharsis* to I. A. Richard's "stable poise," theories of formal wholeness are immobilizing.

It is tempting to extend these claims politically. In the earlier nineteenth century, Shelley and Hazlitt as Longinians supported political radicalism, against which Coleridge the Aristotelian stood conservatively.[18] In the 1930s, Walter Benjamin's Longinian politics of agitation opposed Lukacs's Stalinist Aristotelianism.[19] Such analogies have been very important in recent decades in making certain critical positions seem more, or less, attractive. I have argued elsewhere,[20] but can only assert here, that culture is related to politics—and a task of what I call "realist" criticism is to study and specify such connections—but that there is no reason to think that the relation is a simple analogy. There are more complex figurative relations than that of metaphor; relation does not consist only in likeness. If a notion like "reification" means anything, it means that Marxists cannot assume a transparent resemblance between sectors that have been socially produced as distinct.

One value in studying Flaubert is to recall us to these difficulties. Jonathan Culler's deconstructive reading of Flaubert hails his "achievement" as "revolutionary," but it goes without saying that the effects are limited within the institution of literature. Jean-Paul Sartre's Marxist analysis brings home the success of *Madame Bovary* as ideology: it helped to constitute a class fraction of the upper bourgeoisie who shared a position toward the second Empire of cynical support, which the book allowed to reach articulation. In a further twist, Fredric Jameson's Marxism is more difficult, dubious, and challenging, neither euphoric like Culler nor censorious like Sartre. While dismissing the anarchist political claims of the deconstructive reading, Jameson would see in the socially formative power that Sartre exposes just what a left wing critic should most value—if only one makes the allegorical transformation that cancels the empirical content in favor of a utopian projection of a world wholly different.[21]

I would like to conclude with a final observation that I hope has been clearly implicit—yet I shun ellipsis to spell it out. In the last few years the narrative responsibilities of intellectuals have become a major topic for debate and exhortation, whether in the work of establishment historians like Lawrence Stone and Bernard Bailyn, of maverick philosophers like Alasdair MacIntyre and Richard Rorty, or of radical critics like Jameson and Edward Said.[22] In trying to come to terms with the complexities of this issue, I find it salutary to explore the comparable, though far from identical, cases of the novelists of the nineteenth century. Like them, as cultural intellectuals we are participating in a hegemonic practice, more deeply than we can ever fully know, yet we also understand ourselves in our activities as teachers, scholars, and writers to be doing "counter" work that not only aims but somewhat succeeds at making an opening where alternative views and practices may emerge. From a certain demographic perspective, it is a surprising fact that the novel of the nineteenth century reached a smaller proportion of the population than college English courses do in the United States today; that is, that statistically the novel was more elitist than contemporary literary higher education. On the other hand, there is an immensely greater state investment in authorizing higher education now than there ever has been in fiction. I offer these contrasts only to suggest that the differences are interestingly complex, rather than easy, and to return to my fundamental emphasis. The refinement of textual inquiry can aid but should not replace the questions of uses and effects: rhetoric, yes, but realism too.

NOTES

1. See, for example, Lionel Trilling, "Manners, Morals, and the Novel," in *The Liberal Imagination* (London: Secker and Warburg, 1950); and Harry Levin, "Society as Its Own Historian," in *Contexts of Criticism* (Cambridge: Harvard University Press, 1957).

2. See, for example, Paul de Man "Semiology and Rhetoric," in *Allegories of Reading* (New Haven: Yale University Press, 1979); and Fredric Jameson, "Magical Narratives: On the Dialectical Use of Genre Criticism," in *The Political Unconscious* (Ithaca: Cornell University Press, 1981).

3. To supplement this discussion of anti-representationalism, see Jonathan Arac, "Introduction," in *Postmodernism and Politics* (Minneapolis: University of Minnesota Press, 1986).

4. On the intellectual excitement of 1966, see the retrospective remarks

by Frank Kermode introductory to his *Art of Telling* (Cambridge: Harvard University Press, 1983).

5. For Nietzsche, see *The Genealogy of Morals*, first essay, second section; and for Woolf, "Mr. Bennett and Mrs. Brown," in *Collected Essays* (New York: Harcourt, 1967), 1:325.

6. See, for example, Hans Robert Jauss, "Literary History as a Challenge to Literary Theory," in *Toward an Aesthetic Reception* (Minneapolis: University of Minnesota Press, 1982).

7. See, for example, Mikhail Bakhtin, *The Dialogic Imagination* (Austin: University of Texas Press, 1981).

8. In quoting *Madame Bovary*, I use, with modifications, the revision of the Aveling translation by Paul de Man (New York: Norton, 1965) and refer to the novel by section and chapter, followed by page references to the French text in the Pléiade edition (Paris: Gallimard, 1951).

9. *The Arte of English Poesie* (1589), 136.

10. Here I alter de Man's edition, which replaces the ellipsis with a repetitive stammer. On the interpretation of Charles's cap, contrast Jonathan Culler, *Flaubert* (Ithaca: Cornell University Press, 1974) to Victor Brombert, *The Novels of Flaubert* (Princeton: Princeton University Press, 1966).

11. On the continuing power of classical rhetorical models, see Michael Riffaterre, "Flaubert's Presuppositions," in *Flaubert and Postmodernism*, éd. Naomi Schor and Henry F. Majewski (Lincoln: University of Nebraska Press, 1984).

12. For the negative reading, see for example, Tony Tanner's chapter in *Adultery in the Novel* (Baltimore: Johns Hopkins University Press, 1979).

13. Gustave Flaubert, *Correspondence*, ed. Jean Bruneau (Paris: Gallimard, 1973), 2:783.

14. See discussion by Jacques Seebacher, in Claudine Gothot-Mersch ed., *La Production du Sens chez Flaubert* (Paris: Union générale d'editions, 1975), 318.

15. Roman Jakobson, "Linguistics and Poetics," in *Style in Language*, ed. Thomas Sebeok (Cambridge: Technology Press of MIT, 1960).

16. Henry James, paraphrasing Hippolyte Taine's "elaborate satire," "The Opinions of M. Graindorge," in *French Poets and Novelists* (New York: Macmillan, 1878).

17. For the trial in English, see, for example, the New American Library Signet Classic edition; and for discussion, Dominick La Capra, *Madame Bovary on Trial* (Ithaca: Cornell University Press, 1982).

18. For such contrasts, see Paul Fry on Shelley and Aristotle in *The Reach of Criticism* (New Haven: Yale University Press, 1983); and David Bromwich on Hazlitt and Coleridge in *Hazlitt, the Mind of a Critic* (Oxford: Oxford University Press, 1983).

19. See, for example the documents translated in Ernst Bloch et al., *Aesthetics and Politics* (London: NLB, 1977).

20. See Jonathan Arac, *Critical Genealogies* (forthcoming, 1987), and "The Politics of *The Scarlet Letter*," in *Ideology and Classic American Literature*, ed. Sacvan Bercovitch and Myra Jehlen (Cambridge: Cambridge University Press, 1986).

21. Culler, *Flaubert*; Jameson, *Political Unconscious*; Sartre, *L'Idiot de la Famille* (Paris: Gallimard, 1971-72), e.g., 3:206. See also an important essay published after mine was completed: Lawrence Rothfield, "Discursive Intertextuality: The Case of Bovary," *Novel* 19 (1985): 57-81.

22. Lawrence Stone, "The Return of Narrative," in *The Past and Present* (Boston: Routledge and K. Paul, 1981); Bernard Bailyn, "The Challenge of Modern Historiography," in *American Historical Review* (1982); Richard Rorty, *Philosophy and the Mirror of Nature* (Princeton: Princeton University Press, 1979); Alasdair MacIntyre, *After Virtue* (Notre Dame: University of Notre Dame Press, 1981); Edward W. Said, "Permission to Narrate," *London Review of Books* 6 (1984); Fredric Jameson, "Postmodernism; or the Cultural Logic of Late Capitalism," *New Left Review* 146 (1984).

8. The Reality of Theory: Freud in His Critics

DANIEL T. O'HARA

They cannot free themselves from him because their revenge is not yet complete. . . .[1]

I

Over the last two decades especially, psychoanalysis has suffered a progressive loss in scientific credibility and cultural legitimacy. Strangely enough, however, its founder Sigmund Freud, has gained in speculative validity and critical authority during the same period in the discipline of literary study. Freud has in fact become the cornerstone of a literary conception of reality generally informing American critical theory. Obviously, I cannot hope to do justice here to this historical irony. But what I can do is to suggest, in outline, some of its dimensions and to examine a few of its more curious and clearly representative manifestations in some detail. The following paper is thus intended as a preface to a much larger study of the paradoxical appropriation of Freud by American critical theorists in our increasingly postmodern and post-psychoanalytic age.

Before beginning this project, however, I need to specify a little more precisely what I mean by that much over—or is it, under?—determined word in my title, "reality." I think the following rather long quotation from Freud can serve as a convenient locus of meanings the various shades of which continue to haunt the profession:

> . . . The super-ego continues to play the part of an external world for the ego, although it has become a portion of the internal world. Throughout later life it represents the influence of a person's childhood, of the care and education given him by his parents and of his dependence on them—a childhood which is prolonged so greatly in human beings by a family life in common. And in

all this it is not only the personal qualities of these parents that is making itself felt, but also everything that had a determining effect on them themselves, the tastes and standards of the social class in which they lived and the innate dispositions and traditions of the race from which they sprang. Those who have a liking for generalizations and sharp distinctions may say that the external world, in which the individual finds himself exposed after being detached from his parents, represents the power of the present; that the id, with its inherited trends, represents the organic past; and that the super-ego, which comes to join them later, represents more than anything the cultural past, which a child has, as it were, to repeat as an after-experience during the few years of his early life.[2]

In terms of that to which my title and subtitle allude, then, the reality of theory which Freud represents in his critics is the persistence of the literary tradition in which they were trained and to which they return repeatedly, in order to work through it once again. I will of course be recurring to this conventional, even professional definition of "reality" in the course of this paper. You can think of it as an exercise in social psychology.

II

It is remarkable, really, to behold how greatly the base of rational, empirical, and scientific validity for psychoanalysis has shrunk since the early 1960s. Paradoxically enough, it is the work in philosophy, in experimental psychology, and in cultural history of those researchers and scholars who take Freud and the discipline he founded most seriously that exemplifies best this curious development. An essay in philosophical critique, a collective research project in psychology, and the first text of a multi-volume cultural analysis of the history of sexuality will serve as our cases in point.

Robert C. Solomon in "Freud's Neurological Theory of Mind" (1974), for instance, argues persuasively that it is only insofar as Freud's psychological model of the mind continues to be based upon his early neurological formulations of psychic processes as outlined in the 1895 *Project for a Scientific Psychology* that psychoanalysis retains any vestige of the rationality, comprehensiveness, or predictive capacity of a gen-

uine science. In thus defending psychoanalysis from charges of being
wildly speculative made by Anglo-American philosophers of science,
Solomon, who believes that the scientific validity of psychoanalysis is
greater than these charges allow, demonstrates nonetheless that the range
of its scientific plausibility is considerably smaller than Freud was able
to recognize. For Solomon shows that as "Freud increasingly despairs
of confirmation of his structural model by neuroanatomical research,
he separates his models from neurology, but only in a formal gesture
(like the apologetic and humble comments in the preface of a book)
which he never really accepts."[3] That is, despite his assertion to the
contrary and despite their narrow scientific basis, Freud always expects
that his theories will be fully confirmed by later experiment, by the
kind of biological and neurological science in which he was first trained.

Without delving too deeply into the complexities of Freud's original
neurological theory of mind, in which the psychical apparatus is represented as a Newtonian machine for conserving and transforming into
mental representations physical forces and energy currents via definite
material particles (different kinds of neurons) located in specifiable
regions of the central nervous system, one must conclude, on the basis
of Solomon's own analysis, that the conception of psychoanalysis as
a new and distinct science discovering a new and distinct order of nature with its own laws is ill-founded, perhaps even illusory. One of
Freud's critics in the history of science, Frank Sulloway, in his monumental study *Freud, Biologist of the Mind: Beyond the Psychoanalytic Legend*
(1979), has delved more deeply into all this and, following Solomon's
principle of reducing psychoanalysis to its tiny, fragile neurological core,
takes the next step which Solomon never does, which is to prove conclusively that virtually all of Freud's major contributions to a psychoanalytic theory of mental operations are based primarily on a shifting
series of illegitimate analogies with a now generally superceded
nineteenth-century version of science, and particularly of biology and
neurology. The tiny, fragile core of valid science, of real knowledge,
is thus very tiny and fragile indeed. And all the rest of psychoanalysis
is one gigantic category mistake.[4]

Similarly, in *The Scientific Evaluation of Freud's Theories and Therapy*,
a collective research project involving many experimental psychologists
edited by Seymour Fisher and Roger P. Greenberg, all that the most
loyal partisan of Freud can discover is carrion comfort. For these
researchers have found that the only verifiable hypothesis among Freud's
speculations on the causes and cures of mental illness, of the classical

neuroses, is his theory of the aetiology of paranoia. By giving a battery of the latest tests to different groups of paranoiacs over several years, these researchers have determined that Freud's view of paranoia as being caused by or resulting from repressed homoerotic impulses is scientifically plausible.

The paranoid individual, you will recall, is unable in Freud's scenario to deal with his latent homosexual feelings and so must first convert his unconscious wish to love another man into its inverse formulation. Then, he is compelled to project it as a categorical fear of all others in a monstrous act of hysterical self-justification. "I want to love that man," becomes in short, "everyone is plotting against me." This confirmation of Freud's conception of paranoia by the experimental psychologists is highly ironical in several ways. Most ironical, however, is the fact that in this instance Freud is generalizing essentially from the single case of Schreber, a patient he never personally treated but whose memories he read and whose analyst he consulted with.[5] This means that Freud demonstrates here not so much the scientific plausibility of psychoanalysis as his expertise in the art of interpreting texts. In crediting his theory of paranoia, therefore, these psychological researchers are actually further discrediting the scientific validity of psychoanalysis as a theory of neurosis and a method of treatment, even as they are also clearly confirming Freud's status as an intuitive hermeneut of some genius.

One could speculate in this connection that Freud may prove his mettle in the case of paranoia because his so-called new science of mind, so severely undermined and drastically curtailed in its philosophical and empirical claims to truth as it is, has much in common with the delusional systems of the paranoid personality. Certainly, the work in cultural history and the sociology of knowledge done by Peter Gay and Michel Foucault, not to mention the savage critiques of psychoanalysis made by such revisionary analysts and social theorists of conformity, alienation, and sexual revolution as R.D. Laing, David Cooper, Norman O. Brown, Herbert Marcuse, and, most recently, Jeffrey Masson in *The Assault on Truth: Freud's Suppression of the Seduction Theory*, all have argued in ways which suggest the fittingness of this comparison. Of these cultural critiques of Freud and psychoanalysis, however, the arguments of Michel Foucault are the most worth considering, because of their inherent cogency and their considerable (if often consciously denied) influence.[6]

In *The History of Sexuality, Vol. I*, Foucault mounts a devastatingly appreciative critique of Freud and psychoanalysis. Foucault shows how Freud's sexual theories of personal identity and social formations take their central place in the history of modern culture as the climax in a long series of systematic interventions in the life of the human subject by discursive practices—scientific, medical, administrative, philosophical, and ideological. These disciplinary interventions work to implant in the bodies of individuals a form of sexuality which constitutes the modern articulation of subjectivity itself. This discursive constitution of the subject conceives sexuality as the repressed, guilty secret of the self, a secret about which one is coerced by the culture to speak endlessly, in the manner of a latter-day rite of confession in and through which one first comes to recognize oneself as an individual. Foucault refuses to imagine a dialectical history of sexual openness, sexual repression, and sexual liberation for the last three hundred odd years or so in modern culture. Rather, he employs a genealogy of power which is also an archeology of knowledge that disperses this kind of dialectical history by exposing the facile ideology of repression and liberation informing it as a seductive cover for the production by the bourgeoisie of a micro-physics, an analytics, of power-knowledge, an archive of discursive and disciplinary techniques intended to legitimate their claim to represent the authentic future of man and to authorize their drive to materially supervise and regulate the bodies of those others who are members of generally excluded or suppressed classes and groups. The bourgeois claim to the right kind of sexuality, in other words, has come to replace the aristocratic claim to the right kind of blood. And the modern Western state, whatever its philosophical orientation or ideological proclamations, functions to administer *all* the resources at its disposal for the benefit of the classes and groups strong and smart enough to rule by means of the proliferating mechanisms of representation available to them in their culture since the Renaissance.

In this context, Freud becomes something quite different than either the provocative scientific liberator from repression he was once thought to be or the unwitting ideologue of the patriarchy he is often still called. Rather, for Foucault, Freud is a master strategist in the modern war of ideas by which human beings define themselves as cultural and sexual subjects. It is usually claimed, Foucault remarks at the conclusion of this volume, that Freud had "at last, through a sudden reversal, restored to sex the rightful share which it had been denied for so long." Actually, Foucault goes on to antithetically argue, that in a move of genius "worthy of the greatest spiritual fathers" of the Church, Freud has given "new impetus to the secular injunction to study sex and transform it into discourse"—as that compound of knowledge and power, constitutive of the individual subject, termed "sexuality."[7] In this way the human subject in the West has been more effectively particularized, so as to be better administered and managed than ever before, all in order to serve more efficiently the interests of power.

From the point of view of even its most appreciative critics, therefore, psychoanalysis as a theory of the human subject and of culture and as a modern institution of knowledge and administrative technique now appears to be as rationally defensible, empirically verifiable, and ideologically disinterested as Babylonian astrology. (And like Babylonian astrology, the question of its truth-value has little or nothing to do, in the final analysis, with its effectiveness as an ideological weapon.) This last fact—the potential ideological effectiveness of psychoanalysis— explains in part why American literary critics have repeatedly seized upon Freud and his works to justify or authorize their elaboration and refinement of theories of reader-response (Norman Holland), of change in poetic and cultural history (Geoffrey Hartman and Harold Bloom), of fictional representation and narrative structure (Fredric Jameson), and all the rest. For a variety of reasons—institutionalized marginality, radical psychological alienation, and profound political disaffection—literary critics in America believe that they live in a time bereft of authentic imaginative achievement of major cultural significance, and so they have returned to Freud again and again, in order to conceive of a standard of excellence, a measure of genuine authority, a principle of literary reality, as it were, which would be appropriate for the professional nature of their discipline of study. Consequently, their theoretical speculations are unanchored, really, to specific literary texts of our cultural moment, or to particular social groups, or to larger historical forces and movements in the world today. The pathos of this ironic turn of events is as considerable as it seems irrevocable. It is a situation worthy of a work of fiction—a work of minor fiction no doubt.

                                    III

Be that as it may, I suspect that before going on to discuss the literary critical exploitation of Freud during this period of decline in the prestige of psychoanalysis, I should say something further regarding not only that use of the term "reality" previously discussed but, as well, the selection of critics to come. By "reality" in this context I mean only to refer to those perceived conditions of intellectual production which define the agreed-upon limits, possibilities, and standards of achievement for any particular interpretive community in the profession (or for that of the profession as a whole), as these conditions are enacted and enunciated in representative texts of some influence within a certain period of time. I admit that this definition is at once highly "conventionalistic" in nature and completely unsatisfactory as a philosophical concept. Nevertheless, its advantage lies in its capacity for isolating—at least—the role which Freud and his works have played in literary appropriations of psychoanalytic insights for speculative purposes by American critics of the first rank over the last two generations. Which role is of course, that of a measure, a principle of intellectual achievement, maturity, and excellence. This "reality function" played by Freud obviously incorporates an "ideal" function as well—just as that initial quotation from *An Outline of Psychoanalysis* predicts. I like to think of Freud playing the role of "reality" for literary intellectuals in terms of a categorical imperative to go and do likewise if they can: that is, to emulate Freud's founding performance of a modern intellectual discipline, an institution which has reshaped the lives of millions of people in the century. Like other ethical or moral or ideological standards of reality and value, of ego-ideals as it were, this literary conception of "reality" represented by the legend of Freud and his achievement is as influential and formative as the compelling obsessions of the paranoid's delusional system. The true mark of the paranoiac, by the way, is his constitutional incapacity to accept the fact that other people may have different views of the world.

With this provisional and makeshift definition of "reality" in mind, I have decided to limit my examples to the work of three literary critics who have appropriated Freudian insights for their theoretical speculations in ways I find most representative of those white male literary intellectuals, generally from economic and social origins defined in some way as inferior, who respond to the diverse pressures of cultural assimilation by attempting to form a rhetorical style and an ideological stance which can be oppositional in nature, ironical or provocative in function, and yet becomes essentially conservative in effect. I confess to a clear failure of distinterestedness in this respect: I can think of many of my friends who fit this profile. . . .

IV

. . . and most of my critical "fathers."

Lionel Trilling discussed Freud and his influence in modern culture five times over a period of nearly thirty years. The two most famous essays, written in the 1940s and collected in *The Liberal Imagination* (1950), are of course "Art and Neurosis" (1945) and "Freud and Literature" (1940). They are followed in 1955 and 1965 by two somewhat different versions of his address before the New York Psychoanalytic Society and the New York Psychoanalytic Institute on the occasion of the first Freud Anniversary Lecture. These versions are entitled, respectively, "Freud and the Crisis of Our Culture" (in this form it was published as a separate monograph) and "Freud: Within and Beyond Culture" (this is the central essay of the 1965 collection *Beyond Culture*). This latter essay has an equally compelling, perhaps even more provocative companion piece, also included in this volume, which is called "The Fate of Pleasure." Since this essay deals in part with Freud, I suppose it constitutes the sixth time Trilling treats one of his masters. Finally, early in 1972, Trilling writes again on Freud in modern culture, in the last chapter of the published version of his Charles Eliot Norton Lectures at Harvard for 1970, *Sincerity and Authenticity*. In three great waves, then, Trilling makes Freud possible for serious literary study in both senses of the phrase.

By brilliantly summarizing the possibilities and limitations of psychoanalysis for literary study, Trilling first makes Freud available for selective use by the critics of his and subsequent generations. Trilling legitimates and implants his Freud in the profession as much by his manner and tone as by the content in "Art and Neurosis" and "Freud and Literature." He does so, as well, by assimilating, via irony, Kenneth Burke's earlier and now familiar critique of psychoanalysis as an essentialist nineteenth-century pseudo-science that reduces the variety and mix of human motives to one single libidinal kernel or atom of sexual energy and desire. That is, Trilling accepts this kind of critique of psychoanalysis only to turn it around to Freud's literary advantage. For, Trilling argues, this outmoded pseudo-scientific essentialism, Freud's positivism and biologism, cannot really touch, ironically enough, the essential Freud. The essential Freud is the Freud who discovers that the language of the unconscious psyche is the same as the language of poetry and literature. This is the Freud who really counts for Trilling.

Trilling is the first American literary critic of any stature in his time to stress in an influential manner that the four forms of dream distortion—condensation, displacement, representability, and secondary elaboration—constitute "a science of tropos,"[8] a psychoanalytic rhetoric, which Burke himself will go on to describe later as consisting in four basic figures of symbolic action, namely, metaphor, metonomy, synecdoche, and irony.[9] By so emphasizing the protoliterary critical side of Freud, Trilling is then free generally to admit the dangers inherent in any systematic approach to literature—the dangers of reductiveness and polemical arrogance. In addition, in these two early essays, Trilling suggests that Freud's work amounts virtually to a grand epic, a novel in the classic tradition of the genre, on the subject of modern culture's inevitably tragic impact upon the self and its ever-dwindling fund of vital energies. Trilling in these two ways legitimates Freudian perspectives and Freudian texts for literary study, in order to appropriate Freudian ideology—the rhetoric of maturity, of the reality-principle, of sacrifice—as a means of legitimating in turn his representative call for social and cultural conformity in the period of the Cold War. In this fashion, too, Trilling authorizes the entire class of liberal intellectuals, literary or not, for whom he speaks.

Freud thus serves Trilling's institutional and ideological purposes well in the post-World War Two period. For he enshrines for an influential generation of American scholars and their almost equally influential students, a conception of analysis, of social reality, and of cultural (as opposed to political) achievement intimately associated with a view of life as necessarily entailing sacrifice, especially the sacrifice of the dream of revolution. A quotation from his classic essay on James's *Princess Casamassima* can serve to indicate the subtle ideological function Freud plays in Trilling's formative literary criticism:

> Inevitably, of course, the great irony of her fate is that the more passionately she seeks reality and the happier she becomes in her belief that she is close to it, the further removed she is. . . . She cannot but mistake the nature of reality, for she believes it is a thing, a position, a finality, a bedrock. She is, in short, the very embodiment of the modern will which masks itself in virtue, making itself appear harmless, the will that hates itself and finds its manifestations guilty and is able to exist only if it operates in the name of virtue, that despises the variety and modulations of the

human story and longs for an absolute humanity, which is but another way of saying a nothingness. In her alliance with Paul Muniment she constitutes a striking symbol of that powerful part of modern culture that exists by means of its claim to political innocence and by its false seriousness—the political awareness that is not aware, the social consciousness which hates full consciousness, the moral earnestness which is moral luxury.[10]

Such a tragic vision, made possible by Freudian insights, of the fate of the intellectual in modern culture is imaginatively consistent with the personal and professional situations of cultural assimilation and political bad faith of this class of liberal writers Trilling represents, whose maturity is measured by how much distance they can put between themselves and their salad days of fellow-traveling. In a sense, the hatred Trilling expresses in this passage is as much self-hatred as hatred of a particular class of once intimate colleagues and comrades-in-arms, as it were. Trilling's first phase of appropriating Freud for literary study in America sets the pattern for later, more theoretical but no less ideological uses of psychoanalysis and Freud to authorize an acceptance of things as they are which is equally repressive and sentimental.

Trilling in the two versions of his 1955 address to the New York Psychoanalytic Society and the New York Psychoanalytic Institute appropriates Freud in a second way which can be characterized as now more adversarial or oppositional in stance. As the title of his 1965 collection, *Beyond Culture*, may suggest, Trilling discovers in Freud a principle of reality, still tragic in outline, but more biological than cultural in content, and associated less with sublimation and the vicissitudes of instinct in civilization than with the inevitable and inescapable extinction of all possibility represented by the hypothesis of the death-instinct. This new perspective sanctioned by Freud speaks to Trilling of a recalcitrant core of instinct at the center of each individual making possible an ultimate vantage-point within the mind which is truly beyond culture and from which all cultures and their products, including those of one's own, can be ruthlessly evaluated. (In light of the previous citation from Trilling on James's *Princess*, this development makes for a certain irony.) By shifting thus from the Freud of *Civilization and Its Discontents* back to the Freud of *Beyond The Pleasure Principle*, Trilling provides American literary critics in the late 1950s and early 1960s with an institutional and ideological rationale for their current use of Freud

in their work and for their possible deployment of a psychoanalytic critique of the repressions—sexual and otherwise—of the time. Trilling, in
providing himself and his peers with another Freudian license for their
positions and arrested social consciences, unwittingly authorizes as well
the fellow-traveling of literary intellectuals with that neo-Romantic
counterculture to emerge in the Vietnam era—which he would detest
so vigorously in his final and finest work.

"The Authentic Unconscious" in *Sincerity and Authenticity* (1972)
composes the final movement in Trilling's seminal appropriation and
dissemination of Freud in our literary culture. It represents a dialectical
return to the argument for acceptance drawn from *Civilization and Its
Discontents* that informed those famous early essays on Freud included
in *The Liberal Imagination*, but with the added wrinkles of the more recent adversarial essays written in the baleful light cast by *Beyond the
Pleasure Principle* and its antithetical naturalism, and to be found pervading the atmosphere of *Beyond Culture* (1965).[11] What Trilling puts
forth as his ultimate position on the matter of Freud in modern culture
is a vision so forbidding and horrific, so celebratory of intellectual self-
destruction, as to rival the awful pronouncements of Urizen in Blake's
Prophetic Books on the petty spectacle of the necessity of human pain
in this world. Trilling reads Freud in *Civilization and Its Discontents* as
proving that there is no realistic possibility of ameliorating the suffer-
ings which arise from the sacrifices of pleasure and desire demanded
by the requirements of culture. Neither social revolution, nor therapeutic
intervention, Trilling has Freud say, can transform the human condition sufficiently to rid us of this inexorable asceticism. Moreover, the
final cause for this situation is not really cultural anyway. The final cause
is the institution in the psyche of that hypercritical agency, the superego,
which exceeds the demands of civilization in its severity and which can
never be effectively muzzled short of psychosis, whether individual or
collective in nature, in any genuinely social context. Trilling appears
indeed to relish the prospect of failure necessarily facing all quixotic
hopes of social renovation of any kind:

> In 1930 Freud published his most fully articulated statement of
> what his theory of the mind implies for man's destiny. *Civilization
> and Its Discontents* is a work of extraordinary power. For social
> thought in our time its significance is unique. It may be thought
> to stand like a lion in the path of all hopes of achieving happiness

through the radical revision of social life. . . . Freud, in insisting upon the essential immitigability of the human condition as determined by the nature of the mind, had the intention of sustaining the authenticity of human existence that formerly had been ratified by God. It was his purpose to keep all things from becoming 'weightless'. . . . Different individual temperaments committed to incompatible cultural predilections, will respond to *Civilization and Its Discontents* in diverse ways, but all will take into account, positively or negatively, its powerful representation of the momentous claims which life makes upon us by very reason, it seems, of its hardness, intractability, and irrationality. The fabric of contradictions that Freud conceives human existence to be is recalcitrant to preference, to will, to reason; it is not to be lightly manipulated. His imagination of the human condition preserves something—much—of the stratum of hardness that runs through the Jewish and Christian traditions as they respond to the hardness of human destiny. Like the Book of Job it propounds and accepts the mystery and the naturalness—the natural mystery, the mysterious naturalness—of suffering. At the same time it has at its heart an explanation of suffering through a doctrine of something like original sin: not for nothing had Freud in his youth chosen John Milton as a favourite poet, and although of course the idea of redemption can mean nothing to him, he yet acquiesces, and with something of Milton's appalled elation, in the ordeal of man's life in history.[12]

I have quoted here at length in order to let you savor the sublime enmity which emanates from Trilling at the end—an enmity directed against a revolutionary use of Freud, against a permissive society, and, finally, against historical change and life itself. *Sincerity and Authenticity* is in many ways the swan song of a dying class in literary culture.

The reasons for Trilling's self-indulgent disillusionment are several and complexly interrelated, and, I suspect, still representative of much of our profession and its sub-discipline of critical theory. The most visible objects of Trilling's assault are such revisionary psychoanalytic thinkers and critics as Herbert Marcuse, Norman O. Brown, R. D. Laing, and David Cooper (even Michel Foucault comes in for a weary swat or two). All these critics of Freud and modern culture appear to Trilling as providing arguments and theories which authorize the counter-cultural revelling in all forms of excess, sexual, political, social, and even chemical. Trilling believes that these critics license, finally, madness as the most authentic of irrational responses to an essentially irrational and sick—an actively mortifying—society.[13]

But Trilling is really after other and more intimately threatening game than this—to him—ragtag band of scholarly misfits and chronic malcontents. For he is quite clearly after himself and that group of primarily literary intellectuals he has liberally represented for so many years as the genteely prophetic voice of their consciences. This circle of cultural critics is largely Jewish in origin, liberal but anticommunist in propensity, and generally ascendent in the humanities, without too many serious challenges during the Cold War period in America. Trilling is after, that is, the class responsible for disseminating the best that has been thought and said in his generation by his generation—all those progressive, adversarial ideas and values which the students of the Vietnam era turned against their academic fathers and against all aspects of modern American civilization in an outburst of apocalyptic discontent. Freud in this context sanctions Trilling's turning of the lash of his imperial scorn back upon himself and his class—a sublimely ironic passion play of imaginative self-flagellation which he recognizes as being such even as he appears to be compelled by the force of his own rhetoric to climactically enact:

> Who that has had experience of our social reality will doubt its alienated condition? And who that has thought of his experience in the light of certain momentous speculations made over the last two centuries, of which a few have been touched on in these pages, will not be disposed to find some seed of cogency in a view that proposes an antinomian reversal of all accepted values, of all received realities?
>
> But who that has spoken, or tried to speak, with a psychotic friend will consent to betray the masked pain of his bewilderment and solitude by making it the paradigm of liberation from the imprisoning falsehood of an alienated social reality? Who that finds intelligible the sentences which describe madness (to use the word that cant prefers) in terms of transcendence and charisma will fail to penetrate to the great refusal of human connection that they express, the appalling belief that human existence is made authentic by the possession of a power, or the persuasion of its posses-

sion, which is not to be qualified or restricted by the co-ordinate existence of any fellow man?

Yet the doctrine that madness is health, that madness is liberation and authenticity, receives a happy welcome from a consequential part of the educated public. And when we have given due weight to the likelihood that those who respond positively to the doctrine don't have it in mind to go mad, let alone insane—it is characteristic of the intellectual life of our culture that it fosters a form of assent which does not involve actual credence—we must yet take it to be significant of our circumstance that many among us find it gratifying to entertain the thought that alienation is to be overcome only by the completeness of alienation, and that alienation completed is not a deprivation or deficiency but a potency. Perhaps exactly because the thought is assented to so facilely, so without what used to be called seriousness, it might seem that no expression of disaffection from social existence was ever so desperate as this eagerness to say that authenticity of personal being is achieved through an ultimate isolateness and through the power that this is presumed to bring. The falsities of an alienated social reality are rejected in favor of an upward psychopathic mobility to the point of divinity, each one of us a Christ—but with none of the inconveniences of undertaking to intercede, of being a sacrifice, of reasoning with rabbis, of making sermons, of having disciples, of going to weddings and to funerals, of beginning something and at a certain point remarking that it is finished.[14]

This powerful if finally pathetic summary statement of his career is also, clearly, another (shall I say?) more "authentic" *imitatio Christi*. It is intended to belittle everyone else for not appearing to be as perspicacious as the great Lionel Trilling. Actually, however, it functions more as a sad prophecy of how far literary intellectuals will go in the coming years to discover some standard of cultural or social necessity, some measure of aesthetic and moral excellence, some principle of tragic reality which can legitimate their function in American society. For literary critics and critical theorists in the coming years, in order to establish themselves and secure their authority, will generally propose a vision akin to Trilling's here: a self-victimizing apotheosis of fate or destiny or necessity in some form or other which can ironically justify their marginal and alienated existences as the last guardians of the Judeo-Christian tradition who thereby know best how to revise it. Legitimate heirs all, they claim—as all actual usurpers do.

V

Speaking of fateful self-victimization and critical usurpation naturally brings us now to Harold Bloom and his set of Freudian appropriations. Recently, of course, Bloom has written several essays on Freud, including "Freud and the Sublime: A Catastrophe Theory of Creativity," "Freud's Concepts of Defense and the Poetic Will," (both of which are reprinted in *Agon: Towards a Theory of Revisionism* [1982]), and "Reading Freud: Transference, Taboo, and Truth," which appears in a recent festschrift for Northrop Frye.[15] In addition, the central chapter of *The Breaking of the Vessels* (1982), is entitled "Wrestling Freud" and this title tells its own tale. Finally, Bloom's recent essay, "Criticism, Canon-Formation, and Prophecy: The Sorrows of Facticity"[16] focuses climactically upon Freud and his last work, which was left unfinished by its author's demise, *An Outline of Psycho-analysis*. But in truth everything Bloom has ever written since at least "The Internalization of Quest-Romance" (1968) is saturated with Freud and psychoanalytic formulations.[17] It should come as no surprise, therefore, that Bloom has been promising for some time now a book, *Transference and Authority*, devoted to Freud.[18]

One obvious irony of this incredible speculative productivity on Bloom's part lies in the comparative simplicity of its shaping principle, which all the subsequent accretions and modifications, the various methodological applications, do little to substantially complicate. Bloom's theory of influence-anxiety argues first, last, and always that the dynamic of literary and even cultural change is the revisionary skepticism of the Oedipal son. Even when, in reaction to charges of oversimplification, Bloom denies that he transposes wholesale to literary history the lineaments of the family romance as characterized by Freud, he nevertheless continues to speak of the intertextual dimensions existing between earlier and later poets and writers in language essentially Freudian and Oedipal in nature. The precursor, great original, or poetic father and the ephebe, belated poet, or weak son define a realm of discourse between them, in which weak sons to appear strong must misread in their work the work of their imaginative progenitors by finding there a defect, a weakness, the absence of some effective defense, which only the fabulous creative potential of the sons can correct, fulfill, or remediate. In this revisionary manner, weak sons may seem to overcome the burdensome influence, the repressive memory, the belittling sublimity of their mortifying fathers. Where strong precursors are, there facilitating muses must come to be—at least according to Bloom's aesthetics of envy, betrayal—and emasculation.

It wasn't always this way, however, for Bloom. After an initial prelude of reading closely if provocatively for the time the Romantic poets in three generally well- received books,[19] Bloom's first phase of appropriating Freud for theoretical and ideological purposes begins in 1968 with "The Internalization of Quest-Romance," and continues in the other essays collected in *The Ringers in the Tower* (1971). In this essay Freud authorizes for Bloom a naturalistic humanism akin to that of Wordsworth's healing vision of nature and mind in a fragile creative harmony which nature must finally destroy, however much the imagination trumpets its apocalyptic hymns of protest and self-praise to the contrary, along the individual poet's own evasive way to death. Bloom, in short, appropriates a Freud similar to, if still milder than, the Freud of Trilling at the end—a Freud who sanctions a stance beyond culture and the modern moment of crisis, from which the agitation for social revolution in the late 1960s and early 1970s must ironically appear irrelevant if not silly. In this way, Bloom legitimates the growing marginalization, alienation, and political disaffection endemic to the literary culture of the time. Just as Trilling in this period finds in Freud's biological fatalism a vehicle for castigating the opposing self and its adversarial culture, so Bloom also discovers in Freud a means for transcending the present moment—at a cost nearly as great as that entailed by Trilling's espousal of a self-destructive aesthetic humanism.

Similarly, in his theoretical tetralogy of the mid-seventies—*The Anxiety of Influence* (1973), *A Map of Misreading* (1975), *Kabbalah and Criticism* (1975), and *Poetry and Repression* (1976)—Bloom, like Trilling in his second phase, continues to embrace Freud for his authorization of a position beyond culture, but like Trilling at the conclusion of his essay "Freud: Within and Beyond Culture" (1965) Bloom comes to realize that all such transcendent vantage points are the ficitonal productions of the specific historical and psychological circumstances and desires inspiring the attempt at transcendence. Consequently, Bloom must go beyond even Freud and resurrect a Gnostic principle of vision,

from the heights of which he, like Trilling before him, can condemn
the modern, which is now defined by Bloom as beginning with Wordsworth, then with Milton, and finally with the ascendency of orthodox
Christianity in the Western world.

In his most recent essays, Bloom has appropriated Freud in a way
resembling most strikingly the Freud in Trilling's earliest essay on the
topic from *The Liberal Imagination* ("Freud and Literature" [1940]). For
Bloom now discovers that our culture, essentially literary or figurative
in nature, has been defined by the primarily literary or imaginative
achievement of Sigmund Freud. Freud, in other words, is our most comprehensive mythologist, our Milton or Moses:

> Freud wants us to believe that the superego represents all our aban-
> doned object affections, as well as the revenge that the abandoned
> take upon us. Literary facticity, as I seek to describe it, assimilates
> the superego to the id and makes the most powerful texts—the
> Bible, Shakespeare, Freud—a kind of drive within us as well as
> a partly internalized spirit of revenge. When the present is al-
> together changed into the past in the agon of reading, then fac-
> ticity has triumphed over the reader's Sublime, which is to say,
> it has voided the function of criticism. So powerful is Freud's own
> facticity for us that it prevents us from seeing the extent to which
> his reductive authority has augmented our inability to be strong
> critics. . . . Criticism cannot teach us to be Freud, or even how
> to avoid imprisonment by Freud. The function of criticism at the
> present time, as I conceive it, cannot be to liberate us from the
> brute factuality of our dependent relation to culture, whether that
> culture be biblical or Freudian. But criticism alone can teach us
> to stop literalizing our cultural dilemmas. Education when it is
> most authentic, centers upon the precise project of showing the
> student just what degree of freedom is possible for her or him in
> relation to the presentness of the cultural past. The most cirical
> of educations never will be capable of totally convincing us that
> the figurations of the past *are* figurations and not literal entities.
> Yahweh and the superego will go on haunting us, whether we are
> persuaded that they are ironies or synedoches or whatever. The
> strong critic does not arrive to exorcise the colors of our involun-
> tary imaginings, but she or he does stand at the threshold of
> culture's haunted mansion to admonish us to enter, not even as

the most alert among spectators, but as agonists armed with the past's own weapons, the only weapons that will defend us honorably against the force of the past.[20]

Just as Trilling in the 1940s looks to Freud at first for a principle of cultural reality—the sublimation of aggressive instincts via poetic displacement in dreams and other imaginative productions—which would justify and foster the tragic humanism he finds in the intellectual's position in modern life; so Bloom most recently paints Freud as the ultimate revisionary educator, the neo-Romantic creator of the modern mind, whose work is as much an authoritative fact for us and the way we see things and function in the world as the Bible has been for traditionalists. For, according to what Bloom says here, it is Freud who best can teach us how to fail with nobility and honor—that is, to fail, as he believes we must, in our struggle with the greatness of the past, precisely by our recognition that we cannot help but deify or demonize the past, even as we lie imaginatively against all the vicissitudes of our life in time. If Trilling's original use of Freud inspires the liberal imagination of American literary intellectuals during the Cold War; then Bloom's latest turn of the revisionary screw with respect to Freud exploits the most sublimely belittling elements of the Freudian idiom in a manner apparently intended to put an end to all projects of "inspiration," whatever their nature, that are not as fiercely reductive as his own now-all-too-typical project of disillusionment.

Coming full circle as we do here by closing this dialectical history I feel I must ask, what is it that compels American critics in their speculative appropriations of Freud and his works to propose an increasingly self-conscious literary conception of reality which speaks always of sublimity and heroism, but always at the expense of pleasure and so, ultimately, of life?

VI

I think that the recent work of the American Marxist theorist, Fredric Jameson, provides the suggestion of an answer to this far from rhetorical question. In a now classic exposition of Freud's leading French interpreter, entitled "Imaginary and Symbolic in Lacan: Marxism, Psychoanalytic Criticism, and the Problem of the Subject" (1977), and in his tremendously influential magnum opus, *The Political Unconscious*

(1981), Jameson appropriates Lacan's revisions of Freud's theories of the unconscious, of repression, and of the dream-work for a socially symbolic understanding of the subject and the various narratives in and through which Lacan like Foucault and Derrida in their different ways, claims, that the subject is constituted.

Baldly summarized, Jameson's position in both these texts relies upon Lacan's formative revision of Freud. This revision consists principally in Lacan's discovery in Freud of the notion that the unconscious is structured as a language and, consequently, the human subject that speaks, always must stand vis-à-vis the unconscious in a relation of radical alterity or otherness. (That Trilling, like Burke and Bloom after him, also recognizes this notion in Freud goes without saying.) "The unconscious," Lacan says in a currently famous pronouncement, "is the discourse of the Other," and it articulates itself primarily in a register of language Lacan calls "the imaginary." This kind of discourse is an aesthetic or specular one in which the subject is constituted as if in a quest for an illusory union with an idealized self-image. This fiction of a quest which structures the psyche in the discourse of the imaginary arises from the experience of the mirror-stage of infancy, when the child first recognizes as realizable an ideal vision of wholeness and unity by gazing into the glass at its own image.

The Imaginary is thus a kind of discursive misreading which is constitutive of that portion of the unconscious Freud terms the id. Its manifestations appear in our dreams, our fantasies, and our delusions, as well as—in fragmentary and displaced forms—the various symptoms of neurosis. This language of the unconscious contrasts strikingly with the language of authority, rationality, and law which Lacan designates as the Symbolic, and which appears with the passing—or rather, the submerging—of the Oedipus complex, when the individual subject recognizes in the name of the Father the necessity of repression for civilized life. (Needless to say this latter recognition scene is never a once-and-for-all kind of experience.) This register of language, the Symbolic, is a form of discourse constitutive of the Freudian superego and of the more or less "realistic" ego-ideals of cultural achievement and socially symbolic, even ritualistic, acts such as may be entailed in any institutionalized setting. One thinks of the theater, or the Mass, or the asylum and prison, as obvious cases in point.

What Jameson predicts in his 1977 essay on Lacan is that the distinction between these two kinds of disourse or registers of language, these two different idioms, may become useful for critical theory in the

coming years, especially for our understanding of narrative structure and
its social functions:

> We have thus, strengthened by this detour through Lacan's own
> literary criticism, returned to our hypothesis that whatever else
> it is, the distinction between the Imaginary and the Symbolic and
> the requirement that a given analysis be able to do justice to the
> qualitative gap between them, may prove to be an invaluable in-
> strument for measuring the range or the limits of a particular way
> of thinking. If it is always unsatisfying to speculate on what a Lacan-
> ian literary criticism ought to be in the future, if it is clear that
> the "Seminar on 'The Purloined Letter' " cannot possibly con-
> stitute a model for such criticism, since on the contrary the literary
> work is in it a mere pretext for a dazzling illustration of a non-
> literary thesis, then at least we may be able to use the concept
> of the two orders or registers as a means for demonstrating the
> imbalance of other critical methods, and of suggesting ways in
> which they may be coordinated, and an eclectic pluralism over-
> come. So, for instance, it seems abundantly clear that the whole
> area of image-study and image-hunting must be transformed, when
> we grasp the image content of a given text, not as so many clues
> to its ideational content (or "meaning"), but rather as the sedi-
> mentation of the imaginary material on which the text must work,
> and which it must transform. The relationship of the literary text
> to its image content is thus—in spite of the historic preponderance
> of the sensory in modern literature since Romanticism—not that
> of the production of imagery, but rather of its mastery and control
> in ways which range from outright repression (and the transfor-
> mation of the sensory image into some more comfortable concep-
> tual symbol) to the more complex modes of assimilation of sur-
> realism and, more recently, of schizophrenic literature. Only by
> grasping images—and also the surviving fragments of authentic
> myth and delusion—in this way, as that trace of the Imaginary,
> of sheer private or physiological experience, which has undergone
> the sea-change of the Symbolic, can criticism of this kind recover
> a vital and hermeneutic relationship to the literary text.[21]

I have quoted this passage at length in order to suggest as precisely and
economically as possible what Jameson's program for criticism is, and
to suggest further that in The Political Unconscious he has himself attempted single-handedly to enact that program. From a voice crying

in the wilderness, Jameson would become what he has so eloquently prophesized.

To put a complex and comprehensive argument as briefly as space permits, Jameson in The Political Unconscious constructs a comprehensive theory of the novel as a socially symbolic act, in which a dialectic of ideology and utopian vision, corresponding loosely to Lacan's opposition of the Symbolic and the Imaginary, structures as it fissures the narrative line. The result is that the conventions of the genre, whether those of the classic realistic novel or those of the now more popular Romance, function as enabling constraints upon the full expression of the repressed political critique inherent in the complete utopian vision being partially represented and contained by the generic necessities of plot-construction. (In this argument, "reality" appears in the texts of novels as a consciously unacknowledged "absent cause" akin to Althusser's idea of the material conditions of life or to Freud's idea of traumatic experiences, neither of which can be represented directly in a unified conceptual totality.) Conrad's Lord Jim with its disturbing double plot of the Patna incident and the second chance for Jim in Patusan provided by Stein, best exemplifies Jameson's theory for him.[22]

What Jameson has done here is quite typical of poststructuralist appropriations of Freud. It is a highly mediated appropriation for one thing. Freud's theories of the unconscious, of dream-distortion, and of repression and the rest appear in Jameson's texts via their comparatively radical Lacanian revisions. And for another thing, Lacan's "Freud" is combined by Jameson with a wide variety of critical theories and names— Greimas, Propp, Frye, Nietzsche, Marx, Hegel, Althusser, Foucault, the Frankfurt School, Derrida—just to cite a few. These figures and the positions they represent are also present in Jameson in highly mediated and revised forms. The point in saying this is not that Trilling and Bloom are any truer to their sources in Freud or anyone else. Rather, it is that by coming at Freud and company in this way Jameson hopes apparently to recontextualize the psychoanalytic discourse he deploys and thereby avoid the dialectical dead-end of Freud's other, equally prominent American critical heirs. Also symptomatic of our time, Jameson gives a political twist to all his revisionary mediations, Freudian or otherwise.

In any event, where Jameson becomes most representative of this kind of criticism is where he also becomes most suggestive of an answer to our question of why American critical theorists celebrate the sublime and heroic at the expense of pleasure and of life, often exactly when they think they are championing the here and now or even, as in Jameson's own case, the newly emerging, possibly utopian, world order:

> History is therefore the experience of Necessity, and it is this alone which can forestall its thematization or reification as a mere object of representation or as one master code among many others. Necessity is not in that sense a type of content, but rather the inexorable *form* of events; it is therefore a narrative category in the enlarged sense of some properly narrative political unconscious which has been argued here, a retextualization of History which does not propose the latter as some new representation or "vision," some new content, but as the formal effects of what Althusser, following Spinoza, calls an "absent cause." Conceived in this sense, History is what hurts, it is what refuses desire and sets inexorable limits to individual as well as collective praxis, which its "ruses" turn into grisly and ironic reversals of their overt intention. But this History can be apprehended only through its effects, and never directly as some reified force. This is indeed the ultimate sense in which History as ground and untranscendable horizon needs no particular theoretical justification: we may be sure that its alienating necessities will not forget us, however much we might prefer to ignore them.[23]

If Jameson's grimly gleeful tone in this conclusion to his long theoretical introduction to *The Political Unconscious* sounds like Bloom at the end of his previously cited essay "The Sorrows of Facticity," or even like Trilling at the end of "The Authentic Unconscious" from *Sincerity and Authenticty*; it is because for all his reflexive revisionary labor, theoretical inclusiveness, and principled social concern, Jameson, too, ultimately defines the Real—Lacan's virtually empty third register of psychic discourse—as Trilling, Bloom, and their "Freuds" do before him. That is, all three critics, sounding vaguely like frontier preachers, define the Real as what Emerson first termed in his finest later essay, "Fate," the "Beautiful Necessity"—that awful figurative representation of reality as the power of death which is always so delightfully fitting for the ascetic spirit of criticism in America to behold.

VII

Perhaps, however, I should allow Freud the last word on this fateful internalization and re-projection of "reality" as a severe disciplinary necessity—which is fatally beautiful only to those possessed by the most perverse of speculative imaginations, so anxious as they are to act upon the world, whether in a humanly meaningful manner or not:

> It is unlikely that such generalizations can be universally correct. Some portion of the cultural acquisitions have undoubtedly left a precipitate behind them in the id; much of what is contributed by the super-ego will awaken an echo in the id; not a few of the child's new experiences will be intensified because they are repetitions of some primaeval phylogenetic experience.
> 'Was du ererbt von deinen Vätern hast,
> Erwirb es, um es zu besitzen.'
> ('What thou hast inherited from thy fathers,
> Acquire it to make it thine.')
> Thus the super-ego takes up a kind of intermediate position between the id and the external world; it unites in itself the influences of the present and the past. In the establishment of the super-ego we have before us, as it were, an example of the way the present is changed into the past . . .[24]

It would appear, according to the logic of this argument, that literary critics and their offspring, critical theorists, must repeatedly become the unconscious gravediggers of the future, doesn't it? My only suggestion at this time, in light of such an apparently perennial development in American culture, is that it may be advisable now to close our Faustian "Freuds" and open our—eyes!

NOTES

1. This quotation comes from the conclusion to the third of the "Contributions to the Psychology of Love," "The Taboo of Virginity" (1918), in Freud, *Collected Papers, Vol 4*, trans. and ed. Joan Riviere (New York: Basic Books, 1959), 235. Freud's point is to suggest how the taboo of virginity and neurotic resentment of wayward wives for their husbands arise from similar psychic origins. All I mean to suggest by using it as my epigraph here is that, perhaps, this similar psychology of resentment may be at work in the appropriations of Freud by his critics.

2. Freud, *An Outline of Psycho-analysis*, trans. and ed. James Strachey (New York: Norton, 1949, 1969), 63.

3. Robert C. Solomon, "Freud's Neurological Theory of Mind," in *Freud: A Collection of Critical Essays*, ed. Richard Wollheim (New York: Anchor Books, 1974), 44.

4. I am not suggesting that Sulloway is specifically indebted to Solomon, only that he follows a similar line of argument.

5. See Part VI, "Paranoid Delusion Formation" in Fisher and Greenberg, eds., *The Scientific Evaluation of Freud's Theories and Therapy* (New York: Basic Books, 1978), 288-346.

6. In an appended bibliographical essay to the first volume of his multivolume study, *The Bourgeois Experience: Victoria to Freud*, which is entitled *The Education of the Senses*, Peter Gay vigorously denies Foucault's interpretation of repression even as he uses it.

7. *The History of Sexuality, Vol, I: An Introduction* (New York: Vintage, 1978, 1980), 159.

8. See "Art and Neurosis" and "Freud and Literature" in *The Liberal Imagination* (New York: Viking, 1950).

9. For an excellent overview of these developments and relationships, see Perry Meisel's introduction, entitled significantly, "Freud as Literature," to his collection, *Freud: A Collection of Critical Essays* (Englewood Cliffs, N.J.: Prentice-Hall, Inc., 1981).

10. *The Liberal Imagination*, 87-88.

11. The tone and thrust of the later Trilling may be suggested by his concluding remarks of the Preface to *Beyond Culture* (New York: Viking, 1965), xvii-xviii: "In our adversary culture such experience as is represented in and proposed by art moves toward becoming an idea, even an ideology, as witness the present ideational and ideological status of sex, violence, madness, and art itself. If in this situation the rational intellect comes into play, it may be found that it works in the interests of experience."

12. *Sincerity and Authenticity* (Cambridge, Mass.: Harvard University Press, 1972), 151, 156-57.

13. There is a certain irony in imagining Mark Rudd and the Yippies storming Trilling's beloved Columbia campus in 1968 with remaindered copies of *The Opposing Self* in their hands to ward off billy-club wielding police.

14. *Sincerity and Authenticity*, 171-72.

15. See *Centre and Labyrinth: Essays in Honor of Northrop Frye*, ed. Chaviva Hosek et al. (Toronto: The University of Toronto Press, 1983), 309-28.

16. "Criticism, Canon-Formation, and Prophecy: The Sorrows of Facticity," *Raritan* 3 (Winter 1984): 1-20.

17. See *The Ringers in the Tower* (Chicago: The University of Chicago Press, 1971), 13-35.

18. Even Bloom's Gnostic Fantasy *The Flight to Lucifer* (1979) is so saturated.

19. The best overviews of Bloom's career are Frank Lentricchia's in *After the New Criticism* (Chicago: The University of Chicago Press, 1979) and Elizabeth Bruss's *Beautiful Theories: The Spectacle of Discourse in Contemporary Criticism* (Baltimore: The Johns Hopkins University Press, 1982).

20. Bloom, "Sorrows," 19-20.

21. Jameson, "Imaginary and Symbolic in Lacan," in *Literature and Psychoanalysis: The Question of Reading: Otherwise*, ed. Shoshana Felman, (Ithaca, N.Y.: Cornell University Press, 1980), 375-76.

22. I have discussed this aspect of Jameson's book at greater length in "The Ideology of Romance," *Contemporary Literature* 34 (Summer 1982).

23. *The Political Unconscious: Narrative as Socially Symbolic Act* (Ithaca, N.Y.: Cornell University Press, 1981), 102.

24. Freud, *An Outline of Psycho-analysis*, 63-64.

9. From Structures of Meaning to the Meaning of Structures

MICHAEL HAYS

During the past ten to fifteen years, a lively struggle has been unfolding on the playing fields of academic criticism. Each side has claimed victory in this ongoing battle between the Anglo-American tradition and its (mostly) French-inspired opponents; but there seems to have been no absolute rout as yet. This is all the more surprising given the general assumption that there is a fundamental difference between the methods and intentions and, therefore, the values of the practitioners of the new and the newer criticism. This "difference" has in fact become one of the code words in the game, signalling to players and bystanders alike the claim of a superior perceptual position available within the critical models derived from Saussure and Lévi-Strauss.

Since "difference" is both a sign and the theme of the newer criticism, its exponents have repeatedly gone on the offensive by demonstrating the failure of traditional critics to discover its traces—the hidden contradictions, the binary oppositions, that subvert their interpretations from within. Scholars loyal to the Anglo-American tradition have countered with attacks on the supposed superficiality of critical methods that only play with "surface" relations between abstractions such as signifier and signified, *langue* and *parole*. Despite the temptation to act as arbiter in this contest, I do not intend to stake a claim with or for either side here. Instead, in keeping with the implicit rules of the game, I want to look at both sides a bit differently than either of the contestants might. My interest is in fact not in what separates them but in what binds them together, and, therefore, my perspective will not be one that emerges from within either of their specific domains, but rather one that will scan the periphery of a possible historical linkage between them on the level of reception and practice.

Interestingly enough, the possibility of making such a connection emerged during the process of thinking about another project—a survey of the impact of semiotics on the criticism of the past fifteen years. The initial shift in my plan came about as I was rereading a 1966 essay by Geoffrey Hartman in which he discusses the similarities between the work of Northrop Frye and Lévi-Strauss.[1] Although Hartman subsequently came to a different and far more critical view of Frye's work,[2] this initial conflation of Frye's project for a universal critical system with the structuralist model elaborated by Lévi-Strauss seemed to suggest a desire both to remain within and flee from the Anglo-American critical scene. If so, we might ask what there was in the criticism of Frye and his contemporaries that could appeal to such a desire.

Raising this question led first of all to remembering that Frye was far from the only academic of the fifties and early sixties who was interested in setting up a "universal" critical model. His archetypal quartet is only the most overtly formalist of a number of critical enterprises that sought to define the literary-critical space in terms of some "unified theory" (S, 14) of oppositions. The others that I discuss are merely examples that came to mind most readily because their titles also announce a preoccupation with binary relations, supposedly one of the hallmarks of the "later criticism": Isaiah Berlin's The Hedgehog and the Fox; M.H. Abrams' The Mirror and the Lamp; George Steiner's Tolstoy or Dostoyevsky; and Maurice Valency's The Flower and the Castle.[3] Why this nascent interest in binary oppositions before and outside the structuralist revision? And how are these antinomies different than those uncovered by contemporary (post) structuralist criticism? These questions lead us to an investigation of the manner in which Anglo-American critics of the fifties and early sixties organized both the resistance to and the reception of structuralist theory.

In the earliest of these books, The Hedgehog and the Fox (first published in 1951 and reissued in an expanded version in 1953), we find that Berlin is above all concerned with the "great chasm" that separates two ways of looking at the world. There are those who "relate everything to a single central vision, one system, more or less coherent" and "those who pursue many ends, often unrelated and even contradictory, connected, if at all, only in some de facto way. . ." (HF, 1). According to Berlin, these two points of view existed side by side in Tolstoy, and the tension of their difference produced in him a devastation that led to what Berlin calls Tolstoy's final, "tragic" condition (HF, 81).

In order to explain this tragic conflict between Tolstoy's desire to expound a "unifying pattern [for] the world" and the "differences which divide and forces which disrupt [this]world," Berlin, instead of examining Tolstoy's context in nineteenth-century Russia, turns to a distinction made by the Greek poet Archilochus:[4] "The fox knows many things, but the hedgehog knows one big thing" (HF, 1). Berlin uses these terms not simply to depict Tolstoy's divided psyche, but to represent the "deepest differences which divide writers and thinkers, and, it may be, humans in general" (HF, 1). He then goes on to name the authors, the tradition that precedes Tolstoy (and by extension, us as well): Plato, Lucretius, Nietzsche, and some others were hedgehogs, while Herodotus, Aristotle, Pushkin, and Balzac were foxes. Thus, what "divides" Tolstoy is not particular to him or his time; it emerges as a "natural" division between "humans in general," a division that has always existed and has always permitted grand literary and philosophical achievements. The dangerous opposition discovered in Tolstoy's work, the dissolution of the notion of historical and intellectual continuity when confronted by the force of historical difference, is thus overcome in advance, re-covered by a (Western) tradition that proposes unity even in difference. Tolstoy's "tragedy," therefore, lies merely in his inability to opt for one or the other of these two equally viable, here parallel rather than contradictory or mutually exclusive segments of that tradition. The struggle between irreconcilable positions implicated in the intitial opposition, the struggle between objective and subjective, order and disorder, unity and difference, is reduced to a case history.

   This aspect of Berlin's work is especially interesting since it points to the context out of which his work arises. The "case history" is a typical attribute of the thinking that emerged with nineteenth-century positivism, as is the closed, ordered movement of The Hedgehog and the Fox. This unexplored frame of reference (the nineteenth-century roots of Berlin's discourse) is also the source of a fundamental contradiction in the book: the claim of timelessness which Berlin makes for the tradition he elaborates is bound within a knowledge formation that is itself historical. But here, as in the other works I will be discussing, the goal is not to confront this problem of knowledge/history, but to escape its uncertainty by circumscribing its manifestations in specific, nonbinding instances of discord which, being singular, cannot jeopardize the system of meanings proposed by the critic. Here it is Tolstoy's psyche, not the tradition we have inherited, that is in contradiction with itself. In other words, "Tolstoy" serves not to reveal but to displace and hide the problem that underlies Berlin's text— the threat to a system of knowledge that had provided a sense of order and continuity for the critic's discourse and for the critical institution in general. I will come back to this point later.

The problem of the possible subversion of "unifying patterns" of knowledge is taken up again but in somewhat less dramatic terms in Abrams' *Mirror and the Lamp* (1953), which focuses "two exhaustive modes. . . . imaginative [read subjective] and rational. . . ." (*ML*, p. 335). Here the problem is discovered in a different place—in a temporal rather than a purely psychic space—but the gesture of discovery nonetheless encodes the same critical move. Both Abrams and Berlin select a site, distant in time and place, within which to locate and circumscribe the effects of a critical and historical awareness that could undermine the possibility of generating unified structures of knowledge and meaning. As the closing lines of the book indicate, much of Abrams' effort is directed at demonstrating that this problem of meaning is indeed not his own, or ours, but lies in the past as an object of historical investigation. "It was . . . in the Victorian period . . . that all discourse was thrown into the two exhaustive modes of imaginative and rational. . . ."

But before he can arrive at this confident summation, Abrams must begin by securing a place for his own discourse. He therefore introduces an "orientation of critical theories," which he asserts is necessary in view of the "incommensurable" critical positions available as he writes. This move is justified by the claim that in order to grasp the complexities of Romantic thought—the conceptual conflict he embodies in the figures of the mirror and the lamp—"our first need" is to find a frame of reference "simple enough to be manageable, yet flexible enough so that without undue violence to any one set of statements about art, it will translate as many sets as possible onto a single plain of discourse" (*ML*, 5). Thus, the complexities and contradictions that he suggests pervade our own critical world are to be reduced to a single denominator in the name of clarifying those of another.

The language in which Abrams expresses this desire to order several sets or systems of meaning within a large set is itself quite interesting, since it indicates that he has at least a proto-semiotic awareness that such "sets of statements" can be manipulated and "translated" precisely because they are closed systems, subsets within the larger set of the critical institution. Today, such a point of view would no doubt lead to some further thoughts about the necessarily artificial and even fictive nature of all such structures,[5] but here this incipient awareness is used against itself—not as a means of opening up a discussion of the multiple and contradictory structures of meaning embedded in the "incommensurable" criticism to which he refers, but as a means of justifying the enclosure and reduction of this multiplicity within a single critical construct, Abrams' own, which seems to require no such scrutiny.[6]

Freed from the present and from the problem of incommensurability, Abrams proceeds into the past. The critical disjunction is relocated in the Romantic period. There, Abrams finds it announced in the move away from a theory of the work of art as an imitation of something found in the external world to a notion of the artwork as a manifestation of the artist's subjectivity. The problem raised by this shift is indeed a serious one, since implicit in it is the possibility that not just the artist's work but discourse in general is forever locked away in a subjectivity that can find no corresponding objective ground. But even this difference is not explored before first being given a "universal" background. Abrams provides this background by discovering the "archetypal analogies" that precede and thus already contain the possibility of a distinctly romantic criticism (ML, 31). These archetypes are anchored in the past in such a way that the romantics' "new" subjectivity and the immediately "prior" theory of mimesis emerge (as did the oppositional structures in Berlin's work) as recent avatars of the classical tradition. Aristotle is the ground for mimesis, while Plotinus is credited with being the "chief begetter of the archetype of [projected subjectivity]." Both the "romantic theory of knowledge and the romantic theory of poetry can be accounted the remote descendents of this root image of Plotinian philosophy" (ML, 42, 59). A further step in Abrams' analysis next manages to fix the source of both positions in Aristotle alone (ML, 27). Origins, lineal descent, and the possibility of a simple narrative accounting for critical differences are the enabling notions embedded in these lines and, for that matter, in the entirety of Abrams' text. By proposing this image of continuity before narrating the Romantics' confrontation with the epistemological and, finally, ontological dilemma of a rupture between the self and the external world, the narration, framed as it is by an unproblematic tradition, is granted a closure and conclusiveness that might otherwise be called into question by its own subject matter. Disorder, both that lurking in criticism of the present and that of the romantic past, is submerged in the serenity of a discourse firmly grounded in the idea of an original order. Having established this connection Abrams

can suggest a unity of artist and text at the very moment that this relation is being called into question. In his reading of the Romantics,
neither the artist-subject nor the text is granted the power to reflect
or represent the external world, but nonetheless Abrams is now free
to propose a relationship of organic unity between the two, one that
provides a sense of order both for the artist and for life itself (*ML*, 69,
218-25).

Even more than Abrams, George Steiner announces what seems
then to have been the need to "impose order and interpretation on
the chaos of experience" (*TD*, 6), not just literary/critical experience
but that of life in general. In order to set about this task, Steiner too
has recourse to the opposition between rational (objective) and irrational (subjective) modes of perception. From the outset he naturalizes
this opposition by suggesting that the poles of this binary correspond
to "two types among men's souls."[7] The first type is represented by
Tolstoy, while the second is embodied in Dostoyevsky, the "contemner
of rationalism" (*TD*, 346).

Of course, it is amusing to note that Steiner discovers in Tolstoy
only one half of the problem that Berlin located fully within Tolstoy's
being, but this difference in their use of "Tolstoy" is, in the long run,
much less interesting than the similarity in the problems that lie behind
their choices of representative figures. According to Steiner, it is the
obligation of the critic to confront the "chaos" that has invaded contemporary experience and to bring it under control. This can best be
accomplished if criticism turns to the past and to a "remembrance of
our great lineage" that will deny the instability of the present (*TD*, 4).
We must be made aware that "tradition and the long ground-swell of
unity are no less real that that sense of disorder and vertigo which the
new dark ages have loosed upon us" (*TD*, 5). Not the current problems
of language, text, and history, but "the meaning of language when it
is in a condition of beauty or of truth" (*TD*, 5), not the present but
an ideal past is the *telos* toward which Steiner's text will move. This,
as I will try to show, is the same program that inspired Berlin and
Abrams, but in their work it remains a more or less hidden agenda.

The notion of a coherent past and the inscription in it of stable
authorial presence, not the absolute reality of any given author, is the
deciding factor here. The works of Tolstoy and Dostoyevsky become
for Steiner the means of proclaiming the archetypal patterns that have
governed and, therefore, must still govern the history of Western culture.

Though the two novelists stand in contrariety "even beyond their deaths" (TD, 347), this antinomy is rendered harmless by construing it as an embodiment of the difference between the epic and the drama. In other words, once the initial opposition has been subsumed within their names and further reduced to a question of genre, each of these authors can serve to reveal a part of that "long ground-swell of unity" embodied in our literary tradition, "the matchless tradition [that] unfolds from Homer to Milton, to the splendours of Athenian, Elizabethan and neo-classical drama, to the masters of the novel" (TD, 4-5). Once again the initial problem is evaded in the name of an unassailable (and unexamined) continuity. The function of the critic in this case is not to examine the present, not to "atomize" that which already seems in jeopardy, but to provide a calming discourse able to mediate between the reader and a less threatening image of "transcendent dignity" (TD, 6-7).

Four years later, in *The Flower and the Castle*, Maurice Valency undertook much the same project.[8] Although he centers his text on another set of authors (his emphasis on the drama leads him to choose Ibsen and Strindberg), the primary difference between him and the other critics I have mentioned is his even greater emphasis on the need to secure the present within the past.

After opening with a brief discussion of what had happened in the drama during the preceding century, Valency announces that

> long before Ibsen, the ancient edifice was crumbling. By the middle of the nineteenth century the system of values which had stood firm during the long twilight of the Renaissance seemed to be so thoroughly decayed that it would no longer support the weight of doubt. Yet to this day it has not toppled. Ramshackle as they are we still inhabit the ancient mansions. . . . (FC, 2)

Where Joseph Wood Krutch and others whom Valency cites thought Ibsen and Strindberg "marked the end of the ordered, rational, comfortable world" (FC, 4), Valency uses these same playwrights to describe a different relation between the present and the past. "Before Ibsen, nobody wrote like Ibsen. But Ibsen did not make a new departure. . . . He marks . . . neither the beginning nor the end of a tradition" (FC, 4). Instead, Ibsen represents for Valency the "orderly movement of progressive thought since the time of Rousseau," that is, the rational point of view over against which he places Strindberg as respresentative of an irrationalist "reaction" (FC, 4). But even this reaction is not new or somehow destructive of order; on the contrary, it "illustrates the development of a highly moral nature . . . which, after great spiritual tribulation, found its faith and made peace with God. The process and the type are classical. St. Paul prefigured both" (FC, 5). Thus, Valency can go on to claim, repeating the formula within which he had enclosed Ibsen's work, that, "before Strindberg, nobody wrote like Strindberg; but Strindberg also said nothing new" (FC, 6).

Once again, a possible threat to rational order and to our belief in the continuity between the past and the present has been contained before the fact. "Ibsen" and "Strindberg" invoke the possibility of change and difference only to erase it. They reembody the distinction between the objective and the subjective, the mimetic and the "imaginative," and once again this opposition is construed not as a problem of understanding but as a sign of differences in individual being: "from the plays of Ibsen it is possible to reconstruct Ibsen, and the plays of Strindberg are Strindberg himself" (FC, 7). This move to contain difference within the individual subject and the tradition is certainly not suprising, given what we have already seen; it is all the more striking therefore that Valency also seems impelled to draw our attention to other events that are subversive of his entire project. Toward the end of his book he notes that "the analytical tendency of impressionism. . . . brought about, ultimately, a dissolution of the subject, and what had begun as an attempt to represent nature more truly ended in the destruction of the conceptual basis of nature itself" (FC, 368).

If we take this statement at face value, it not only renders Valency's discussion of Ibsen and Strindberg problematic, it also calls into question the herculean efforts our other three critics have undertaken in order to protect the notion of the subject, and critical discourse itself, from the threat of dissolution implicit in the binary oppositions with which they began. Thus, Valency's brief comment opens a way into the problem and the critical trajectory that lies behind, or better, submerged in, the works I have discussed here. He had already given an unintentional summary of this movement in his introduction, while assuring his readers that they need not turn to the seemingly more problematic drama of the twentieth century: "The texture of the drama has loosened. Its forms have developed. Its subject matter has been several times renewed. New currents are felt; new departures announced." But these can remain unexamined since "essentially nothing has altered"

(FC, 1). "Anyone who understands what [was of concern to Ibsen and Strindberg] will have gone a long way toward comprehending the rest" (FC, v). This "rest," all that is problematic for the present, all the literary, critical, and historical events that might cast into doubt a discourse aimed at stabilizing the critic's own world, is ignored in order to establish a narrative continuity in the name of Ibsen and Strindberg. But despite Valency's valiant effort to contain the tensions of language and meaning, subject and object within the characters of this narrative, they constantly reemerge and draw our attention away from the figures he discusses to the critic himself and to the problems that his text serves not to solve, but to deny.

It is these gaps and contradictions that we must examine, therefore, if we want to understand the connection between Valency, Steiner, Abrams, Berlin and their historico-critical context. What strikes one most of all in reading their works is the incongruity between the difficulty embodied in the initial binary—in each case a juxtaposition of the rational and the irrational, an antinomy announcing the possibility that rational, referential assertion, the establishment of a single coherent system of meaning, is impossible—and the simplicity with which it is resolved. The epistemological aporia is not confronted as such, but is instead lodged within an individual as his mode of being, and then further enclosed in a double structure that displaces the problem into the past and into the noncontradictory linearity of the Western tradition. The seeming rigor and clarity of this movement is belied, however, by the surprising and unexplained intrusion of other problems, problems in critical interpretation, ruptures in the crtitic's own history and process of understanding, that remain unexplored. Such problems as the "destruction of the conceptual basis of nature," are, of course, the real, if hidden objects of these works, each of which sets out to deny them existence by containing them within the closure of its own discourse.

It is in this sense that we can best understand Valency's and Steiner's insistence that the "function of art has been to bring order out of chaos" (FC, 8). It is not really in art but in the critics' interpretations that such order is achieved. In each of the cases examined here, it is the historical account provided by the critic's narrative that supercedes and contains the possible disorder located in its subject matter. This subject matter, rather than being allowed to stand as a possibly exemplary model for the exploration of the epistemological and

ontological problems that it proposes, is instead used to deny such problems any general validity. But this denial and the desire that lies behind
it must surely belong to the narrator of these "histories" and not to
the material itself. Thus, we can assume that the critic, not the artist
or the work of art, is the actual center of each of these texts. It is the
critic himself that needs, and therefore "reveals," a unity between the
tradition, the text, and the artist's inner life. Steiner provides a clear
indication of this need when he claims that the "job" of the critic is to
"mediate" between the author and the reader in order to expose the
"heroic efforts of the human spirit to impose order and interpretation
on the chaos of experience," and capture "man's transcendent dignity,"
a dignity Steiner lodges within the "tradition and the long ground-swell
of unity" it serves to represent (TD, 5-6). Likewise, Berlin finds in Tolstoy
the "insight that reveals the nature and structure of [the social, moral,
political, and spiritual] worlds . . . not a makeshift substitute, an empirical *pis aller* to which recourse is had only so long as relevant scientific techniques are insufficiently refined; its business is altogether different: . . . it distinguishes the real from the sham, . . . [the] movement
of events, or changing pattern of characteristics as something 'inexorable,' universal, pervasive. . . ," even in the face of historical disorder
(HF, 70-71).

The question that arises here is why these critics need to declaim
so vigorously about the existence of a universal structure of meaning.
If Berlin and his peers felt no challenge to their own assumptions about
the nature and structure of their world, about their techniques for
demonstrating these "universal" qualities, would they need to insist
that this challenge had already been met earlier and elsewhere? An
answer to the first of these questions emerges, albeit indirectly, in
Abrams' work at that moment when he justifies his own ordered return to the past with a reference to the complexities and confusion of
critical language in the present. The current problem of language, the
"diverse terms," or "terms with diverse signification" (ML, 5), the
polysemy that would cast doubt on the stability and validity of the critic's
own discourse, not that of the Romantics, is the hidden locus of the
book. Thus, the "archetypal analogies" Abrams proposes, which serve
to "interpret, systematize and evaluate the facts of art" (ML, 31), actually announce the critic's own need for a system of abstractions with
which to insulate the critical process from its own history, from the
possibility of the world appearing "inchoate" (ML, 31), or as Steiner

put it, from the "disorder and vertigo that the new dark ages have loosed upon us" (*TD*, 5).

This desire also lurks behind each of these critics' attempts to demonstrate a coherence between the artist's psyche and his work. These efforts, which I have described above, serve, according to Berlin, to provide a "vision of the unity of experience, [a] sense of history that prevents our acts and thoughts from being self-defeating" (*HF*, 72). Furthermore, this vision is intended to supply a "depth" of meaning superior to that supplied by the "surface" readings produced by reason and science alone (*HF*, 78). Again we sense a note of personal anxiety. Why this fear of reason as a possible source of disunity and self-defeat? There is no room here for a detailed answer to such questions; I can only point toward two related problems. The first, and most obvious, is that inscribed in the titles of their works: the binary opposition that, were it in fact to be examined as a current problem of meaning forma-tion, would lead to the destruction of the epistemological ground upon which traditional Anglo-American critical practice had been built. If there is no certain connection between the self and others, between the self and the external world, then the possibility of a criticism "in depth," a coherent representation of the connections between the in-dividual, life, and art, is dispersed into a series of non sequiturs, subjec-tive gestures of desire for a unity that exits only as a fiction of the past or as a utopian ideal. The critic would then find himself bereft of the possibility of laying claim to any systematic knowledge of enduring ar-tistic "values"; deprived of his raison d'etre, he would be a mere fab-ricator of cultural fictions.

This threat to the traditional critics' activity is serious enough by itself, but when combined with the events of recent history, it takes on an even more ominous character. To grasp this connection we need only to be aware that the "dark ages," to which Steiner refers without further elaboration, and which all of these critics wish to fend off, are not simply the years of disorder that now pass unexamined under the names "World War II" or "the Holocaust." They are also the subse-quent years during which critics and intellectuals on both sides of the Atlantic fled from recognition of the complicity of their own discourse in the production of those particularly destructive "visions of unity"— from an awareness of the intellectual as well as ideological failure of their idealism.[9] Thinking about these questions might well seem "self-defeating," to borrow Berlin's phrase, since such thoughts would call into question the historical and institutional roles of the critic as well as his criticism. Indeed, with the validity of his own self-image at stake, the critic might well wish to flee once more into the production of a coherent past and the idea of a stable subject-object (artist-art work) relationship. Certainly, this would be a less painful move to make than would a turning away from the idea of universals to an examination of the critic's own history and ideology, or even to the "surface" of texts, since this latter gesture, too, would seem to jeopardize the project of meaning production that, as Steiner points out, had been the goal and the justification of the critic's activity up to that moment.

The sense of urgency that arises in the works of these critics can, therefore, best be understood not as a heightened desire to generate such structures of meaning for the artist and his art but as the result of their need to legitimate themselves and their practice. It is not, as Berlin's discussion of Tolstoy would have it, a problem of the artist as subject, but of the critic as subject—his ability to reestablish his position as coherent reader and interpreter, as mediator between art and artist, past and present. The degree to which Berlin wishes both to deny and, surreptitiously, to solve this problem is indicated by the rigor with which he displaces and isolates it in Tolstoy as his "tragedy." This term itself is a token of the difference between the beginning problematic and its textual avatar. It comes from the vocabulary of "universals" used to link the literary tradition to life itself. But however much Berlin and his readers may sympathize with the Tolstoy he presents, the "tragedy" he describes remains entirely Tolstoy's own. The term is too strong insofar as Tolstoy's experience of psychic conflict in no way implicates us or the world. On the contrary, as indicated earlier, Berlin has taken pains from the beginning to isolate this particular conflict of rational and irrational perspectives in a single individual, while otherwise granting a transparent history of coexistence to the poles of the binary. Berlin's references to the tradition serve to demonstrate the absence of any problem, the absence of this possibly tragic condition from our world, yet at the same time the term is retained. It is the echo of a fate from which the critic has escaped, and *The Hedgehog and the Fox* as a whole is the path by which the escape is made good. An ideal discursive continuity has reduced the dangerous recognition of historical and subjective discontinuity to a generic trope.[10]

Valency comes the closest of any of these critics to reopening these questions, though not intentionally, to be sure. In the lines I quoted earlier, he alludes to the possibility that both the notion of historical continuity and the subject had already been cast into doubt. Later, he also mentions the "two great wars, a long series of social and political cataclysms, the unexampled widening of knowledge" (FC, 363), that belong to the historical context from which his book emerges and that, if examined, would raise further questions about our received ideas concerning life and art. Of course, Valency does not go into detail about these events. "Ibsen" and "Strindberg" do not reveal more about them or their background. Instead they stand for the notion that "essentially nothing has altered." But because his is a book that claims to describe the modern drama, Valency is forced to mention, if only in passing, those other, later, dramatists that might be construed as tokens of a rather radical change in understanding. Thus it is that he twice refers to that "group of avant-garde dramatists who are now lumped together as 'absurdists' " (FC, 8,397). Who these playwrights are, why they were given this sobriquet and by whom are questions that ought to be dealt with, but cannot be, since they would challenge the most fundamental of Valency's positions. Such questions do not lead us confidently back to the tradition and to the assertion that "nothing has changed," but lead us instead to a recognition of the historical discontinuities and institutional imperatives that lie hidden in such claims. Furthermore, in the plays themselves the notions of epistemological and ontological continuity are revealed to be narrative gambits with which we fend off knowledge of a defeated subjectivity and of the metaphysical void which surrounds it. Therefore, these plays (and with them the critic's own present) are deftly put aside. They are turned into examples of a dramatic practice that is the heritage of the "charming irresponsibility" of Jarry: "What these works involve is principally a gesture of derision, the artist thumbing his nose at art, a relaxing, but not especially profitable artistic recreation" (FC, 8-9). Only in this manner can Valency escape a confrontation with the problems of the individual, of language and history as they are posed by the "derision" in the works of a Beckett or a Genet, for example.[11]

   If the other critics mentioned here are more successful at masking such questions, it is only because they have chosen to locate their critical enterprises in a terrain that seems more distant and, therefore, more secure. But for how long can such fundamental problems of understanding be ignored when they are already inscribed in the binary antinomies that open and pervade their texts? Already in the sixties another mode of analysis had begun to emerge, one in which such oppositions were explored quite differently—not in an effort to overcome them, but to reveal them as the structures that precede and organize the "meanings" granted to written and verbal texts and to other cultural artifacts as well. But works such as *The Raw and the Cooked, Les mots et les choses,* and *Writing and Difference* did not penetrate the world of Anglo-American criticism until some time later.[12] But did they then put an end to the critical practice and to the contradictions that underly the work of Berlin and the others I have discussed? It seems to me that the answer to this question is both yes and no, since this new appropriation of the binary opposition has frequently been put to work in Anglo-American criticism not in order to discover the historical nexus in which such contradictions arose, but to free the critic from the burden of both meaning and history.[13]

This transition was already underway in the works I have been examining, however. As we have seen, the hidden problem in each of them is not the difficulty they have in maintaining the structures of meaning that they wish to uphold (as and in the name of the tradition); it is, rather, the threat to criticism and the critic posed by the subversion of these structures. The events of history, both cognitive and cultural, belie not only the linearity of the critic's narrative but also the centrality of his role as narrator. In order to evade this problem, Berlin, Abrams, Steiner, and Valency all resort to the tactic of reducing alternative artistic and critical positions (that is, the evidence of historical and epistemological difference) to a single set of binary parallels. In so doing they also elevate the role of the critic to a position of absolute authority. It is the critic and not the artist or the work of art that assumes responsibility for the production of meaning—for the structures within which the text is incorporated and assumes its "value."[14] Indeed, the process of structuring itself acquires an importance far greater than that of any "meaning" granted the individual text, since the structure into which the critic inserts that text always contains the larger sense under which individual artistic variants are subsumed.[15] Frye's *Anatomy of Criticism* is, of course, the preeminent example of this development during the fifties, but the works I have discussed so far are more interesting and more poignant demonstrations of the difficult passage undertaken by the critic at this time in his move out of history into the security of his own abstractions.

Each of these structures of meaning, "the tradition" for example, can now be understood as a pseudonym for the critic and his practice, a projection into time and space of the critic's own desire for presence and continuity. At the same time, once a particular "name" no longer serves to assuage the anxiety of the critic, once there are too many gaps in the narrative it underwrites, too many "difficulties" which the critic must gloss over as do Valency and Abrams when they erase the vicissitudes of contemporary drama and criticism, that name can be "translated" and assigned a different sense, since what is essential here is the totalizing process, the act of discovering and naming structures, and not the names themselves. This is one of the most striking and successful aspects of the criticism of the period. Freed from the burden of history, whether their own or that of their subject matter, these critics could produce ever more systematic and reassuring structures and, at the same time, an ever greater need for their presence, since it is their discourse alone that identifies these structures and thereby "clarifies" their meaning.

"Archetypal analogies" or simply "archetypes," two terms that emerge in the fifties, can be read as tokens of this possibility. They insist on the critic's presence, his discovery of an all pervasive though hidden structure, while working to release him from the awkward moments found in the works discussed here. Gone is the troubling need to create a contextual history that might compel the critic to question the conceptual realms named "tradition," "subjective," "objective," "present," "past," "author," and "text"—a history that might ask these terms to comment on each other and on the critical process as well. In lieu of this possibility, the new discourse and its concomitant abstraction bespeaks a critical mode in which all such terms can still be named, but without the critic taking any responsibility for them. The shift is from language that proposes itself as a narrative, a language of referential content, to language that focuses on the forms in which the work of art and the discourse of others have appeared. It is of course at this point that we begin to see more clearly the connection between the criticism of the fifties and the newer criticism that burgeoned in the seventies. It is also here that I must return to the place at which I began and to Geoffrey Hartman's essay "Structuralism: The Anglo-American Adventure."

This text is an important milestone in our mapping of the transition of the critic and his discourse. In it, Hartman himself makes the passage I have just described and announces it in such a way that there seem to be far fewer knots in the skein from which he produces his critical web. By conflating the work of Lévi-Strauss with that of Frye and other Anglo-American critics, he bows to the past and a certain aspect of the critical tradition while describing the new method as a theorizing of formal relations that had "always" been important within a sector of the tradition (*BF*, 5-6). At the same time, Hartman asserts the need to turn away from the specifics of the work of art, the "arti-fact" still attached to place and time, toward the search for totalizing forms and a "unified field theory," one that is "not subject to this or that culture (a corpus of texts, a geographically or historically delimited area) but [is] the very process of mediation . . ." (*BF*, 4, 13). Culture is no longer to be identified with certain historical moments or texts and instead becomes the process of discovering mythic structures; and interpretation, as I have already indicated, becomes the act of naming these structures. It is the critic himself, who, despite Hartman's stan-dard references to the work of art as the instrument of mediation, is clearly the author of all meaning here. "Whatever literary structure is in itself, it must be spatial *to the critic*" (*BF*, 13; italics in the original). This is Steiner's critic/mediator come full-fledged. We should not be surprised therefore that Hartman was soon able to dismiss Lévi-Strauss as well, arguing that "literature. . . . must be of a more liberal and chancy" form than that suggested by Lévi-Strauss, who would relate all such forms to social function.[16] Not surprisingly, after eliminating these connections, Hartman closes his essay with a nod toward Auer-bach's theory that we are moving toward the end of history. He covers over the traces of his own activity by giving it a past and a necessity that lie outside critical activity, ironically enough in the very history that he has begun to erase. Neither is it surprising that a few years later Hartman would give an almost messianic tone to this activity by send-ing the critic into the wilderness.[17]

Of course, Hartman was not alone in his efforts to reground critical activity and, thereby, the critic himself within the secure space of lin-guistic abstractions. If we wish to understand the reception of struc-turalist and poststructuralist criticism in these terms it would be worth-while to turn to the work of Jonathan Culler as well. In his *Structuralist Poetics* we can see a movement similar to Hartman's carried out within the realm of the newer criticism itself.[18] There is no room here to discuss Culler's analysis of the numerous critics that are the objects of his study; fortunately, a number of scholars have already provided insightful critiques of his work.[19] What is most important to my discussion is in any case not the specific points he makes regarding this or that critic, but the fact that the linguistic model, which in the hands of Barthes, Jacobson, Lévi-Strauss, and especially Foucault, raises questions about the relationship between language and society, is reduced to a discovery principle for literary texts alone. That such texts are also manifestations of a larger structural set, a social text, and that literature might also inscribe the perplexities of particular historical encounters between these two levels of text production is in fact of no interest to Culler here, since, despite claims to the contrary, connecting literature and society is not his real aim. That, after all, was the problematic relation from which the prior generation of Anglo-American critics had already fled in order to establish a secure space for the critic/mediator.

Structuralist Poetics refines this move by focusing on the importance of the linguistic "surface" of the text and the complex discourse that has evolved as a means of describing this space. This sets the stage for the central chapter where it is claimed that the "task of criticism" is to produce literary competence. "That achievement requires acquaintance with a range of literature and in many cases some form of guidance," despite the fact that "acquiescence [to such guidance] may occasionally be disgruntled yielding to a higher authority" (*SP*, 121). Submission to the critic's authority, to the critic as "guide," emerges here as the absolute priority for knowledge itself, and at the same time, the critical subject, no longer in jeopardy of colliding with the destructive forces of history, can reassert its magisterial presence.[20]

That this new critic harks back to the old is apparent not only in the language that Culler uses to describe the critic's role but in his references to Frye as well. It is the desire to empower the critic to "formulate the broad laws of literary experience" (*Anatomy of Criticism*, 14; *SP*, 119) that binds together all of the critics I have discussed here.[21] This legislation, which proposes a world outside and above the realm of historical experience, was known to earlier critics simply as "the tradition," and it is back to this tradition that Culler returns us both here and in his later work. His reading of Abrams' *Mirror and the Lamp* as a forerunner of poststructuralist criticism in fact proposes the same genealogy that I have been suggesting, but with a contradictory outcome.[22] While this essay tries to make of Abrams a "father" of the newer linguistic criticism, the gesture itself clearly fixes the latter as the descendent of an Anglo-American tradition that has been able to maintain itself here by reasserting its demands from within the space that had once been occupied by its possible alternative—the historical and epistemological knowledge that formed the hidden problematic in the works of Berlin, Abrams, Steiner, Valency, and a number of other critics in the fifties. And what might at first have appeared to be a radical "difference" on the level of critical discourse, turns out here, and on the level of criticism as an institution, to be a mere shifting of weight. The critical subject no longer maintains its position by revealing structures of meaning; now its presence is announced by the discovery of the meaning of structures.

NOTES

1. "Structuralism: The Anglo-American Adventure," *Yale French Studies* (1966), reprinted in *Beyond Formalism* (New Haven: Yale University Press, 1970), 3-23, hereafter cited in the text as S.
2. See "The Sweet Science of Northrop Frye," first published in the *English Institute Essays* (New York: Columbia University Press, 1966), reprinted in *Beyond Formalism*, 24-41.
3. The editions referred to in my discussion are as follows: Isaiah Berlin, *The Hedgehog and the Fox: Essays on Tolstoy's View of History* (New York: Simon & Schuster, 1953), hereafter referred to in the text as HF; M.H. Abrams, *The Mirror and the Lamp; Romantic Theory and the Critical Tradition* (New York: Norton, 1958), hereafter ML; Georg Steiner, *Tolstoy or Dostoyevsky: An Essay in the Old Criticism* (New York: Random House, 1961), hereafter, TD; Maurice Valency, *The Flower and the Castle: An Introduction to the Modern Drama* (New York: Grosset & Dunlap, 1966), hereafter, FC.
4. Berlin's unconscious solicitation of the *archia* can be noted, but must remain undiscussed here; however, see Jacques Derrida, "Violence and Metaphysics," in *Writing and Difference*, trans. Alan Bass, (Chicago: University of Chicago Press, 1978), 79-153.
5. See Umberto Eco, *A Theory of Semiotics* (Bloomington: Indiana University Press, 1976).
6. Jonathan Culler has provided a rather different reading of Abrams' text, one that will play a role later in my own discussion. See his *The Pursuit of Signs: Semiotics, Literature, Deconstruction* (Ithaca: Cornell University Press, 1981), 153-68.
7. This line is cited from Berdiaev, who thus becomes the guarantor of Steiner's postion.
8. Although Valency's work does not have the same stature today as

that granted the other works dealt with here, or that of formalist orderings of the drama such as Frye's, its great virtue is that it exposes the underlying historico-critical anxiety that these other contemporary works manage to mask more or less effectively through the rigor with which they apply their critical abstractions.

9. Further comments on this subject can be found in chapters 2 through 6 of Paul Bové, *Intellectuals in Power: A Genealogy of Critical Humanism* (New York: Columbia University Press, 1986) and in Fritz Stern, *The Politics of Cultural Despair* (Berkeley: University of California Press, 1961). See also my "Tracing a Critical Path: Peter Szondi and the Critical Tradition," published as the Foreword to Peter Szondi, *On Critical Understanding* (Minneapolis: University of Minnesota Press, 1986).

10. This same sort of reduction seems to be operative in most contemporary discussions of genre as well. Inherent in these discussions is a notion of generic immutability and continuity that wishes to deny its own historical grounding as well as that of its subject matter.

11. In fairness it must be noted that Valency does grant Ionesco and Beckett the *occasional* expression of a serious artistic viewpoint (*FC*, 9).

12. Claude Levi-Strauss, *Le cru et le cuit* (Paris: Plon, 1964), trans. as *The Raw and the Cooked* (New York: Harper: 1969); Michel Foucault, *Les mots et les choses* (Paris: Gallimard, 1966), trans. as *The Order of Things* (New York: Pantheon, 1971); and Jacques Derrida *L'ecriture et la difference* (Paris: Seuil, 1967), trans. as *Writing and Difference* (Chicago: University of Chicago Press, 1978).

13. Among the works that indicate the opposite movement, that is, towards a historical appreciation of poststructuralist methods, are: Edward Said, *Orientalism* (New York: Pantheon, 1978); Jonathan Arac, *Commissioned Spirits* (New Brunswick, N.J.: Rutgers University Press, 1979); Frank Lentricchia, *After the New Criticism* (Chicago: University of Chicago Press, 1980); Margaret Ferguson, *Trials of Desire: Renaissance Defenses of Poetry* (New Haven: Yale University Press, 1983).

14. This had no doubt always been the case, but only when the critic turns fully away from history in order to defend critical practice itself rather than some extracritical socio-aesthetic norm, does the critic's role as mediator assume the position of absolute priority in the dissemination of "meaning."

15. A thoroughly unselfconscious proclamation of this type of critical move can be found in W.K. Wimsatt, "The Concrete Universal," in *The Verbal Icon*, (Lexington: University of Kentucky Press, 1954), 69-83.

16. "Toward Literary History," in *Beyond Formalism*, 264.

17. Geoffrey Hartman, *Criticism in the Wilderness: The Study of Literature Today* (New Haven: Yale University Press, 1980). Hartman has moved beyond this position as well, and although his latest work might well be analyzed from

the same point of view as that I have applied here, there is no space to do so in this discussion. In any case, Hartman serves here primarily as an example of the transition to and reception of the discourse and methods of the French structuralists.

18. *Structuralist Poetics: Structuralism, Linguistics and the Study of Literature* (Ithaca: Cornell University Press, 1975), hereafter *SP*.

19. See, for example, Frank Lentricchia, *After the New Criticism.*

20. In his most recent work, Culler has shifted from the idea of critic as guide to a notion of "community" which alters the status of the interlocutors in the critical game, but this later shift does not really bear on the process of assimilating the newer criticism to the needs of the older during the 1970s.

21. It is interesting to note that some critics on the left feel equally obliged to pay homage to Frye, and thereby reanchor themselves and the tradition, even as they claim to be departing from it. This certainly seems to be the case in Fredric Jameson's *The Political Unconscious.* A discussion of Jameson's use of Frye can be found in Cornel West, "Fredric Jameson's Marxist Hermeneutics," *boundary 2*, 9 (1982/83): 177-200.

22. See Jonathan Culler, *The Pursuit of Signs*, 153-68.

10. When the Sorcerer's Apprentice Becomes the Defeated Master: Frankfurtians

FABIO B. DASILVA

Thematically, the key issue in this essay regards the mode of the negation of the negation not simply as an intellectual mode but rather as that of the structural strictures in which, still under the clarity of Western Enlightenment, the *form* of such critique collapses into a new stage, where reason and life remain at a distance rather than bridged. Thus, the question becomes simultaneously why we got here through the mainstream of Western culture (reason-egocentrism), and why each of the solutions given have become, in a label for the Frankfurtians, "melancholy."

I take a clue from the last major work of Husserl, *The Crisis*, and through such a clue I would like to examine in some detail (inasmuch as is possible within the limitations of an essay), the key moments of negation that brought us the Frankfurtians. In a nutshell: the shifts from Descartes, to Kant, to Hegel, and to the Marxism of Horkheimer.

Thus, I propose to take into account the transformations that structurally took place through "inversion" from Descartes' centrality of the ego, to Kant's critique of the relations of consciousness and nature, to Hegel's critique and the resulting dialectics of the subject and object, and to the Frankfurtians' (through Marx's shift from idealism to materialism) critique leading from Structure to de-structuration.

Moreover, since in the classical essay by Horkheimer, "Traditional and Critical Theory," the question of *value*, and in latu sensu that of morals or ethics, emerges as frontally significant for the critical program of the Frankfurtians, I choose to look in some detail to that question and that sphere in the work of each of these thinkers.

The following graph may help in plotting our course:

Intellectual moments of inquiry indicating structural "inversions"				
1	2	3	4	5
Descartes	Kant	Hegel	Marx (a) infra-structure ◇	Horkheimer
cogito	homo noumenon /		base	state ↓
S ←—	S \	S ←–→ O	_____	managerial society
will	homo phenomenon	historical teleological	(b) B class ↑ ¦ – –> ↓	masses \ /
	will	will	P class	S
			will of collective subject	enlightened individual will

Notes:
– – → direction of reflective measurement or relationship
S   subject
O   object
B   bourgeois
P   proletariat

DESCARTES

Truth and Error

Such is the title of the fourth meditation—an old theme in philosophy that all those who want to fight skepticism have to face. Parmenides simply negated the existence of error, since it is impossible to speak of the non-being. Plato, to fight the sophists, on the contrary, faced the need to prove the existence of error or non-being. Descartes, having proved in the first meditations the existence of God and of thought itself, moves to "la connaisance des autres choses de l'univers" and considers it necessary to face the problem of error. The veracity of God is a fundamental point. Without eliminating the idea of the Malevolent Genius of a misleading God, there would remain the doubt to prejudice all possibility of knowledge of man. That is the reason why already in the second paragraph of the fourth meditation he moves to demonstrate that it is impossible for God to mislead us. Thus, it is also true that the faculty of judgment that was given us by God is of such nature that we will never err, once we use such faculty as necessary. "And there would not remain any doubt about the subject, if, it seems to me, we could not take this consequence, to wit, that I never can mislead myself, because since everything that exists in me comes from God, and since he did not place in me any faculty to err, it seems to me that I can never err."[1] But, against that there is the experience we have of an "infinity of errors" we can commit.

To solve the problem Descartes makes a series of general considerations that can be summarized in the following way: (a) the affirmation that error has nothing in itself either real or positive; it is only a "lacking," so that one errs only because the capacity that God has given one to discern the truth of error is not infinite; (b) if I dispute that error is not simply a lack of some perfection that is not given to me, but rather the privation of a knowledge *that seems to me that I should have* (since if God has given me the capacity for knowledge, it should be "perfect in its genus"), Descartes would respond from a viewpoint which is absolutely the same as that of Christian philosophy, to wit, that "I should not feel uneasy if I am not capable to understand why God has done what has been done"[2] and that "I cannot without temerity attempt to discover the opaque aims of God"; and (c) finally that, facing these problems, "we must not consider one sole creature, independently, when we want to know if God's works are perfect, but rather consider beings in their totality, since that which taken independently might appear imperfect when taken as a whole can be very perfect while being considered as a part of an entire universe."[3]

After such an introduction Descartes moves to consider the problem by searching the explanation of error in the nature of the human spirit itself. It is exactly this section that interests us here, since it is in it that there appears quite clearly, once again, the conception that in the life of the spirit the activity of will dominates the simple faculty of understanding, going beyond it in extension, and keeping its independence from understanding even when apparently it is determined by the strength of clear and distinct ideas.

A constant effort of will is required to move the mind from the contemplation of sensible imaginary ideas created by the mind itself (in which the mind enjoys itself since its cognitive function is nothing more than to see and to contemplate) to a clear and distinct understanding of ideas themselves. We might add that clarity itself depends upon the *attention* with which the spirit contemplates an idea.[4] Descartes' position is reinforced by other texts.[5] The clarity and distinctiveness of ideas can break down through an action of will, which deliberately leaves aside the reasons to see them as clear and distinct, and also deliberately searches for other reasons so as not to accept or not to see their clarity.

That is what happens with mathematics, which in the "Rules" are admitted as inconclusive truths, and later in the "Meditations" (in view of the hypothesis of the doubt) become also an object of doubt.[6]

Thus we find that in Descartes the significance of will is located in judgment itself, that is, in the linkage of two ideas. The fundamental text regarding this subject is the fourth meditation.

It is necessary to differentiate in judgments, says Descartes, two elements: the predominantly intellectual and the volitional. In the first place let us note what he says regarding the place of understanding in judgment: "by understanding I not only not affirm or negate anything but simply conceive the ideas of the things that I can affirm or negate."[7]

In another text Descartes points out that understanding by itself is only receptive or passive.[8] One can thus see the convenience or the possibility or even the necessity for linking the two elements of intellect and volition in the concept of judgment. But, by themselves, they cannot bring about such unity. As a faculty, in any case, understanding is perfect in its genre, and one could not say that there is any error in it.[9] It is true that there is an infinite number of things of which understanding has no idea, says Descartes, "but we cannot say that because of that it is deprived from such ideas as that of any thing that is due to its nature."

I cannot really prove that God should have given me necessarily a wider understanding than I have; nor can I, on the grounds of my limited understanding, conclude that God is imperfect and circumscribed in his power, because "I must not think that He should have necessarily to place in each one of His works all the perfections that He placed in some others."[10]

Thus, understanding, although this cannot be attributed to God's imperfections, has a limited character; materially limited, because there is an infinite number of things that shape it and because many others are seen by it confusedly, and also formally limited, because as a consequence of its finite character it cannot understand the infinite.[11]

The second element needed for judgment is volition, the act of will, found in agreement or negation. The intervention of the "faculty to elect" or free will[12] is necessary in order for judgment to be realized. Thus Descartes differentiates the two elements or the two aspects of judgment. It is true that in another text already discussed he declares that the "actions and passions of the mind are two manners of being of the same substance."[13] However, it is not enough to attribute to the philosopher a vision of the human spirit similar to that destroyed by modern psychology, namely a soul with separate faculties. Nevertheless, while still presenting intelligence and volition as modes of being of the same substance, it is clear that Descartes attributes to will a number of characteristics that place it at a higher level in relation to understanding. This becomes even clearer in the discussions on freedom where, for Descartes, will and free will are synonymous.

Freedom

The study on freedom appears in the fourth meditation in relation to the doctrine of error. The scope of will, greater than that of understanding, is what explains the doctrine of error, which is nothing more than the result of what Descartes in the "Discourse" calls precipitation or prevention. One and the other are abusive forms of the action of will: the first is the acceptance and affirmation, in judgments, of the consonance between two ideas regarding which we do not have a clear and distinctive idea; the second is the affirmation of ideas, also confused, that comes to us from education or habituations acquired in childhood. In any case, precipitation and prevention demonstrate that there is no determinism of clear and distinct ideas; will can act regardless of whether the ideas that constitute the matter for its deliberation are clear or confused.

With respect to the explanation of error Descartes says: "I cannot myself complain that God has not given me a will or free will quite wide. . . ."[14] But let us focus these remarks on his ideas regarding will and free will. We can note, first of all, that Descartes gives no proof for such an affirmation; he roots it on his own experience:[15] "I experience it so widely and so extensively that it is not enclosed by any limits."[16] And, further on: "There is nothing but the will or only the freedom of will that I experience in myself which is so great that I cannot conceive another idea that would be in any way wider and more extensive."[17]

What comes out of such texts will clarify the sense of such *experience*. Examining introspectively the faculties of his spirit, he verifies, with respect to all of them, that they are limited: (a) for being of small extension; (b) and for simultaneously being possible to represent the existence of another spirit in which such limitations do not exist. Regarding the first aspect of experience, it seems clear that Descartes wants to refer to the fact that there are an infinite number of things that we do not understand or conceive. In the same way, when we examine memory or imagination, our common experience tells us that we cannot remember or imagine the whole of our past. Moreover, such experience can only be realized by positing the idea of another faculty "much greater or even infinite." And by "the fact alone that I can represent my idea, I know without any difficulty that it belongs to the nature of God."[18] Thus, it is clear that Descartes makes here an approximation between primordial experience and the "cogito."

In brief, one finds in Descartes a parallelism between the experience of free will and the experience of the evidence of the "cogito." The "cogito" is the experience of the limits of our understanding, as well as a clear and distinctive idea, which understanding grasps through an effort of will.

To conclude, one sees that Descartes has a conception of will and freedom that seems to many (for instance Gilson) the result of an effort toward adaptation. Such a conception, far from incorporating contradictions and inconsequences, is perfectly understandable within the Cartesian system, and moreover constitutes a necessary element of that system, since the theory of will and freedom is intimately linked to his ideas on method and to a metaphysics related to the nature of God and man.

Finally, such a conception undoubtedly aims at attributing to human will not absolute primacy but a priority that consists in the affirmation of the active character of the will and of the passive character of understanding; the formally unlimited character of the will and the limited character of understanding; the affirmation that it is on the grounds of the wider character of the will that one can attribute to man the quality of being an image of God.

KANT

As we have seen in the analysis of the preceding section, Descartes' philosophical and moral voluntarism starts to break out of ontological voluntarism and to orient itself toward a more empiricistic direction But such a development is not enough. To give all its strength to the theory of volitional intuition one must also eliminate every bearing of theology, every metaphysical construction which is superimposed on the direct experience of the will. To make the Cartesian tendency triumph it will be necessary to renounce definitely the psychology of God and concentrate upon that of man.

Everthing that is truly innovative and original in the Kantian conception of the autonomy of the moral sphere derives from Kant's moral voluntarism grounded upon the theory of the volitive intuition of man.

Each intuition affirms itself in spite of the premises of Kant's general philosophy that negates every possibility for a nonsensible intuition. Intuition enters continuously in contradiction with the rationalistic and intellectualistic conclusion of his morals—the generality of the categorical imperative, the principle of identity and noncontradiction of moral conscience, the unity of reason in which theoretical and practical reason are reconciled thanks to the primacy of the latter. Kant's concept of the moral is necessarily based upon volitional intuition.

For Kant the significance of the data of moral life, irreducible to any moral construction and upon which we can reflect a posteriori, is grounded upon the independence of the good in relation to the true and the autonomy of moral will in relation to every criterion that it has not given to itself. Thus, Kant opens his *Foundations of the Metaphysics of Custom* with an appeal to a "Critique of Practical Reason." Thus he calls Rousseau the "Newton of morals," since he has freed it from all the intellectualistic prejudices of the Liebnizian and Wolfian schools. Nevertheless, such data of moral life are not, after Kant, graspable by sentiment, which remains sensible and passive, but through the will itself, which is immanent to conduct. Moral intention which inspires conduct is itself already will and action. That is the reason why "of everything that it is possible to conceive in the world and even in general besides the world, there is nothing that could, without restriction, be taken for good if it is not good will."[19] Good will, then, is not merely the aptitude to reach a given end, but rather it is good as an end in itself. A will that is good in itself as an end, independently of the aims that it proposes to itself, constitutes the first datum of real moral life, irreducible to intelligence and prior to every theoretical knowledge—is this not a volitional intuition, an insightful will?

Kant demonstrates this in a number of passages of the *Critique of Practical Reason*. "It is a *fact* that pure reason affirms itself in us effectively as practice; . . . such fact is linked in an unbreakable way to the conscience of the freedom of the will."[20] Such fact (*Faktum*) is one of the "givens" (*Datum*) not resembling in anything the sensible data that cannot be grasped except in the frame of time and space. We find here a telling contrast between "practical reason" and "pure reason" (or theoretical reason) through a reference to the *inexplicable fact* of nonsensible, immediate experience. The immediate consciousness of freedom, implied by the awareness of moral duty, breaks the Kantian reduction of every experience to the experience of the sensible submitted to the categories of understanding: it leads him to recognize a kind of pure intuition, the intuition of will grasping directly the moral principles which are otherwise unprovable. "The effectiveness of pure will, or what is the same, practical reason, *is given to us* as that of a presence."[21] Such presence, identical after all to that of positive freedom as absolute spontaneity, is an "incomprehensible" element for theoretical reason,[22] and even "totally incomprehensible" (*völlige Unbegreiflichkeit*)[23] since the possibility of freedom cannot be explained (*lässt sich nicht weiter erklären*).[24] That does not mean that we cannot reflect in a theoretical manner a posteriori on such freedom experienced immediately in the will; it means simply that it is given immediately in a nonintellectualized experience, which we cannot deduct or induct from anything. On such a given Kant reflected with such intensity that he ends by constructing it, by involving it in the unity of reason and, what is even more, by attributing it to the "things in themselves."

The quoted texts do not leave any doubt. Kant finds himself always pushed toward a volitional intuition that seems to identify itself with the pure will, itself identical to good will or to the moral will of man.

In the development of his moral philosophy Kant gives many different meanings to the notions of pure will and freedom. In some of these meanings he seems to contradict directly the theory of volitional intuition. On the one hand man is, according to Kant, "will guided by the simple representation of duty";[25] while on the other hand he regards every representation as evidently of an intellectual order, and therefore considers the pure will as intellectualizing will, as reasonable will. And, as duty is a general law, inasmuch as it forms the universal legislation of the will, the pure will seems like a will determined by the general form of the law which is characteristic of reason as a whole.[26] Thus, "It is the only and same reason that, in the theoretical domain or in the practical domain, judges on the basis of a priori principles."[27] Pure will is thus the reasonable will penetrated by judgment. The autonomy of the will would not be thus the irreducibility and the independence of moral certainty, but rather its capability for submitting itself freely, while prescribing its law, to the unique certainty of reason. But then, in what regard would the autonomy of morals in Kant be distinguished from the "freedom of the wise man," of the Stoics and Spinoza? Why affirm that the will alone can be good and that practical reason opposes itself to theoretical reason? It is not sufficient to argue that such a law, cast in the form of a subjective maxim of the will and affirming itself as legislative, does not represent anything except a "will being" (Sollen), and is not a law of nature. On the one hand, we cannot see from where such specificity derives, and on the other hand, such specificity is destroyed inasmuch as everything is reduced to the unity of reason submitting to the will. Kant's position can only be explained first by reference to his view that man is at the same time homo noumenon and homo phenomenon, thing-in-itself and empirical being; and secondly, by his argument that the things in themselves, unknowable by intelligence, are themselves pure wills. Herein we find two different and opposed senses of the notion of pure will: intuitive will and will guided by the representation of duty. Both are aspects of good will, the pure will of the homo noumenon opposing itself to the empirical will of the homo phenomenon. Finally, pure will is conceived as absolute spontaneity and the free causal agent of the things in themselves.

The pure will of the homo noumenon is alone effectively free, since it is not subject to the causal determinations that rule the phenomenal world. In that sense it has no need of duty and of representations; moreover in it "I want" and "I must" are identical since it is legislated.

The duty does not appear, Kant himself says, except because man belongs to two worlds simultaneously. It is the call of the noumenal will, which is free, to the phenomenal will, which is not. We could not speak, according to Kant, of volitional intuition except by reference to the *homo noumenon*, whereas the will of the *homo phenomenon* not submitting itself to the general law of reason, is nothing but arbitrary, blind will. By virtue of his noumenal will and its insights, man submits himself to his intelligence, its representation of duty and its consequent judgment.

But why does *homo phenomenon* submit to the general law? And why does he search for a contact with the pure will of the *homo noumenon*? What is the moral basis of these moves? Kant presupposes that every pure and absolute spontaneity (even of the things in themselves as such), or free causality (i.e., cosmological freedom, that he discusses in the third antinomy of the *Critique of Pure Reason*, and that he transposes in the *homo noumenon*), is a spontaneity that is determined by one law: *Freiheit unter dem Gesetze*. In the same way it seems evident to him that empirical will, submitting itself to a general law that gives itself to itself, enters into contact with the absolute spontaneity of the noumenal will, and that, through such an imperative, a consonance is established between one and the other of these two wills. Thus, the empirical will is liberated, raising through the intermediary of moral autonomy beyond the causal determination of the phenomenal world, toward absolute spontaneity which is at the same time legislative of the thing in itself.

Kant's solution implies three metaphysical theses of a purely constitutive character: the rupture of man between *homo noumenon* and *homo phenomenon*—the will as the true nature of the *homo noumenon* and the thing in itself in general; the identity of creative will and absolute spontaneity, attributed to the *homo noumenon*; and the attribution of legislative powers to the thing in itself.

The combination of these three theses leads Kant to reject voluntary intuition, the first basis of his morals, in the noumenal world. He finds thus the link between the empirical will of man and moral principles, by the submission of will to intelligence under the aspect of the representation of the general form of the moral law.

It is enough thus to reject one of these constitutive metaphysical theses to invalidate the Kantian solution. If one denies that the absolute spontaneity of creative will is identical to legislative determination (and such a denial ensues from the antinomy between the "trans-intelligible" character of creative freedom and the generality and intellectualist stability of every legislation), the submission to the categorical imperative will not lead to any contact with the pure will of the *homo noumenon*, and the moral life in the phenomenal world becomes radically impossible. The same thing occurs if we reject the separation, the break between the *homo noumenon* and the *homo phenomenon*. Moreover, if we were to reject a world of things in themselves (even when interpreted as pure will or spontaneity) we would also eliminate every reason to negate the possibility of the volitional intuition of the sensible man: the limitation of the will of the real agent to the alternative between the arbitrary and the submission to the general law would thus appear artificial.

The whole morality of Kant furthermore has no other beginning than his presupposition of a secret affinity between the phenomenal and noumenal will of man, parallel to that between these two and the metaphysical will of the thing in itself. Such affinity is grounded on the thesis of the primacy of practical reason; the effort of human will would lead, through intermediary steps, to the grasp of the true nature of the thing in itself, which is inconceivable for intelligence, because such nature is itself will. Kant, like Descartes, but without direct reference to God, thus identifies *psychological* and *metaphysical voluntarism*, and such identification serves as a basis for his moral voluntarism. But, metaphysical voluntarism is a kind of monism of certainties and consequently, of intellectualism. From such a situation emerge the contradictions of Kantian morals, grounded as they are upon volitional intuition that he continuously negates.

Such intuition, rejected at every moment in the noumenal world, reappears nevertheless in a permanent fashion and takes revenge upon his system. Because, all considered, the contact itself in man between noumenal and phenomenal personality is established not so much through the representation of the categorical imperative but rather by the intuition of duty and the freedom that it implies. The duty is grasped by the empirical good will as an appeal, as Kant himself says. Kant always returns to immediate conscience, not only of duty, but also of freedom as *presences*, as the *givens* of empirical human conscience. This is certainly the sense of Kant's famous dictum: "Two things fill man's soul with an always new astonishment and respect: the starred skies above him and the moral law within him." Volitional intuition finds itself thus at the same time at the beginning and throughout the development of Kant's moral philosophy.

The theory of volitional intuition implied in Kant's moral philosophy could bear fruit once its internal contradictions are resolved. This would require a rejection of the theory of things in themselves and the separation of men into noumenal and phenomenal. For this it is sufficient to realize that man's empirical will is prior to arbitrary will and that will as decision and creation precedes will as choice between duties. In other words one has to affirm the primacy of intuitive volition or pure will. In sum, it is necessary to realize that creative will goes beyond all legislation and all determination by law. It was up to Fichte to eliminate these contradictions and the confusion of psychological and moral voluntarism with metaphysical voluntarism.

HEGEL

We find a significant presentation of Hegel's morality in the section of *Phenomenology of Spirit* where he discusses the human spirit as it has been "purified" by the Terror, or Revolution. In theoretical terms, Rousseau, when reinterpreted by Kant, leads us to moral consciousness or "self-certain Spirit." The term "certain" (*gewisse*) contains in German a strong echo of the word "conscience" (*Gewissen*). This term is central for both Rousseau and Kant. Hegel's criticism of Kant is that the appeal to the conscience, in the form of the categorical imperative, is a quasi-mathematical transformation of morality into universal rules, or of spiritual form lacking in content. In Kantian thought, consciousness is moral and nature is amoral. This is why Kant attacks eudaimonism, or the view that moral virtue is connected to happiness. Hegel on the contrary, rejects this ascetic doctrine of pure duty to formal law. As is obvious from his allegience to the modern doctrine of desire, Hegel maintains that the individual has a right to insist upon satisfaction. The individual works toward the rational goal of historical as opposed to heavenly happiness. Socrates is said to have brought philosophy down from heaven into the cities of men. Hegel attempts and revises this by revealing the necessity for mediation in desire and obligation.

Hegel is in a way a "Greek" in his criticism of the Kantian thesis that nature is amoral. But his point should not be exaggerated; more cautiously, nature, as assimilated into history, is the "substance" of the State, which is in turn rendered subjective by Spirit or religion. Man therefore finds happiness in actual deeds performed within history; in this sense, man is a "political" animal, since history is essentially political history. Kant cannot separate morality from happiness without transcending the world of nature, which he refuses to do, since his avowed intention is to harmonize Spirit and nature. For epistemological as well as moral reasons, Kant must insist that sensuousness is *compatible* with morality, while insisting simultaneously upon the opposition between sensuousness and pure consciousness. The unity of morality and nature both must and cannot appear in nature. The fulfillment of morality leads to a contradiction which seems to rob it of its holy character, to make it unachievable. In order to avoid this, or to account for the requisite harmony of consciousness and nature on the one hand and the harmony of reason and sensuousness on the other, we are forced to postulate a divine legislator. What is *in-itself* is brought together with what is *for-itself*. What must be true of consciousness, yet cannot be true of its human form, is conceived as true of the divine consciousness. I receive my reward of happiness in the divine kingdom of virtuous spirits for the sake of actions performed in the natural kingdom of human spirits. Therefore, the moral consciousness finds its fulfillment in thought only: in the postulated unity of the divine legislator.

The Kantian moral consciousness falls into the abyss of the emptiness or negativity of its own purity: the "difference" between the noumenal and phenomenal domains. And yet, Kant's effort to reconcile nature and consciousness is very close to the Hegelian interpretation of the exteriority and interiority of the Spirit. For Kant, however, Spirit or the transcendental ego is known only as a "condition for the possibility of" nature and consciousness. This "condition" is neither alive nor dead, neither subject nor substance, but the visible aspect of the invisible or spontaneous "Absolute" which is, as the name implies, all too separate from its own consequences. The hidden or invisible is rendered visible not in a concept but in a *postulate* of what *ought* to be. Consciousness as consciousness remains a form of alienation. The self places its significance in moral activity. A moral act can only be performed in the natural world. As such, however, it is subject to natural rather than moral laws. And so, as moral, it is amoral: another instance of the dialectic of the inverted world. In slightly different terms, the self poses its own objective significance in the moral act, and is therefore identical with its own essence. Since, however, the absolute essence of pure morality cannot be externalized or objectified, the moral act is not essential or real in itself, but only via the postulation of self-consciousness. As Hegel puts it, consciousness "pretends" to make by its activity what can never occur in the concrete temporal present. This pretense is a displacement of consciousness, at first into its (unreal) acts, but next in a "Beyond" that lies always beyond the perimeter of activity.[28]

The law of this world (accepted by Kant) is Newtonian mechanics. If moral activity were to fulfill itself in this world it would negate itself (since morality requires freedom). The moral consciousness pretends that it is in harmony with actuality, it pretends that its perfection lies in the given finite act as an expression of obedience to conscience. But underneath this pretense is still another pretense. The disharmony of nature and consciousness, and the worthlessness of the finite act in comparison with the true end of the highest good, *make morality a sham.* In order to conceal these results, moral consciousness must then pretend that morality is achieved in itself, as opposed to nature or as purified of all sensuous content. But this is contradicted by the fact of activity; sensuousness is the necessary medium which brings consciousness into actuality. Instincts and inclinations are the engine of moral activity and do not work contrary to it. This engine functions in accordance with natural laws. Once again, moral consciousness is displaced by its dissimulations, or driven from one postulate to another in its search for the *summum bonum.* But each new world is merely the image of its predecessor. There is no progress toward moral perfection, but only toward the *Nichts* or inaccessibility of the end. Moral action is revealed as impossible. We cannot earn our happiness but, at best, receive it as a gift of divine grace. The real good is thus not morality but happiness or blessedness.[29]

Since morality is either impossible or self-deceptive, it cannot be wrong to achieve happiness through immoral acts. More accurately, there cannot be any real distinction between "moral" and "immoral" acts, because all activity is a function of amoral nature. This incoherence or lack of seriousness in the self-interpretation of moral consciousness is now manifest. In an effort to define itself as the absolute, consciousness is forced to pose the absolute as outside itself: as divine legislator. Either morality is nothing but a nihilistic dream, or else, according to Hegel, it must be fulfilled within the "natural" world (as mediated by history), and thus be opposed to "pure" morality. In order to free itself from hypocrisy, the moral consciousness must admit that it was not serious in its interpretation of activity, which leads to the alienation from its own essence. This lack of seriousness is the correlative of taking the world, as the arena of activity, too seriously. The moral consciousness now flees from its representation of the world and its correlative "Beyond." It flees from the external reality of the senses back into itself, which is now interpreted as *pure consciousness*. In this form, moral consciousness turns to itself as pure universal beauty and becomes the *beautiful soul*.[30]

Hegel, as it were, anticipated Kierkegaard's opposition of the ethical and the aesthetic by showing how the ethical is transformed through its own logic into the aesthetic. Pure consciousness is an intermediate stage in this transformation. In order to represent itself as "pure," moral action as subjective self-certitude must be immediate intuition. There can be no interval between the moral agent and the reflexive act of discursive interpretation. The individual act of pure consciousness is the content of the universal form of consciousness itself, which thus finds itself universally present in all of its deeds. Consciousness can act because it is initially silent, whereas moral consciousness as the moral worldview speaks first (or tries to explain its goodness as a postulate of the pure practical reason) and is subsequently silenced.[31] This silencing of moral consciousness is equivalent to a denial of the reality of its activity. The significance of consciousness resides in activity. Since it cannot speak coherently of this activity, consciousness cannot recognize itself therein. Furthermore, consciousness cannot be recognized by the other individuals who constitute the world of moral activity, because this world is in fact a mutual deception. Hegel refers to this detachment of the subject from the world of acts and deeds as the transference of objective predicates to the subject.[32]

The subject now knows itself to be the subject and object, or an objectively enduring activity. Its own certitude takes precedence over the variety of circumstances and duties characteristic of moral action. Consciousness is pure duty; it is free to fill the subjective dimension of pure duty with *any* content, to do anything or to reject anything. For whatever it does must be right: immediate certitude of the self as the highest good cannot be wrong in any mediate determination of itself. Or rather, the consciousness is free from every determination: "In this way, consciousness is altogether free from every content; it absolves itself from every deteminate duty, which claims to be valid as law. In the force of its self-certitude, it possesses the majesty of absolute autarchy" or the power "to bind and to dissolve."[33]

We have now reached a crucial moment in the argument of the

Phenomenology. The subject turns inward, or discovers itself as the ground of certitude in every interpretation of the world. Initially however, this discovery is a kind of silence and so the inverse of an interpretation. Silent self-certitude is no better and no worse than another. In historical terms, the results of the Enlightenment are a development of discourse to the point of logorrhea and to nihilism. In turning away from discursive nihilism, however, the subjective spirit turns into silent nihilism. This is the moment of the negation of negation. In order to resolve the conflict of silent deeds, spirit must begin to speak again. As Hegel puts it, speech allows spirit to be for another what is in itself.[34] Without speech, consciousness would not exist for another because all agents would be identical or indistinguishable in the common silence of their respective certitude.

Silence prior to the experience of Western history would be innocence or ignorance. Silence in the midst of cultivated enlightenment would be a surrender to nihilism. Silence after speech has been completed, or all possible interpretations have been offered, is *potential wisdom*. What I am calling here the complete silence of total discourse is the presence of pure spiritual negativity in and as its moments, each of which is both positive (as determinate or asserted) and negative (as contradicted by its opposite assertion). Of course, silence understood as the separation of universal subjectivity from its discursive moments is still radically defective. The self-certain subject must begin to speak *again*, or to justify itself, and therefore in effect to repeat or reappropriate everything which has already been said, in such a way as to demonstrate its own presence (as negative activity) within each and every discourse. This process of discursive recollection requires us ultimately to repeat the entire course of the *Phenomenology*, but at the level of the Absolute, or as Hegel says in the *Logic*, from the standpoint of God, just before he creates the world. We have to acquire the divine standpoint in order to reappropriate or render intelligible the whole speech of phenomenology.

As Hegel says in the *Phenomenology*, consciousness is the "moral genius that knows the inner voice of its immediate knowledge as a divine voice."[35] The explanation or justification of self-certitude is grounded in the immediate knowledge of the self as doing God's will. The justification initially points beyond the self as immediate to God, or to the complete expression of the goodness of the certain self. This means that the justifying speech is initially theology or religion. We are not yet at the level of logic or the Absolute. This is clear from the fact that immediate intuition or self-certitude, in justifying itself, necessarily calls upon a God who is both the self and the completion of, or higher than, the self. Man is still alienated from God.[36] The negative moment is still detached from its content because it is in the process of assimilating that content. Therefore, the absolute certitude of conscience is now seen to be absolute non-truth.[37] "It is the absolute self-consciousness, in which consciousness sinks out of view." This is what Hegel means by the beautiful soul. Consciousness, at this stage, lives in dread of betraying the silent certitude of its own purity through action and political existence. In order to preserve the purity of its heart, it flees contact with reality. Consciousness longs for activity but is vitiated by its very actualization, like a formless dust that loosens itself into the air.[38]

The beautiful soul comtemplates itself as pure universality, expressed in discourse but unlimited by action. It is the totality of the moments of culture, and thus a recollection of everything that has been done and said thus far, but it lacks responsibility toward the historical and political world. The beautiful soul is both judge and judged; it is the universal which particularizes itself *as* itself. Differently stated, the individual believes himself to be universal, or to determine the content of action by his immediate self-certitude. But action, or the interpretation of action, is no longer universal. The agent is thus condemned by his own guilty conscience as soon as he acts. Since self-justification is itself an act, the act of justification is at once the act of condemnation. Both action and the failure to act are equally good and evil.[39]

On the other side of the same conflict, the universal element is not action but thought. In fact, the individual consciousness becomes aware of its own particularity by an intuition of itself as universal, and so, paradoxically, as other than the universal. The universal is universal as particular: its intuition is determinate, and therefore a (discursive) *judgement* rather than an intuition. I cannot intuit *myself* except by distinguishing myself, or specifying myself *as* thus-and-such. The general form of such an ostensible intuition is thus "S is P." Judgment is neither merely intuition nor action, but the discursive account of the significance of each other. Hegel expresses this in terms of morality as follows. Every moral act is accompanied by particular motives, such as the desire for fame, love of honor, the pursuit of happiness, and the like. An act from pure duty is impossible, because pure duty condemns every act. The judgment that arises originally from the priority of the universal to the particular now insists that the universal must serve the particular. Hegel refers to this as a "morality of valets" (a phrase later adopted by Goethe). To the valet, no man is a hero, not because there is no hero but because the judge is a valet.[40]

Of course the reference to valets is a preparation for the reconciliation between subject and object, or spirit and external world. Judgment (or the interplay of judging valets) replaces silence (the nobility of the master) or consciousness as the medium of universality. In other words, we are now prepared for the labor of conceptual thinking. But this is to anticipate a later stage.[41] Hegel's meaning can be stated as follows. The separation between man and God cannot be overcome by any form of pure morality, whether explicitly political or mystical intuition. It will yield only to the labor of the concept: the judgment replaces self-justification. In order to understand God, man must first understand himself. At first, man regards himself as the "image of God," but this is a preliminary and defective formulation. It is true that God is first accessible to man within his own consciousness. But that consciousness is not an image; it is a mode of the divine and so the divine itself. The doctrine of the image, on the contrary, is an eternal mask of the hidden god. To this extent, then, man must "return to the earth," by turning inward and engaging in the laborious process of self-understanding. But this process is identical with a turning outward, or an exhibition of oneself in the concrete political reality of history. Morality must be rendered articulate. This does not mean that it ceases to be moral; on the contrary, discourse is genuinely articulate only if it includes the moral dimension or is teleological. And this is why Hegel develops a logic of *judgment* rather than of propositions. Logic judges practice, and in a certain sense posits or constitutes it. The judgment of practice is not the condemnation but the assimilation of the particular. The teleological "cunning of reason" is thus at work even, or especially, in the disputes of valets, who will come to discover their spirituality by the work involved in rejecting it.

The dialectic of nature and consciousness, or the analysis of modern individualism, articulates the various worldviews or interpretations of Spirit as actual in human history. In a sense, all the fundamental steps have been accomplished except for the conceptual activity of self-consciousness, which grasps the completeness and hence the significance of what has been accomplished. The modern ego understands itself to be the Whole; it understands the subjectivity of substance. But within the ego there is still a dualism of the universal and the particular (in other words, pure consciousness and worldly activity). In religious language, there is still a dualism between God and man, albeit *within* the absolute ego. God has not yet revealed himself in conceptual terms as "the appearing God who knows himself as pure knowing," or as the Hegelian version of the Aristotelian divine intellect. Man has not yet conceptually grasped the meaning of the Christian revelation, or the identity of God and man in Christ.[42] Therefore the next chapter of *Phenomenology*, devoted to the penultimate version of absolute wisdom, will be concerned with the structure of the appearance of God to man. This analysis is not "historical" in the sense that it does not mark a new stage in spiritual development. Instead it studies all that has been accomplished from the religious standpoint. Religion is a *representation* of the relation between the universal and the particular. It is therefore couched in the language of imagery, and therein lies its defect. The detachment of the image from the original can only be overcome by the transformation of imagery into conceptual knowledge. This does not, needless to say, lessen the importance of religious representation, but defines it. It would not be altogether inaccurate to say that religious representation is the Hegelian analogue to the sensuous content in Kant's doctrine of conceptual judgment.

HORKHEIMER

The Pessimism of Critical Thought and Its Openness to the Totally-Other

In his introduction of 1968 to the republication of essays published in the thirties in the *Zeitschrift für Sozial forschung*, Horkheimer confronted the issue according to which critical theory had broken with the determinations that originally inspired it. With an explicit reference to the accusations raised by student members of the SDS who charged that critical theory had transformed itself into a pure doctrinal speculation, incapable of producing a politically revolutionary action, he answered that "to take from critical theory the consequences for political action is the element that makes it serious," but he also adds that "nevertheless, there is no universal recipe, except that of the need to clearly understand one's own responsibility."[43]

The events of world history in the thirties and forties had contributed to make Horkheimer always more diffident of ideology, which tended to present itself as taumaturgical; the advent of fascism and the scope of the war following the economic crisis of '29 had in fact ruptured the Marxist prognosis, according to which economic collapse would necessarily produce the revolution. Furthermore, reducing the ideals of socialism to instruments of power, Stalin had brought to light the ambiguity of behavior to which the same principles which had inspired the communist revolution could give rise.

The experience of fascism, of the war, and of Stalinism had revealed that power has its roots not so much in this or that system, but much more in the concessions of instrumental reason, which modeling consciousness according to the logic of domination risks subsuming within itself the project of human liberation. If each theory brings its opposite, such as fascism and communism, if theories are instrumental in the disguise of will to power, man cannot expect to be able to bring about emancipation through the elaboration of general theories, in contraposition to theories that openly tend to oppress him, but rather through an analysis oriented toward the identification of concrete totalitarian tendencies, implicitly contained in specific theoretical projects and in the various political structures. Thus, human liberation passes through the moment of critical reflection, that makes it possible to identify (as in theories) the emancipatory dimension of a historical moment, and the actions for the realization of a more rational order against the latent tendencies of domination.

According to Horkheimer, the thinker who more than any other had been able to unveil the ambivalence of theory and practice was Kant. He in fact understood the difference between the nature of things and their phenomenal character, since phenomena and essence belong to two different spheres of existence. The irreconcilable contraposition between the thing-in-itself and its manifestation had also been brought to light in Jewish thought, which had stressed the need to reconsider negative theological intentions.

Through the re-evaluation of the negative present in history, man places himself in the position to understand, through pessimism, that he experiences the situation in general, that the way toward the affirmation of the ideals and their historical concretization is unalienable, and thus starts to consider reality not on the basis of an ideology, but rather on the basis of the concrete behavior of men. He is convinced, in fact, that truth is not expressed in dogmatic formulae or in positive

propositions, which are always shown to be empty formulae when compared to the events themselves. Truth can be only reached if one becomes aware of the impotence, transience, and conditioning of one's
own being and actions. The thought itself of the unconditional is constituted, moreover, exactly from the experience of conditioning. The
critical grasp of reality becomes possible only when the subject grasps
the difference between ideal aims and their historical realization—in
fact, when he risks to project a different world and to understand the
limitations of the present without at the same time suppressing it ideal-
istically or dogmatically. The consciousness of the finite thus evokes
the infinite, not as a fantastic projection of a dream but rather as the
emerging horizon on the terrain of a history suffered in the pain of the
negative, and perceived as nostalgia of a different world. Hope always
leads to delusion; nevertheless, one always also gives oneself over to hope.

The conception of the evil of the world, recognized not through
the idealist transfiguration, in which the negative is posited as a necessary
moment for the complete realization of history and which comes even
to participate of the positivity of such sense, but rather through the
experience of pain and of the finitude of existence always frustrated
in its expectations, led Horkheimer to reconsider the philosophy of
Schopenhauer and to bring back elements of the ideological matrix of
his thought as a youth. The events that had characterized the history
of contemporary society came in fact to confirm the truthfulness of
Schopenhauer's thesis according to which "from the scientific knowledge of nature . . . follows the negation of man."[44]

Schopenhauer's philosophy, which developed around that theme,
makes evident that the solitude of modern man is rooted in his own
history, and thus cannot be imputed to the phenomena of massifica-
tion, to which the contemporary period has condemned man, but is
rather part of the atavic destiny of each individual. This position was
prepared for by German idealism but finds its earlier roots in Christianity. In fact, by proposing the immortality of man and his superiority over the world, Christianity implicitly affirms the irrelevance of non-
spiritual reality, and consequently makes the individual open to the
passive suffering of events, while depriving him of worldly rights, and
thus annuls him as a historical entity. With good reason Schopenhauer
could state that the I resolves itself in death, and that even if that is
a vehicle for a new reincarnation, it does not necessarily restitute to
the individual the human form of existence, since a life without the

sense of its own history could not be said to be fully human: "in face of the decay of the social significance of the individual, the relativization of the *I* by Schopenhauer" thus corresponds to "the social tendencies of the present."[45]

The process of the annulment of the individual finds its confirmation throughout human history and particularly in the present period; not only Nazism and mass society but also Stalinism and the Chinese revolution operate with the ruthlessness proper to the great powers, that always tend to suppress any space for individual autonomy. Thus human freedom finds itself the menace of the immanent logic of this same historical process.

Such a conception had already been developed by Horkheimer in the *Eclipse of Reason*, where he had sustained that "the transformation of reason as spiritual substance resulted from an internal need. Theory today must reflect and express the process, the socially conditioned tendency toward neopositivism, and the instrumentalization of thought purely as an impossible attempt toward salvation."[46]

In front of a historical situation that aims at promoting an always more integral administration of total existence, theory has no other possibility except that of analyzing the trends of history, to unveil the ways and the instruments of the continuous movement toward man's annihilation, and the causes of the terror against the people and the death of hope and unfulfilled rights. Even if the identification and denunciation of the means, placed in the hands of instrumental reason to bring about its strategy of domination, are not sufficient to arrest the suicidal trend of history, it will serve at least to show to man the funereal consequences of such ills.

The Dialectics of Freedom and Equality

The standing social apparatus, while generator of domination of the individual and the whole of humanity, is the historical subject that realizes the intent of absolute spirit of Hegelian philosophy.

Illustrating in the *Eclipse of Reason* the process through which thought becomes instrumental and society is transformed into a collectivity administered by the bureaucratic apparatus and its functionaries, Horkheimer nevertheless made the observation that even in a technocratic world the force of reason is no longer derived from an alienated totality; in fact, even if it is reduced to impotence, it still maintains the ability to express dissent and consequently to make it possible for the individual to continue to aspire toward a rational society. Reason places the individual in a position to bring out, through the acquisition of the consciousness of the difference regarding the intent toward realization and the way through which it becomes realized, the instance of an ulterior rationality.

The analysis, from this perspective, of the motivations that push society toward collectivism, makes it possible now to harvest, in the bosom of humanity, the existence of a "consciousness of social linkages," and there, to maintain "already today the presentiment that will develop the immanent scope of history: the abolition of injustice through inequality is made possible by the technical progress taking place in the industrialized countries, and then in all countries. The more nature becomes radically dominated by society, the less it requires social differentiation, the more the levels of living become similar. . . . If the goal for the elimination of class differences may still require a considerable amount of time, the direction of the course of history toward the return of the meaning of the individual and the realization of the species is indicated by the way and development of technology. . . . It would be unjust to block progress, nevertheless, it is necessary to recognize what comes from it as good and bad."[47]

In technology one finds, even if in a latent mode, the intentionality of reason that tends to establish the equality of man in the world. However, when such intentionality is developed according to an exclusively functional logic, oriented toward the instrumental utilization of resources and not to the promotion of man as such, the result is that the achievement of human equality becomes distorted at the cost of individual freedom. While endowing the individual deprived of personal autonomy and artificially manipulated with the possibility of instrumentality, the technocratic world, nonetheless, does not permit the individual to express himself authentically as man, and permits him to achieve equality solely if he conforms to the parameters established by society which are characterized by mass behavior and the annulment of spontaneity. In the social structure generated by instrumental reason, the reciprocal and complementary requirements of equality and freedom become thus posited antithetically to each other and become the source of conflict for man.

Bourgeois society has attempted to overcome the antinomy of these terms by creating the national state which, placed beyond the interests of the individual, guarantees simultaneously freedom and equality. This solution, though, was shown to be fictitious, because the national state reaches a purely functional consensus regarding the protection of individual interests, and because, as an expression of instrumental logic, it is incapable of bringing about harmony between freedom and equality. In fact the nation tends to absorb the freedom of the individual in the anonymous freedom of the collectivity and thus transforms itself in a motive of terror for all these that intend to maintain autonomy. It is not by accident that the national state, in the majority of cases, marginalizes and fights religion: while turned toward absolute truth religion aims in fact to promote fundamental values, including that of individual freedom, and thus constitutes a radical critique of instrumental reason and an antagonistic force to the state. To the state there remains no other alternative except that of getting rid of religion through marginalization or simply through open attack: "with the passage of competitive capitalism, relatively free, in the context of the state and in the competition of groups, religion that aims at the individual as responsible subject loses at least a part of its significance in face of nationalism. The sense that every action in life comes to acquire in the perspective of eternal values is replaced by the absolutization of the collectivity in which the individual is inserted."[48]

Thus, if in contemporary society the achievement of equality is imposed on the individual through the privatization of his autonomy, it is necessary to conclude that in such a society injustice has found its legitimation. In 1962, in an essay on Kant, Horkheimer affirmed that there had inevitably occurred a regress in world history. Now, in the new form of future society the theoretical and practical ideas of Kant were no longer able to act as a stimulus to promote the "unity of freedom and justice" in our society.[49] Sometime later, in an interview for the journal *Der Spiegel*, Horkheimer stated that he was unable to see how these values could coexist in our time. In the world as it is structured today, "justice and freedom" are in fact "dialectical concepts. The more justice the less freedom; the more freedom the less justice. Freedom, equality, fraternity, all constitute a marvelous expression. But if we want to maintain equality it is necessary to limit freedom, and if we want to give freedom to man then it becomes impossible to grant him equality."[50] These values are incompatible because while freedom makes the individual avail himself of the possibility of affirming himself according to the characteristics that make him different from all others and thus become an "individual," equality presupposes, on the contrary, a power that administers the individual and which will not permit to any one to rise above others. The struggle for social equality contains thus in itself the germ of the loss of freedom.

NOTES

1. *Oeuvres*, ed. Charles Adam and Paul Tanney, 11 vols. (Paris, 1897-1910), 9, 43.
2. Ibid., 44.
3. Ibid.
4. Ibid.
5. "Principles," 1, 45; *Oeuvres*, 9, 44.
6. Ibid., 55-56.
7. Ibid., 45.
8. Note preceeding analysis.
9. *Oeuvres*, 9, 46.
10. Ibid., 45.
11. Fourth Meditation, *Oeuvres*, 7, 57; 1, 4; 9, 44; M. Gueroult, *Apostilas*, 328.
12. *Oeuvres*, 9, 45.
13. See following section.
14. *Oeuvres*, 9, 45.
15. Ibid., 41.
16. Ibid., 45.
17. Ibid.
18. Ibid.
19. I. Kant, *Grundlegung zur Metaphysik des Sitten*, *Werke*, Vol. VII (Berlin: Prussian Academy, 1923), 21-22.
20. I. Kant, *Kritik der practischên Vernunft*, *Werke*, Vol. V (Berlin: Prussian Academy, 1922), first part, first book, #8.
21. Ibid.
22. Ibid., conclusion.
23. I. Kant, *Kritik der practischen Vernunft*, introduction.
24. Ibid., first part, first book, first section.
25. *Grundlegung zur metaphysik der Sitten*, first part, first book, second section.
26. Ibid., first part, first book, first section, #5 to 7.
27. Ibid., second book, second section, #3.
28. G. W. F. Hegel, *Phenomenology of Spirit*, trans. A. V. Miller (Oxford: Oxford University Press, 1977), 432-36; 624-31.

29. Ibid., 436-40; 631-36.

30. Ibid., 440-44; 636-44.

31. Ibid., 449-50; 649-50.

32. Ibid., 450-51; 650-52.

33. Ibid., 456; 658.

34. Ibid., 456-58; 658-61.

35. Ibid., 460; 663.

36. Ibid., 461; 664.

37. Ibid., 462; 665.

38. Ibid., 463; 666-67.

39. Ibid., 463-66; 667-71.

40. Ibid., 466-68; 671-73.

41. Ibid., 471; 677-78.

42. Ibid., 472; 678-79.

43. Max Horkheimer, *Critical Theory: Selected Essays*, trans. Matthew J. O'Connell et al. (New York: Herder and Herder, 1972), vii.

44. Max Horkheimer, "Schopenhauers Aktualitat," in *Neue Zurcher Zeitung* (March 21, 1971).

45. Ibid.

46. Max Horkheimer, *Zur Kritik der instrumentellen Vernunft* (Frankfurt: Frankfurt Verlag, 1974), 8.

47. *Reden anlasslich der Verleihung des Lessing-Preises an Max Horkheimer* (Hamburg, 1971), 28ff.

48. *Zur Kritik der instrumentellen Vernunft*, 348.

49. Ibid., 215.

50. Max Horkheimer, *Die Sehnsucht nach dem ganz Anderen* (Frankfurt: Frankfurt Verlag, 1970), 86.

Contributors

JONATHAN ARAC is a Professor in the Graduate Program in Literature at Duke University. Author of *Critical Genealogies* (1987) and *Commissioned Spirits* (1979), he has also edited *Postmodernism and Politics* (1987) and *The Yale Critics* (1983, with Wlad Godzich and Wallace Martin). While at the University of Illinois at Chicago, he directed a collaborative project (with NEH funding) to redesign freshman literature courses in response to current theoretical concerns.

PAUL A. BOVÉ, a Professor of English at the University of Pittsburgh, is the author of *Destructive Poetics* and *Intellectuals in Power*. He also co-edited *The Question of Textuality*. An associate editor of *boundary 2*, Bové has written numerous articles on contemporary criticism and modern literature.

JOSEPH A. BUTTIGIEG, an Associate Professor of English at the University of Notre Dame, is the author of *A Portrait in Different Perspective* and of numerous essays and reviews on modern literature and criticism. He is currently preparing a critical edition in English of Antonio Gramsci's *Quaderni del carcere*.

FRED R. DALLMAYR is Dee Professor of Government at the University of Notre Dame. He holds a doctorate of law from the University of Munich and a Ph.D. in political science from Duke University. Among his publications are *Beyond Dogma and Despair* (1981), *Twilight of Subjectivity* (1981), *Language and Politics: Why Does Language Matter to Political Philosophy?* (1984), and *Polis and Praxis: Exercises in Contemporary Political Theory* (1984). He is also editor

of *From Contract to Community* and (with Thomas McCarthy) of
Understanding and Social Inquiry.

FABIO S. DASILVA was born in Brazil and received his education at the
University of Sao Paulo and the Graduate School of Social and
Political Studies at the University of Florida. He continued his
postdoctoral studies in Paris, Heidelberg, and Berlin. Dasilva's
research has focused on French and German thought of the nineteenth and twentieth centuries. His publications include *Towards
an Interpretive Sociology*, *The Sociology of Music*, and articles on
phenomenology, aesthetics, and critical theory. He is a Professor
of Sociology at the University of Notre Dame.

MICHAEL HAYS teaches theater history and theory at Cornell University and Columbia University. He is the author of *The Public and
the Performance: Essays in the History of French and German Theater,
1871-1900* and has edited *The Criticism of Peter Szondi*, a special
issue of *boundary 2*. He is now translating Szondi's *Theory of Modern Drama* and completing a book on dramatic form in the modern and postmodern theater. Hays is also an assistant editor of
boundary 2.

DANIEL T. O'HARA, Professor of English at Temple University, is the
author of three books—*Tragic Knowledge: Yeat's Autobiography and
Hermeneutics* (1981), *The Romance of Interpretation: Visionary Criticism from Pater to de Man* (1985), and *Lionel Trilling: The Work
of Liberation* (1987). He is also the editor, with Paul A. Bové and
William V. Spanos, of *The Question of Textuality: Strategies of
Reading in Contemporary American Criticism* (1982) and the editor
of *Why Nietzsche Now?* (1985). In addition, he is an assistant editor of *boundary 2*. He is currently working on a study of Freud's
humanism.

DONALD PEASE who teaches at Dartmouth College, has published on
Hart Crane, Tennessee Williams, Stephen Crane, Blake and
Milton, and Whitman in connection with his continuing interest

in the poetics of modernism. Pease has also written extensively on contemporary critical theory and is an assistant editor of *boundary 2*.

DONNA PRZYBYLOWICZ is an Associate Professor of English at the University of Minnesota. She is the editor of *Cultural Critique* and the author of *Desire and Repression: The Dialectic of Self and Other in the Late Works of Henry James*.

WILLIAM V. SPANOS, a Professor of English at SUNY-Binghamton, is the founder and editor of *boundary 2*. He has published widely on modern literature and criticism. Spanos recently completed his book, *Repetitions: Essays on the Postmodern Occasion*. He is now at work on two other books, one on literary meaning, and the other on humanism and higher education.